DATE DUE			

Álvaro Siza. Private Houses 1954–2004

To Elías Torres

Alessandra Cianchetta, Enrico Molteni

Álvaro Siza
Private Houses

1954–2004

SKIRA

Cover
Casa Avelino Duarte, Ovar
Photograph by Roberto Collovà

Editor
Luca Molinari

Design
Marcello Francone

Editing
Rosanna Schiavone

Layout
Serena Parini

Translations
Antony Shugaar

First published in Italy in 2004 by
Skira Editore S.p.A.
Palazzo Casati Stampa
via Torino 61
20123 Milano
Italy
www.skira.net

Printed and bound in Italy. First edition
ISBN 88-8491-419-1

Distributed in North America by Rizzoli International
Publications, Inc., 300 Park Avenue South, New York,
NY 10010.
Distributed elsewhere in the world by Thames and
Hudson Ltd., 181a High Holborn, London WC1V 7QX,
United Kingdom

Acknowledgements

Álvaro Siza

Luca Dubini
Carles Muro
Alexandre Alves Costa
Rita e Catarina Almada Negreiros
Christine, Jean-Pierre, Matthias Armengaud
Adelaïde De Caters
Marc Dubois
Sandra Jeannette D'Urzo
Sergio Fernandez
Ricardo Granate Rosa Santos
Aurélien Masurel
Marie Annick Maupu
Anabela Monteiro
Luísa Penha
Giacomo Borella
Maria Chiara Porcu
Marco Rampulla
Ana Maria Ribeiro Da Silva
Anja Lautz
Cécile Bonnette
Maria Pilar Casado
Miguel Seguro
Alvaro Negrello
Eduardo Souto de Moura
Alcino Soutinho
Roberto Cremascoli
Andrea Liverani
Chiara Ricci
Filippo Antozzi
Silvia Lupi
José Angel Sanz Esquide
Luca Molinari

Current Owners of the Houses

Photo Credits
The digital photographs are by Enrico Molteni
and Alessandra Cianchetta, 1999-2003.
The large-format photographs are by Roberto
Collovà.

Contents

Foreword

Although it has not yet been presented and taken as a subject for systematic study, the single-family house constitutes a very significant theme in the production of Álvaro Siza. The interest of the volume then is rooted in a clear choice, limited to the single-family house, in an attempt to fill what strikes us as a gap.

The houses presented here were designed and built over a period of fifty years, beginning with the four houses in Matosinhos to the present day, with the house on Majorca currently under construction. Such a number of houses by a single architect constitutes a genuine field for research, in which continuity allows a specific and at the same time general reflection on the theme itself and on architecture at large.

For their rigorous, loving determination, for the tireless and patient research, Siza's houses offer us an exemplary lesson of intellectual greatness. The solutions possess a credibility given by the authenticity of presuppositions and intents: every contingent problem – creating an opening in a wall, resolve a point of access, design a window frame or a piece of furniture – is approached with great sensitivity and skill, without shortcuts. The response and the questions become universal: every solution is added like a tile to a more general *modus operandi* that goes well beyond the relationship to a place and a need, addressing the question of inhabiting, occupying a place, the performance of daily actions in a space. The quality and poetics of these little pieces of architecture is essentially bound up with life and certainly reveals a very profound conception of life.

Our research began with the help of a specialised grant from the Milan Polytechnic and with a series of trips to Oporto (where most of these houses are located).

This was a genuine voyage through the houses, driven by passion and curiosity, in the hope of unexpected discoveries: not a pilgrimage of veneration.

The tours of the houses were documented with a primitive "digital" camera (it was 1999), and were obtained by phoning the owners relentlessly, the help of friends, days of scouting and waiting in the suburban landscape around Oporto.

In conjunction with the tours, the quest for visual and written documentation for each project, found in Siza's and his collaborators' archives, or in the private archives of certain clients, gathered and presented in keeping with a precise and systematic protocol.

Among the objectives was the creation of a book that would be both a tool and a catalogue, as well as a travel guide, a point of departure for later explorations and in-depth studies.

This book, then, is also an invitation to travel, to the subjective experience of the architecture.

The book begins with an essay by Siza, "Living a House": a poetic and vibrant piece that speaks of time and life and which reflects the primary condition of architecture, as a habitat. A short interview from the beginning of the project deals with other related questions.

Then comes an overview of the corpus of houses: the complete array, with clearly abolished chronology, charted geographically to allow easy location, a graphic survey and a clear comparison, beginning with a schematic redesign of each house.

In the graphic survey, the houses are arranged side-by-side so as to offer an immediate comparison, with clear size, orientation, floor plan and plat. In the comparison, there is an analysis beginning with the salient details of each project, arranged by categories, and accompanied by a short explanatory note. These overall designs are to be taken as an instrument to facilitate the process of understanding the houses.

A short essay attempts to describe "the Siza house", suggesting an atmosphere that our tours of the houses has left with us, as a common base note.

The material concerning each house – built or just designed – is organised in a file with the basic information (site, year, client, surface area), the original project "memo", when it exists, along with other possible writings by Siza about the house in question; then the setting, the drawings in precise scale, whatever models and detailed drawings exist; finally the descriptive note about our visit and a sequence of small digital images, a photographic memoir of our visit.

As an invaluable visual complement, a selection of photographs by Roberto Collovà of eleven chosen houses.

Last of all, the apparatus contains bibliographic references to each individual house, a complete list of Siza's collaborators, and a short biography of Álvaro Siza.

I have never been capable of building a house, an authentic house. I am not referring to the design and construction of houses, a minor pursuit of which I am still capable, though I don't know how well.

My idea of a house is a complex machine, in which something goes wrong every day: lamp, faucet, drain, doorlock, hinge, receptacle, and then water heater, stove, refrigerator, television or video; and washing machine, fuses, curtain rods or safety latch.

Drawers stick, carpets tear, as does the upholstery on the living-room couch. A pile of shirts, socks, sheets, handkerchiefs, napkins, tablecloths and kitchen towels lie torn near the ironing board, which has a threadbare covering. There's more: water drips from the ceiling (the neighbour's pipes have broken, the roof leaks, the waterproofing is loose). And the gutters are full of grey leaves, dry or rotting.

If there is a yard, the grass grows too fast to keep up with, your free time is insufficient to master the rage of nature: petals fall and armies of ants swarm over your door sills, there are dead bodies of sparrows and mice and cats. You run out of chlorine for the pool, the filter breaks; there is no vacuum cleaner capable of making the water crystal clear or eliminating insect legs, fine as hairs.

The granite walls and floors are covered with dangerous slime, the paint fades and peels, uncovering knots in the wooden façade. An old man could punch a hole in the window frames with his finger, the glass breaks, the tar falls out and the silicone caulk peels, there is mould in closets and drawers, cockroaches withstand pesticides. When we finally find the oilcan it is empty, the wooden joints come undone, the tiles come away from the wall, first one, then all together.

And if that were all!

Living in a house, a real house, is a full-time job. The owner is a genuine fireman (houses are always catching fire, or they flood, or there are silent gas leaks, and they usually explode); he is a nurse (have you ever seen splinters from a railing get jammed under a finger nail?); he is a rescued swimmer, a master of all arts and trades, a specialist in physics, chemistry, and the law – and not a survivor. He is a switchboard operator, a receptionist, he makes phone calls at every hour of the day, looking for plumbers, carpenters, bricklayers, electricians, and then he opens the front door or the side door for them, following them meekly; he depends on them, though he still needs a complete home workshop, which also falls apart. And so he needs to sharpen blades, buy accessories, oil, organise, dehumidify; suddenly, the dehumidifier breaks, and then the air conditioners, the heat pumps.

All the same, nothing is worse than the torture of books that move mysteriously, by themselves, intentionally mixing up their proper order, attracting dust with their spines and their magnetic thickness. Dust gets into the top of pages, tiny insects chew on them making an indescribable noise; the pages crumble, the leather stains, drops of water from nearby vases with wilting flowers drip on the etchings, sprinkle paintings in a furious process of destruction. The door mat falls apart, there is a deep groove in the wood, straws fall out of the brooms, precious objects break, boards of the tables and other furniture crack open with terrifying creaking sounds, the toilet won't flush, the fireplace fills with soot – one day there will be a chimney fire; in the china cabinet your great-grandmother's crystal goblets break, bottles of fine white wine explode, the corks pop or they rot, you lose the finest vintage in a puddle on the floor.

When, for the first time ever, you fail to immediately replace a burnt-out light bulb, the electricity fails in the whole house, and of course on a Saturday, and the only car available has a flat tire.

So I think it is heroic to own, keep up and renovate a house. In my view, there should be a Guild of Homeowners, and every year they should receive a large cash prize and a medal.

But when this labour of maintenance is not apparent, when the healthy aroma of wax fills a well-ventilated house, and mixes with the scent of flowers in the garden, and when we are in that house – we, visitors irresponsibly unattentive to our moments of happiness – and we feel happy, forgetting our anxieties as barbarian nomads, then the only possible medal is that of gratitude, silent applause; a moment's pause, as we look around, immersing ourselves in the golden air of an autumn interior, at the end of the day.

Oporto, March 1994

Conversation on the Topic of Houses

Enrico Molteni/Alessandra Cianchetta: *The single-family house is a central theme in your work, especially in the early years.*

Álvaro Siza: In the early years, the house was a central theme quite simply because I had no other work, I was only being asked to do small houses. For that matter, even now, designing a small house or other buildings is hardly ideal, because you barely earn enough money to cover your costs. It is a type of work in which the client always has an especially intense involvement in the project. Of course, anyone who wants to build a house for himself wants to express his interests in detail, his own likes, his hopes, etc. And so it is a theme that tends to be examined closely with a certain person, and this condition makes the house a central theme, both in experimental terms and as an exploration in depth of the work of an architect. It is no accident that the development of architecture is marked by the presence of a certain number of famous homes, where the respective architects were allowed to pursue their exploration of the subject; in many cases, thanks to the enthusiasm of the client.

That is why I plan to continue building houses. It is a lighter programme, there is less bureaucratic burden, though it is certainly demanding.

EM/AC: *The relationship with the client, but, in more general terms, with the space and the body, seems to be a fundamental question.*

ÁS: In effect, the ergonomic aspects are quite direct, because, since there is a limitation in scale, normal in a house, the relationship between the body and its movements in space is quite conditional and must be much more precise. In houses, we generally do not have the dimension of the collective space, although certainly, some homeowners have parties, invite people to their homes – but these remain in any case limited situations, with a limited dimension; generally this is a scale that does not extend beyond the direct utilisation of the spaces.

In order for a house to keep from being asphyxiating, it must meet the wishes of the person who will inhabit it, and who may have passing desires, but it is also necessary to attain a certain detachment from all this, a kind of independence. I don't think it is a very good solution to give too direct, precise and limited responses to what a person wants, at a certain moment, because houses have long lives. Often, the tastes of a client change after a few years, become different. The house cannot give a fixed answer, it must have a different destiny; I have already seen many stories…

I remember one house: after a few years, the family became smaller, and the owners told me: "You built an uncomfortable house, it's too big; we would like to retrench and close a few rooms", and so I said, "But don't you remember that your family used to be bigger?" and he insisted: "I want to retrench, it's too much work!" I left it alone and in the end I made no alterations at all. A few years later, the same person came to see me and said: "Mister Architect, you made a house for us that is too small! We can't turn around, we'll have to enlarge it!" and what had happened was that his children had had children of their own, and they came to stay in the house once a week, more or less.

These are issues of size, but of course there are issues of taste, comfort, and these issues change as well! Or else, a person dies, the house is inherited, or it is sold to someone.

On the one hand, then, there is a user, and it is very useful and real, but it need not be a totally conditioning barrier, or else the house may rapidly become obsolete.

EM/AC: *In terms of the organisation of the floor plan, the patio is an element often used that speaks to a sort of introversion, a quest for intimacy, as in the house you built for your brother.*

ÁS: It also depends on the use of the patio, it depends very much on how the house is situated. In the case of my brother's house and other houses, the setting is on the outskirts, not the outskirts of the city, but little lots set in a chaotic and peripheral area. That is why the value of intimacy is so great, defending against the exterior, which can be taken as a visibility/non-visibility, protection from noise, traffic, etc. It is a traditional solution precisely as a response to the need for comfort, but in other, different situations, the patio is not justified. There are other houses that do not have this characteristic.

I have always been intensely interested in transitional spaces: I never like a geometrical volume where I am inside or outside. For various activities, for comfort, intimacy, light, the possibility of having transitional spaces is important. In Portugal we have a strong relationship with the traditions of North Africa, especially in Southern Portugal and Spain, for instance Granada, the enormous gardens of the house of the Generalife where Arabic/Islamic culture strongly cultivated this tradition of the open space, of the open loggia overlooking the garden and the spaces of penumbra. My brother's house is a very specific case and the patio is almost a conquest of space, through the vanishing points and successive alignment of breaking points. This can be quite different however, it does not happen in so typological a manner, but it is certainly an element in the conquest of comfort. A house must also have a community space, even though the house may not have a major representative function.

EM/AC: A Single Multitude, *a collection of poems by Pessoa, could also be used as a title for all these houses of yours.*

ÁS: Yes, when an architect designs a house he does it for someone else, not only because it is a com-mission, but also because the other person, the client, is the one who will actually live in the house. To design is to travel through space, time, occupy this house in your imagination. Therefore, the architect must imagine himself in the client's skin, the skin of his wife, he must become a child, a grandparent, cleaning woman, etc.… hence the quotation from Pessoa, this multiplication of personalities. This multitude is gradually drawing, on the one hand, on the globality, and on the other, a density of the artwork, the space, the walls, a very strong identity. What is designed becomes the design of the father, mother, children, grandchildren, etc.

In short, it is like a reproduction, which is also a translation, of what is, after all, family life.

EM/AC: *Each house, of course, is always a different adventure…*

ÁS: Perhaps that is why I have never built a house for myself, because that would be a different adventure, the adventure of discovering myself, which is always the most difficult one, sometimes painful… don't you agree?

Oporto, 7 October 1999

Enrico Molteni

An Authentic House[1]

"I have never been capable of building a house, an authentic house. I am not referring to the design and construction of houses, a minor pursuit of which I am still capable."
Álvaro Siza

This apparent declaration of modesty shows us that, in reality, for Siza, a house is something that exists outside of architecture.

A house will be authentic only in its full-time *occupation*, in its coinciding with the real life of those who *occupy* it. It is a space that demands to be inhabited.[2] Even though, obviously, it is a question that in theory can be extended to all houses, to all architecture, in reality for Siza this is a decisive and unavoidable question: the quality of these residences (and I must immediately point out that it is a quality that can be understood only when seen directly, in contact with all the house's parts) is closely tied to life itself, to our presence as a human presence.

Inhabitant. The client/inhabitant is in no way typified, idealised, but rather an essential and unavoidably specific condition in the construction of that unique house. Part of a family nucleus, this is an individual linked to the world and to things, a sensible body immersed in reality, which desires "a naïve contact with the world", which lies in the world and knows itself in the world; inhabitant of a fantastic phenomenological labyrinth.[3]

Space. The space of Siza's house is an occupied space, possessed, appropriated – both in terms of *appropriateness* and *appropriation*. It is never a neutral, or strictly functional space, nor is it pure, conceptual, but rather becomes a dense entity, inhabited by affections, habits,[4] sensations that give a meaning both to things and to the body of their inhabitant. Any form of objectivity fails and everything refers to the presence of a body.[5]

Size. In the definition of the spatial limits of the house, of the proportion of spaces, of geometries, the body of the inhabitant will be the reason, the measure of operation: a body that has nothing in common with an abstract, *normative* model. Measurements often become minimal, quite approximate, millimetric,[6] to the same degree that perceptions become more intense, more precise.

In this quality of the small we find all the profound difference both from the house as *existenzminimum* – a rational response for a uniform, catalogable society – and from the house as a work of art, the *villa*.[7]

Organisation. The organisation of spaces, leaving aside the layout of the distribution and the floor plan, will present as a result a multitude of rooms, spaces, each different and not interchangeable, in which labyrinthine paths, secret corners, dark passages, all tend towards a sophisticated and poetic spontaneity. The subdivision into zones and the programmatic distribution will become evident only in a second phase.

In the main, common room, a fireplace represents the household hearth, family life: not the spectacle of fire, the effect, nor the fireplace as a sculptural object.

Materiality. The construction and material quality of the house is resolved without imposing a standardised or experimental system, but its reason is found in a specific environmental quality, a kind of sonority linked to a certain tone, a timbre, like a voice[8] that pervades space.

In each case, then, it will be the coherence and affordability, not so much in terms of technique and construction as much as in tactile and sensory terms that will lead to the choice of materials, the solution of the detail,[9] the colour, incorporating in it, finally, natural elements such as the shadows of leaves and, in a significant manner, the slow process of time.

Garden. A garden is not a representative space that lies between the city and the house, nor is it a space charged with elements, in a caricature. Just as the house is not a volume, so the garden is not a green zone, a free space, but the exterior environment that participates actively in the specific quality of the interior, which it models: light and air change and possess qualities in accordance with the exterior.

Interior-exterior. One fundamental aspect of Siza's houses is the definition of interior-exterior. The structure is understood as a sensitive entity in which the point of passage or delimitation is always a point of great intensity, which can take the form of a threshold, an area of penumbra;[10] it is the transitional space between two different conditions in which exchanges and sensations are multiplied and intensified. Or else this limit can take the form of an extremely sophisticated membrane, a registry of the external and internal world, a very deep and shifting surface.

But the theme of transition pervades the entire house, not merely as a passage from outdoor light and indoor shadow, but also as a passage between one level and another, between high and low, compression and expansion. It is a corporeal and perceptual transition, in which the variations of level are variations of viewpoint: space is not fixed, absolute, or abstract, but it is relative to a movement, a posture, a gesture.

Furniture-objects. In the house, the furniture and objects are selected as emotional presences, they express a non-functional value, a value of comfort or luxury, or a representative value, but they are first and foremost a promise of intimacy.[11] The furnishings are placed in a natural way, they are not pieces of design but often rediscoveries, old furniture, anonymous and private. The well-being is essentially emotional, personal, and the objects underscore this character that pervades the house at every level. Nothing is shown off, nothing is aestheticised. The easy chairs are made of soft, worn leather, the dressers have many drawers of all sizes: the house welcomes and protects our body and, like an ark, houses the traces of our stories in a sort of autobiographical museum, warding off the idea of disappearance and the inevitable dissolution.

Uniqueness. The house is never an abstract model, but the construction of a uniqueness, bound to a concrete and specific moment, to what exists as accidental, to the client/inhabitant as a condition of reference. The multiplicity of situations and sensations is a multiplicity of forms and houses, far from pre-constituted images, built with what is available, at hand, in a healthy and creative opportunism.

You never sense the presence of a modern architect (aesthete, artist, demiurge, etc.); to be more precise, you never sense *that* latent but authoritative presence that invisibly directs the private conduct of the inhabitant, and which makes the inhabitant incapable of experiencing space individually, to establish spontaneously constraints, pleasure, intimacy and surprise. The house is not therefore a haven that protects and defends against the outside world, nor is it a "white" space to contemplate, nor is it an efficient, comfortable machine, but rather the place of memory and sensations.

Privileged moment. These sensations accompany the everyday inhabitant without trauma: the privileged moment, of authentic happiness of the house, is, then, "a moment of reflection, when, immersed in the golden atmosphere of an autumn interior, at day's end, the healthy aroma of wax is mixed with the scent of flowers from the garden."[12]

Milan, 6 January 2004

[1] This text derives from a reading of Iñaki Ábalos, *La buena vida*, GG, Barcelona 2000.

[2] "Because a product becomes a real product only through consumption. For example, a dress becomes really a dress only by being worn, a house which is uninhabited is indeed not really a house" (Karl Marx).

[3] Maurice Merleau-Ponty, *Phenomenology of Perception*, Routledge, London and New York 1962.

[4] "What is a house made of? Of habits, I believe, of the raw material of repetition converted into shelter. Habits include everything: words, jokes, opinions, gestures, acts, even the way you wear your hat. Physical objects and places – a piece of furniture, a bed, a room, a bar, a street corner – all shape the setting, the context of habit, but they are not these things, it is habit that they protect. The mortar that holds up this improvised 'hearth' is memory"; John Berger, *And Our Faces, My Heart, Brief as Photos*, 1992.

[5] Let us think of the presence of the body – whole, a face, the hands – in Siza's designs, as well as wooden *bodies* – modelled torsos and pieces – that make up his sculptures; see Álvaro Siza, *Scultura Architettura*, Skira, Milan 1999.

[6] "I live with intensity only the minimal sensations, and in relation to tiny things. Every detail is stamped monstrously inside of me, in a whole. The exterior world is for me, always, a mere sensation. I never forget my feeling"; *Millimetres (Sensations of Minimal Things)*, in Fernando Pessoa, *The Book of Disquiet*, Serpent's Tail, New York 2002.

[7] "A small house is not a villa. A small house conforms and deforms with the people, and nothing can replace or deprive it of its character of privacy, almost individuality, identification with the body, with undressing and dressing. A villa presupposes interiors as infinite as labyrinths and gardens, however small, and a place. These small houses, instead, are placeless, because the place is interior or is identified with those who live there"; Aldo Rossi, *Autobiografia scientifica*, 1981.

[8] "A voice belongs, first of all, to a body, then to a tongue"; Berger, *op. cit.*

[9] "Details for Siza are neither a decorative occasion nor a technological exhibition, but an intimate dimension of accessibility to the architecture, a way of verifying its substance in tactile terms"; Vittorio Gregotti, "Architetture recenti di Álvaro Siza", in *Controspazio*, no. 9, 1972.

[10] "When we undertake the construction of our home, before anything else we spread out this roof like an umbrella, establishing on the ground a perimeter protected from the sun, and in that penumbra we arrange the house"; Junchiro Tanizaki, *In Praise of Shadow*, 1933.

[11] "Intimacy is a Russian doll: by fragmenting volumes, restricting spaces, it designs one hiding place after another, in concentric circles, an itinerary of objects. The box for living encloses intimacy within intimacy"; Georges Teyssot, "Paesaggio d'interni", in *Quaderni di Lotus*, 1987.

[12] Álvaro Siza, *Living a House*, Oporto 1994.

List of Houses

1. Four Houses at Matosinhos
   1954–57
2. Casa Carneiro de Melo, Oporto
   1957–59
3. Casa Rocha Ribeiro, Maia
   1960–62, 1969–70
4. Casa Júlio Gesta, Matosinhos
   1961
5. Casa Ferreira da Costa / Miranda Santos,
   Matosinhos
   1962–65, 1988–93
6. Casa Rui Feijó, Moledo do Minho
   1963–64
7. Casa Alves Costa, Moledo do Minho
   1964–68
8. Casa Adelino Sousa Felgueira, Oporto
   1966
9. Casa Alves Santos, Póvoa de Varzim
   1966–69
10. Casa Manuel Magalhães, Oporto
    1967–70
11. Casa Carlos Vale Guimarães, Aveiro
    1968
12. Casa Alcino Cardoso, Moledo do Minho
    1971–73, 1988–91
13. Casa Marques Pinto, Oporto
    1972
14. House at Azeitão, Setúbal
    1973–74
15. Casa Carlos Beires, Póvoa de Varzim
    1973–76
16. House at Francelos, Vila Nova de Gaia
    1977
17. Casa António Carlos Siza, Santo Tirso
    1976–78
18. Casa Maria Margarida, Arcozelo
    1979–87
19. Casa José Manuel Teixeira, Taipas, Guimarães
    1980–88
20. Casa Avelino Duarte, Ovar
    1981–84
21. Casa Fernando Machado, Oporto
    1981
22. Casa Aníbal Guimarães da Costa, Trofa
    1982
23. Casa Mário Bahia, Gondomar
    1983
24. Casa Pascher, Sintra
    1984
25. Casa Álvaro Siza, Malagueira, Évora
    1984–89
26. Casa David Vieira de Castro, Vila Nova
    de Famalicão
    1984–94
27. Casa Luís Figueiredo, Gondomar
    1984–94
28. Casa César Rodrigues, Oporto
    1987–96
29. Casa Javier Guardiola, Puerto de Santa
    Maria, Spain
    1988–89
30. *Quinta* de Santo Ovídio, Lousada
    1989–92, 1997–2001
31. Casa Pereira Ganhão, Tróia
    1990
32. Casa Van Middelem-Dupont, Oudenburg,
    Belgium
    1997–2001
33. Restoration of Villa Colonnese, Vicenza, Italy
    1998
34. House on Majorca, Spain
    2002

Graphic Compilation

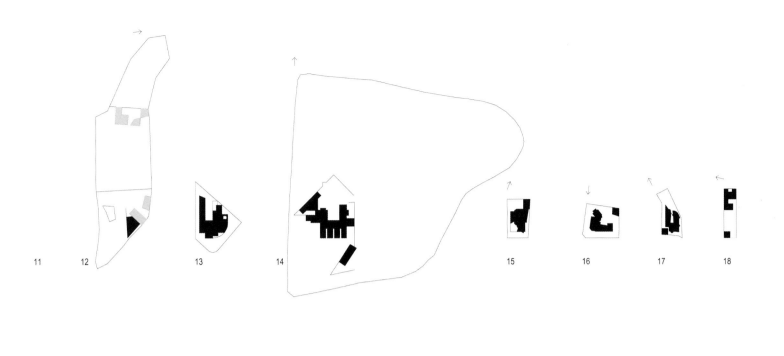

11 12 13 14 15 16 17 18

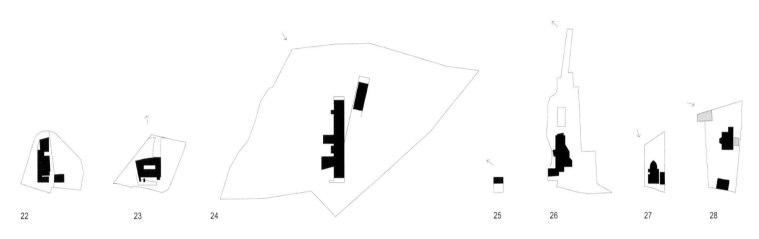

22 23 24 25 26 27 28

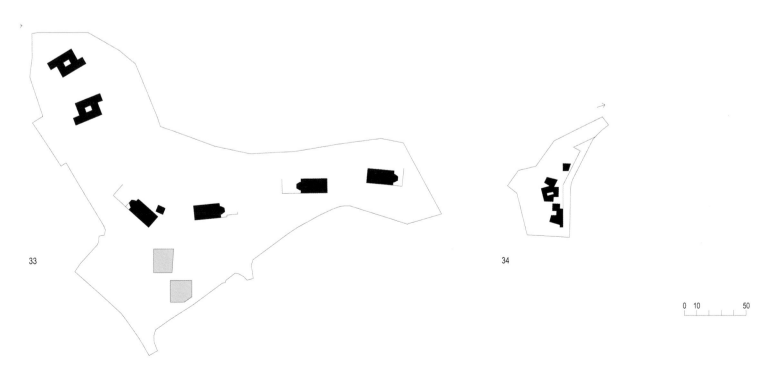

33 34

0 10 50

19

Comparative Chart, by Themes and Principles

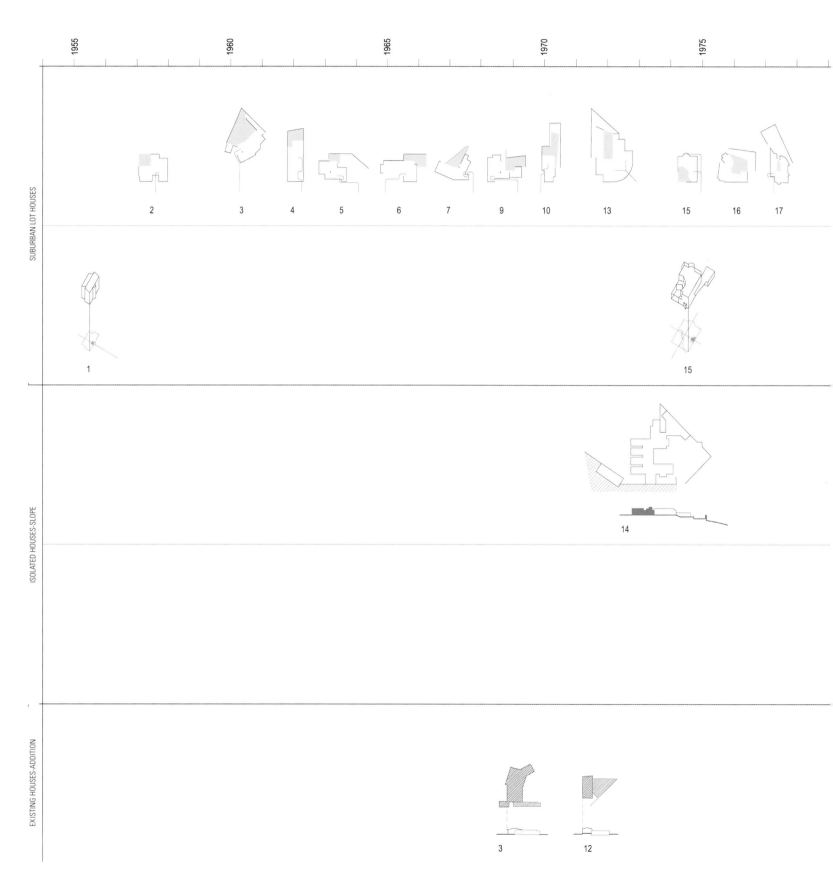

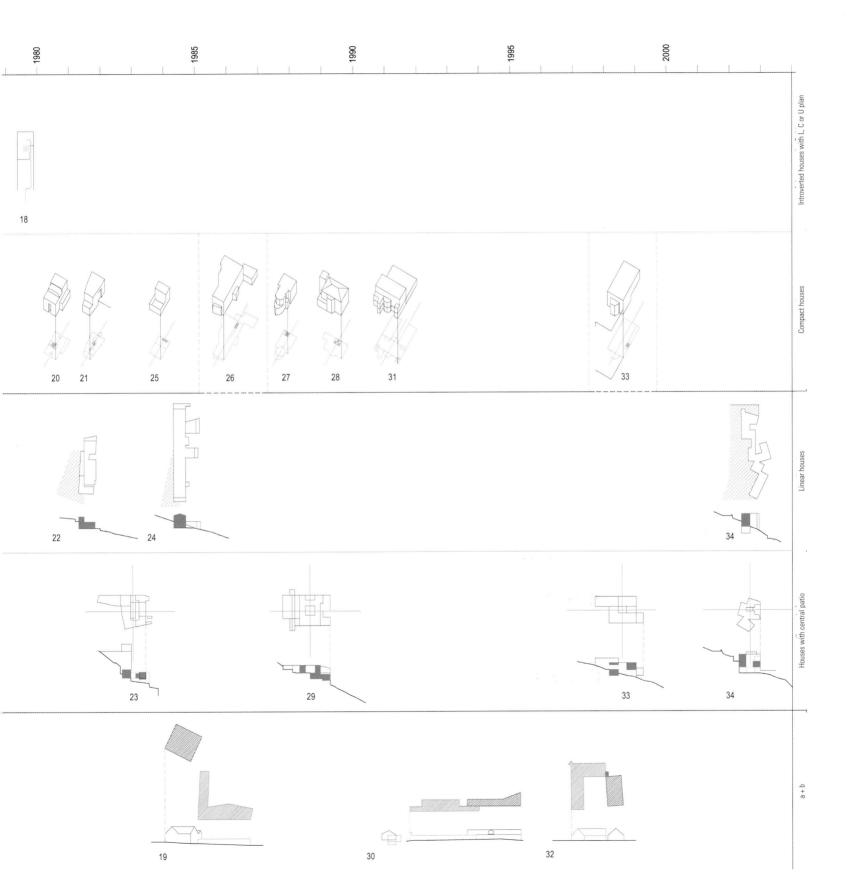

Note on the Comparative Chart

Enrico Molteni

The construction of an overall chart on the theme of the single-family home is intended to visualise the formal generalities of each individual house and, in comparison, to identify those essential elements that reflect the persistence of certain themes and principles. The themes and the principles identified constitute a sort of field of orientation offering easy consultation, a guided glance at the subject, intended, in part, as a primary base for thought. This operation originates out of a working approach, i.e., an approach which would entail the sharing of problems and solutions, closer to practice than criticism: the chart also has an implicitly practical and (auto)didactic aspect. It is necessary to think of this overall chart in terms of design, where nothing is fixed, there is no invention but rather a continuous/discontinuous process of elaboration and research, fine tuning and crisis. Every house, each new piece of architecture is the product of a series of transformations carried out on other houses or pieces of architecture, conceived or built, which are its foundations. This process constitutes in general Siza's system of working, whereby the theme of the house has become the irreplaceable workshop, the special, constant setting for experimentation. In this crucial point it is also possible to include the other pieces of architecture, and, in a sense, all of Siza's architecture.

In the construction of the chart we have utilised simple, architectural-type drawings: floor plan, cross section, axonometric plan. In fact, the type of design identified has the task of portraying – on its own – that which is decisive in each design.

The chart works in two senses. A first level delineates the general themes of each project into types of intervention: suburban lot houses, isolated houses on slopes, existing houses enlarged. A second level identifies the prevalent character and emphasises the typical nature of the solutions adopted, solutions that in relation to the theme are considered as valid

principles that can generally be repeated. It is possible to read it chronologically (1954–2004) and synchronically, establishing a perception that moves transversely and which leads to other aspects and questions, not set forth here. This approach extends the view even beyond the theme of the house.

Suburban lot houses

In a suburban lot, of limited size, there are two prevailing principles: one tends towards the introversion of domestic space, the other towards the volumetric compactness of the structure. The lot, then, is taken in two ways: in its specificity, as a situation, and in its typical aspect, as an abstraction.

Introverted houses. All the early houses are conceived as a way of dividing two worlds, as a separation between domestic life and the outside reality. The placement of the built structure delimits an enclosed space, always within the lot, and the "L" plan, "C" plan, or "U" plan, in the different geometric variations, are defined in close accord to the shape of the lot. This work is focused on the floor plan.

The structure is configured in keeping with a principle of duality, via a counterpoint between an interior section with windows or entirely open and a dominantly closed exterior section. There is not a single construction system, but always a composite and characterised structure, in which use is made of different materials.

Compact houses. The compact house is characterised by its central placement within the lot, configured as a multistorey parallelepiped with a horizontal roof, clearly shown in the axonometric plan. In order to endow each house with identity, the volume is manipulated beginning with primary and symmetrical geometric forms and such architectural elements as bay windows, loggias, awnings, etc. There was a tendency always to resolve the building with the same system, by repetition and declension of well established themes, such as: the ground attachment, terminal protection of the façades,

window and door frames set in the masonry. The theme of the house in the suburban lot is the dominant one and, in general terms, can also be considered the field of action in which Siza's architecture takes form and is fine-tuned. A reading of the sequence of the introverted houses could be viewed, significantly, as the "quest for a language" (in *Poetic Profession*, 1986) or, though this amounts to the same thing, as "Siza's non-style" (Rafael Moneo, 1976). In the same way, the series of compact houses could be taken as emblematic of Siza's language, i.e., of a certain system of expression and construction, typical and recognisable, which, to my view, identifies Siza's architecture at its point of greatest media diffusion.

Isolated houses: slope

The boundary lines and the shape of the lot are of no importance now and the prevailing theme can only be that of the relationship with the topography: the project is resolved both in floor plan and, especially, in cross section. The general characteristics of the compact house continue to have much in common with those of the suburban house, even if in these solutions (26, 33) the volume undergoes transformations primarily in relation to the land and the views. When the construction site, on the other hand, has a sharp slope, two specific schemes are utilised: the central patio scheme, arranging the house against the slope, and the linear development scheme, with the house laying along a certain elevation.

Houses with a central patio. The layout with an enclosed patio appears for the first time in its most expressive version (23) and is later adopted as a typological scheme. The mass, organised on a square form, expands to breathe and the patio, in this sense, is no longer an indicator of introversion, but a way of rendering livable a profound and compact structure set on a slope. The organisational scheme follows successive declensions in which the square is made up of "C"-shaped structures, stacked and in-

verted (33), or else it is elevated like a bridge (23, 34), in which the patio is also a possibility (29). We also find the theme of the projecting structure: smaller structures jutting into the void, or else, into the ground, always as a counterpoint to the line of the slope.

Linear houses. Along the level curves, the house extends horizontally, as a retaining wall, entirely focused downhill. The depth of the structure is limited, open only on one side. This linear scheme can also involve smaller volumes, or empty areas, arranged transversely. In the house on Majorca, the two principles overlap.

Existing houses: enlargement

It is necessary, first of all, to point out, as a decisive and constant element, the relationship with the pre-existing structure and even more with the place, no longer lot or sloping land but a specific and characteristic built landscape. Otherwise, it would be impossible to understand the always different materiality of the structure that is developed in each case. The relationship of scale, form and choice of material are the most important operative questions. The complexity of the theme and the initial conditions prevail over the typological choice; beginning from this point of departure, the addition of a new structure (a + b) is resolved according to different principles: in continuity, adjoining or intersecting, in any case, with a disjunction (3, 12, 30); through a link, by the extension of the same configuration (32); through distancing, the physical separation of the two structures (19).

Afterthought. The critical aspect of the chart lies in its very schematic nature, in its reduction to a single term. As if to say, the doubt that such an operation might also lead to an impoverishment of understanding. This skepticism is perhaps the spirit with which to approach the chart in order to put it into crisis, from one's own point of view and in the light of that which each of us, down deep, seeks or is capable of seeing. Milan, 2 June 2004

Plans and Works

Four Houses at Matosinhos

Avenida Afonso Henriques,
Matosinhos, Portugal

House A
Lot area: 260 sq. m.
Built area, ground floor: 95 sq. m.
+ 20 sq. m. garage

House B
Lot area: 270 sq. m.
Built area, ground floor: 66 sq. m.
+ 20 sq. m. garage

House C
Lot area: 155 sq. m.
Built area, ground floor: 60 sq. m.

House D
Lot area: 100 sq. m.
Built area, ground floor: 50 sq. m.

Residences at Matosinhos

Four residences: two isolated and two set together (rental units), designed together, for reasons of kinship among the clients. If we go back, I realise that I had tried, more than applying a preconceived language, to find a compromise between what I thought and what the clients wanted. I insisted on the abandonment of rigid distribution by zone, giving in where necessary, and defending a "inside-out" solution as the inevitable result of a series of options. This is a sort of limited and naïve realism, as you can guess from what I said before. Clients: captains of fishing boats sailing towards a new richness, but not yet *nouveau riche*.

Álvaro Siza
Oporto, 26 January 1967

Letter to Nuno Portas published in *Siza. Writings on Architecture*, Skira, Milan 1997

Four Houses at Matosinhos

This project was completed before the conclusion of the course, which balanced educational instruction and professional practice.

The anxious attempt to control the design as a whole and the lack of maturity of sight and sound make it hybrid, naïve, fragmented, characterising the "risk" (a word that in Portuguese means both design and danger).

Despite all this, in some sense it is to this first effort that later works refer, as does the sentiment, once broken the apparent coherency of a closed language, of which only long experience can, with other presuppositions, rediscover the lost spontaneity amidst the fragility of the first work.

Álvaro Siza
Oporto, May 1979

1. *Plan of the ground floor (1:250)*
1. Entryway / 2. Service-room / 3. Hall, or great room / 4. Office / 5. Kitchen / 6. Armoire / 7. Bathrooms / 8. Bedroom / 9. Garage
(Source: Álvaro Siza Archives, undated)

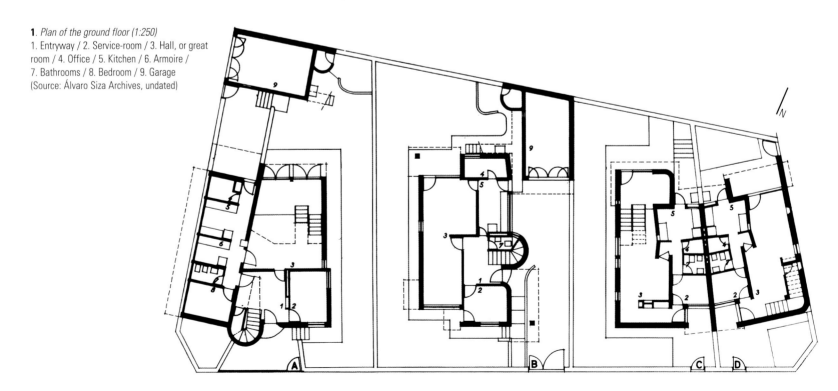

Casa Carneiro de Melo

Avenida da Boavista,
Oporto, Portugal

Client: Emilia Angela Nugent Carneiro de Melo

Lot area: 1480 sq. m.
Built area: 175 sq. m.

Project Description
Site, design and proposal
The house is located on a lot in the area to the south of Avenida da Boavista, overlooking a large green area.

In consideration of potential future construction, study was undertaken and approved of the subdivision of the land in order to establish, without hindering its use as a whole, the most appropriate "site" for this residence.

This subdivision will not be effective immediately, since the land continues to be used for farming; with it, some of the existing residences will be preserved, ensuring an independent access and the isolation of the residence planned through the arrangement of the garden. The intention is to demolish the existing structures near the north wall. The programme, not particularly extensive, which was resolved on a single level, the natural conditions of the land, slightly sloping in a north-south direction, swept by winds chiefly from the north and south-west, a number of considerations linked to the relationship between the residence and the surrounding environment have led to the proposed solution, in which two structures, articulated as "L" shapes, to the north and the west, enclose a space as an external extension of the house, to the south, which the design of the garden and the quality of the pavements complete and specify; this space, though limited, continues to possess something internal. The nexus of the floor plan is a large atrium divided into two parts by a plate glass window, which gives access to three zones: living-room and dining-room (linked by a sliding door), zone for bedrooms and service zone. The first two open onto the exterior space described, while the service zone has a secondary access to the west.
Construction
The selection of materials and building techniques must take into account economic criteria that do not entail, in the future, maintenance costs. Therefore, the roof, made of Portuguese tile, is prolonged in such a way as to protect the external vertical closures from the direct action of the rain and create, at the same time, a porticoed path that contributes to a perfect exterior-interior relationship. The walls in stone and brick will be covered with plaster, the lofts will be stuccoed, the wood painted for the window frames, thresholds, and doors, flooring made of wooden strips and terracotta set on light concrete: these are the materials used. In the bath-rooms and in the kitchen, washable walls and floors, made of waterproof ceramics and mosaics. The design of the bathrooms, to be executed in keeping with regulations, will be presented at the appropriate time.
Plastic analysis
The solution designed, which is based on several of the oldest homes on the Avenida, intends to create an intimate setting for the house, by which is meant the array of interior and exterior spaces described.

This setting demands a certain degree of protection, ensured by the 15-metre setback with the possibility of creating a dense garden in front of the Avenida: a garden that affects the appearance of the house, giving it a tone, softening its lines, anchoring it to the lot.

From the street, through a curtain of greenery that changes seasonally in its density, with varying ranges of colour, it will be possible to glimpse, under the red roof, the white plaster walls: a mass of serene horizontality, barely interrupted by the systematically vertical rhythm of the openings.

Álvaro Siza

Boavista Residence
The characteristics of the ground and the lifestyles of the clients were the most immediate (though today I do not believe they were the real) causes that led me to something like "rendering sociable" the idiom of the residences of Matosinhos. I soon understood that I was not hitting the target, or better that I was not choosing well. I must have missed the target, from what I can see of the influence of this project here in Oporto (this is very secret). As far as the articulation of the programme is concerned, I think that here I tried to combat those aspects that Pedro mentions in the criticism of my works (when mention is made of claustrophobia). Visiting it recently, I found it to be "a house" and not "one of my first projects", though, to me, it is my worst project.

Álvaro Siza
Oporto, 26 January 1967

Letter to Nuno Portas published in *Siza. Writings on Architecture*, Skira, Milan 1997
Siza refers to the article by Pedro Vieira de Almeida, "Un analisis de la obra de Siza Vieira"

1. *Plan of the ground floor (1:250)*
1. Atrium / 2. Living-room / 3. Dining-room /
4. Kitchen / 5. Pantry / 6. Closet / 7.-8.
Facilities / 9. Bathroom / 10.-11.-12. Bedrooms
(Source: Álvaro Siza Archives, undated)

2. *Project elevations and cross sections (1:250)*
(Source: Álvaro Siza Archives, undated)

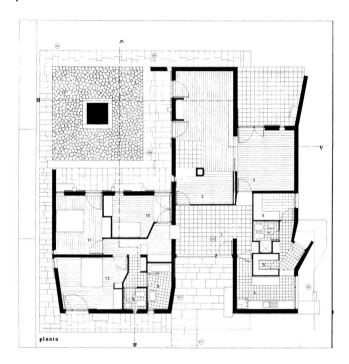

planta

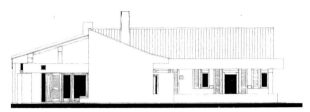

alçado sul

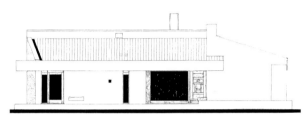

alçado norte

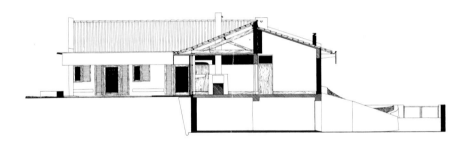

Casa Rocha Ribeiro

Rua de Engenheiro Duarte Pacheco,
Maia, Portugal

Client: Antonio Luiz da Rocha Ribeiro

Collaborators: Alexandre Alves Costa, Beatriz
Madureira, António Madureira, Francisco Guedes
de Carvalho

Lot area: 1380 sq. m.
Total roofed area: 295 sq. m.
Built area: 195 sq. m. + 55 sq. m. portico
Expansion: 45 sq. m.

Project Description

The construction constraints imposed by the roads, the orientation of the land and the desire not to destroy the existing vegetation all led to the layout presented here. The programme requested (atrium, three bedrooms, bathrooms, adjoining living-room and dining-room, kitchen, dining nook, pantry and laundry-room) developed on a single level, completed by the construction of the garage and the studio and by the exterior arrangements.

The roof unified the volumes mentioned, articulated in such a way as to embrace an exterior space through which it communicates directly with the common zone. The presence of this exterior space can be seen throughout the proposal, thanks to a careful arrangement of the windows.

The processes of construction and the materials called for are those used normally in buildings of this sort and in this region: walls made of stone or perforated brick; tile roofs supported on a brick-and-cement loft; beams and pillar of the living-room made of reinforced concrete; wooden window frames, doors and thresholds; ceramics (for the bathrooms and the kitchen, the walls will be sheathed with washable material).

The thermal insulation of the roof will be ensured by a ventilated air chamber, between the loft and the hanging false ceiling, in wood. This ceiling is freely utilised to model and link the interior spaces, with respect to the normative prescriptions concerning the minimum heights (the minimum required, at least half of the surface of each room, and never less than 2 metres).

The pantry and the bathrooms are ventilated from above. The sanitary design will be in compliance with the norms, and the calculations of reinforced concrete will be presented within guidelines.

The intention was to create a discreet and intimate building, which we think we have done through the contrast between the rhythm of the horizontal whole with the surrounding vegetation.

Álvaro Siza
Oporto, 18 March 1960

Residence at Maia

On the interior of a property, in a small town a few kilometres from Oporto. Designed immediately after Boa Nova, I attempted to purify the language in a way that seemed necessary to me. When I am at Boa Nova, I see many things "that it was necessary to remove". At Maia, there aren't too many extra things. I set out, perhaps, from the need to arrange an irregularly shaped piece of land, exactly in the zone indicated for construction, in part because of regulations (distance from the centre line of the road). I also tried to take advantage of the existing vegetation (especially the tree in the courtyard), to find the exact scale, to normalise (and I am not referring to measurements) the design of details, and to become familiar with the clients (Tomé).

Álvaro Siza
Oporto, 26 January 1967

Letter to Nuno Portas published in *Siza. Writings on Architecture*, Skira, Milan 1997

1. *Planimetric plan, with addition*
(Source: Enrico Molteni, 2004)

2. Plan of the ground floor (1:250)
1. Atrium / 2. Access-room / 3.-4.-5. Bedrooms
/ 6.-7. Bathroom / 8. Laundry-room / 9. Pantry /
10. Office / 11. Kitchen / 12. Dining-room / 13.
Hall, or great room / 14. Study / 15. Garbage /
16. Garage / 17. Stone floor
(Source: Álvaro Siza Archives, March 1960,
original scale 1:100)

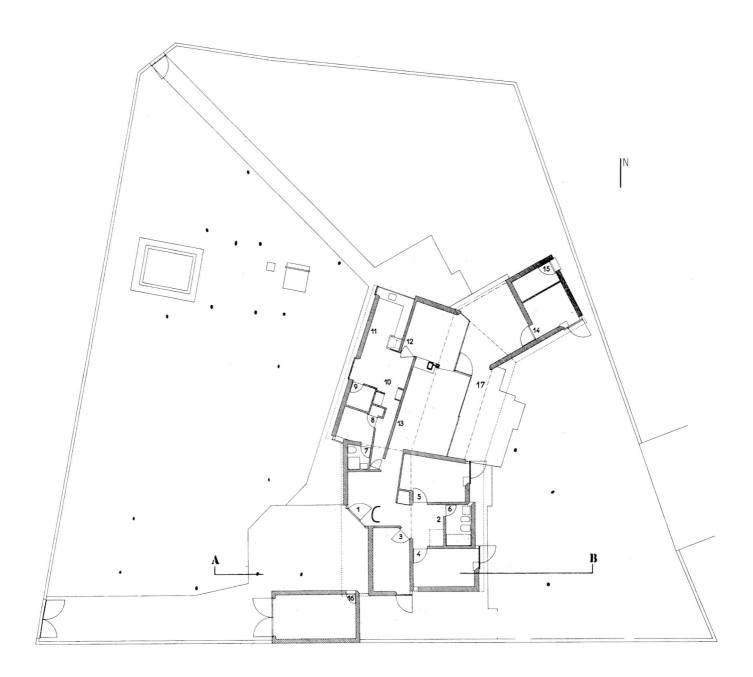

3. *Project elevations and cross sections (1:250)*
(Source: Álvaro Siza Archives, March 1960,
original scale 1:50)

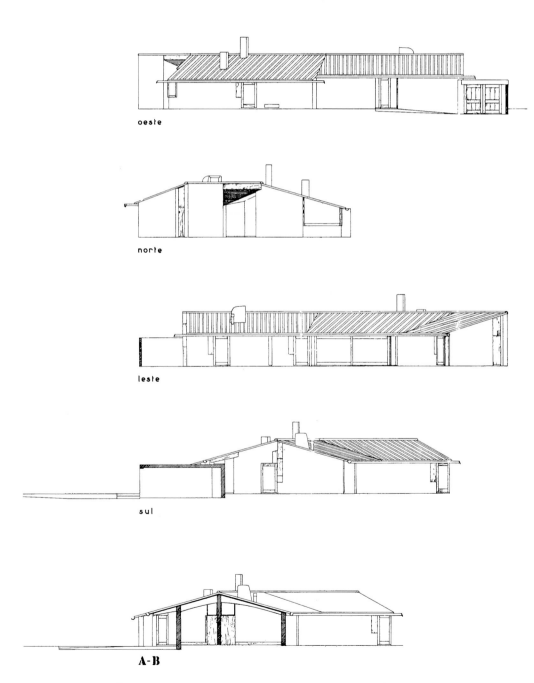

oeste

norte

leste

sul

A-B

4. *Expansion. Details of the windows
on the veranda*
(Source: Álvaro Siza Archives, undated)

Casa Rocha Ribeiro

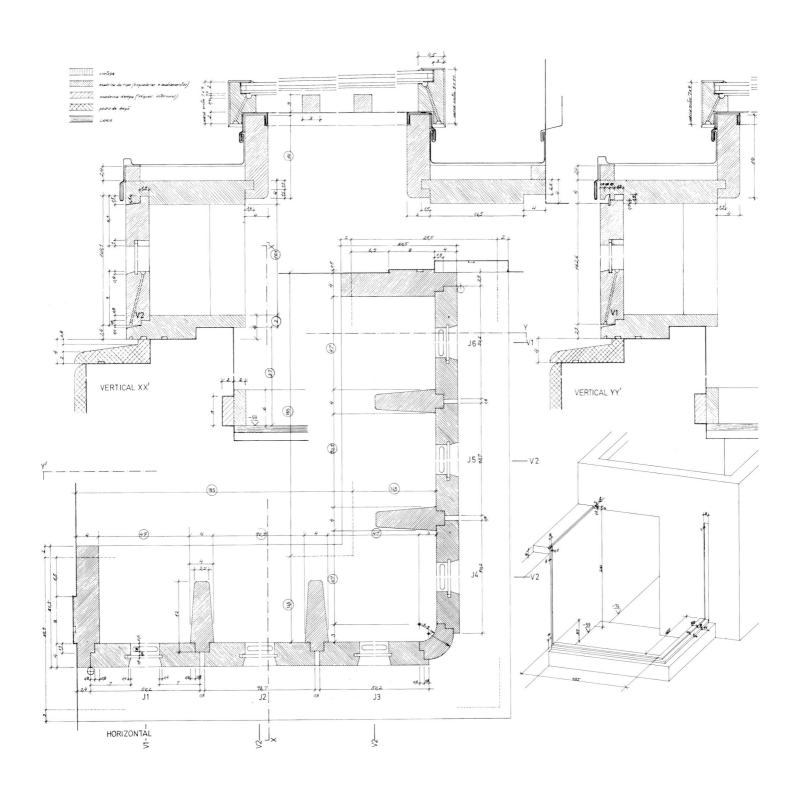

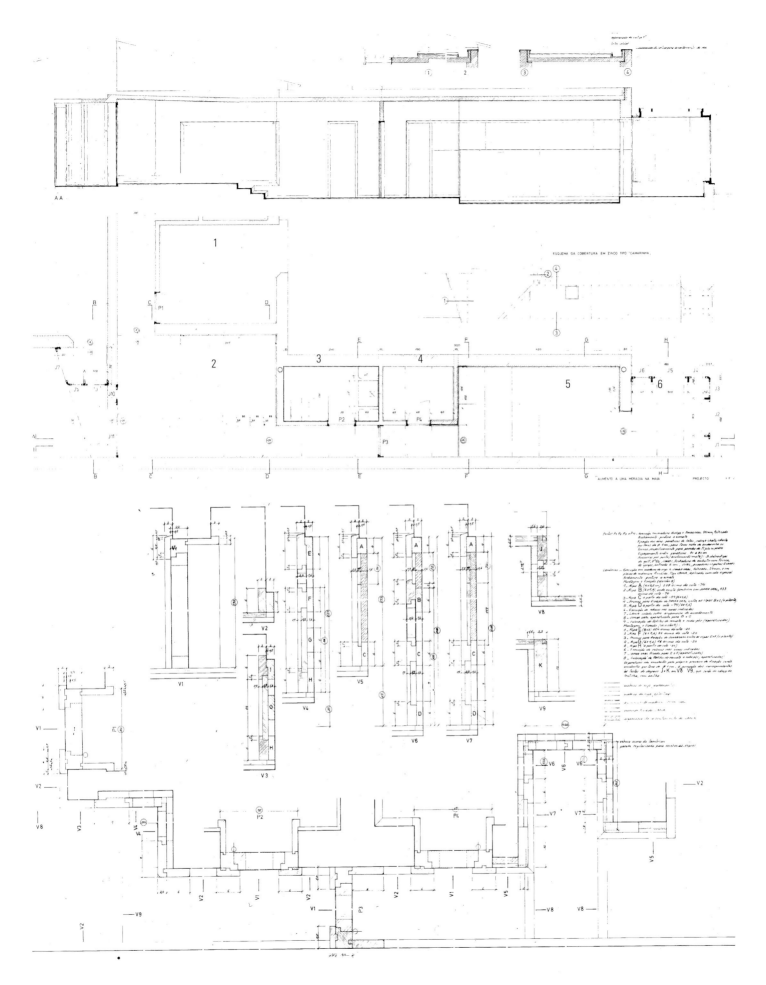

5. *Expansion. Floor plan and cross section (1:100)*
1. Existing bedroom / 2. TV room / 3. Bathroom /
4. Wardrobe / 5. Two-bed bedroom / 6. Study
(Source: Álvaro Siza Archives, October 1969,
original scale 1:50; 1:20)

6. *Expansion. Details of the interiors*
(Source: Álvaro Siza Archives, October 1969,
original scale 1:2)

Descriptive Note

I visited this house on three different occasions: each time I had the opportunity to reflect on an aspect of some new detail, with the feeling that this, more than other houses, is a work marked by an unusually generous dedication to the domestic life. The marvellous little construction shows all its mechanisms and deriving devices, and is lavished with handwork and affection. Inside, as the owner explained to us, it does not seem as if we are on a street in an ordinary urban setting. A sense of protection, intimacy, distance, material quality is what most satisfies the owners, a magistrate and his wife who have lived there for more than forty years. Now they are alone, before with four children, the house was enlarged for the birth of another child. Two grandchildren are visiting the grandmother and play in the garden. The light is warm and faint, evening light. Maia is an anonymous and chaotic place – like many of the areas surrounding Oporto; the irregularly shaped lot is at the corner of two streets. It is broken down into two zones – front and back: the large garden on the street and the small garden-patio on the interior, protected by the house. These two spaces communicate physically through the portico, but they are visually separate. The house seems modest in size, a horizontal volume on one level, with perimeter walls that are just higher than 2 metres and with a slightly angled two-pitch roof. The design of the wooden components – with their heat and colour – has a representative character, beyond the narrow issue of functionality, which contrasts nicely with the simplicity of construction.

The house's floor plan is broken up into functional zones, variously arranged, constituting an arc that surrounds an existing tree, recently replaced. All the rooms open onto the internal garden, with

the exception of the kitchen and the front hall. The quality of construction of the entire house is very high, a piece of craftsmanship that would be unattainable nowadays: we are told that a very good carpenter was vital to the job. Maintenance over the years was easy and inexpensive. All of the openings offered an opportunity for design and quality. Let us consider the large board that covers the entire thickness of the roof, beginning from the central high point: it is inserted into the wall on a line with the plaster as if it were a supporting beam, even though it is a covering element. But this symbolic dimension of the detail, which has a theoretical aspect, slips constantly, and without sharp distinction, into the more intimate aspects of practical mechanisms. This difficult synthesis is one of the explicit goals of the design.

Painstaking details, minutia in resolving junctions, profusion in the work; complicity with the client, to the point of "using" the client as an ergonomic model to fix, directly on the construction site, the height of the glass in the entry door or that of the wooden wainscoting in points of passage. The magistrate shows us the exact measurement of his shoulder and his eye at those points.

Other examples. From the kitchen window, behind the working surface, you can see the corner gate. It has a special design, with abstract lines and fittings between wood and wall, resolved with minimal gaps, highly effective in figurative terms: the fixed part of the gate is in fact raised slightly from the ground and shifted a few centimetres on the high side. The two gaps, we are told, are justified: the one on the side made it possible for the chain of the bell to be pulled out, while the one at the pavement made it possible to see a person's shoes and recognize him, since faces were hidden by the high door. The kitchen has high

openings, above the working counter: the main window is very large, extending to the ceiling, and it is fixed in place. Next to it is a small corner window, which swings out to open ensuring good and unobtrusive ventilation.

The bedrooms: they have French doors that open outwards, a narrow fixed corner window and a blind door with an internal mosquito screen, raised from the ground by a small seat integrated into the frame. This seat linked to the window is a typical element of Portuguese houses. The entire house is custom designed and is close in size to our body; the dimensions are minimal, and the space is perceived as a comfortable, tactile enclosure. The same is true of the ceiling, which links the spaces and extends out to the porches. In just one point, under the peak of the roof, it is broken to show the reinforced concrete structure, and thus to reveal that it is a covering. The same reasoning applies to the visible pillar, only partly covered. The ceiling is, or appears, "Aaltian", as do other details, such as the design of the external pavement. This introduces the theme of references, which are an important part of the project. They are not concealed, nor are they concocted by critics; rather they are signs of a profound and wide-ranging training. The short description that Siza prepared for *Hogar y Arquitectura* is especially significant. Like his designs and architecture, it is exemplary in how it describes a working method. It is a simple operating plan consisting of successive steps of reasoning: respect regulations and standards, adapt the structure to the terrain, establish an ideal scale, rationalise the system of construction, gain the client's consensus.

Another interesting aspect of this house is constituted by the addition, realised after some ten years; on this occasion, Siza

explores the theme of the relationship between the existing and new construction within his own work.

The added structure does not change anything; it presents itself discreetly, but it performs an expressive shift and avoids any direct confrontation on such characteristic structural elements as windows. The horizontal volume is inserted beneath the gutter to obtain a clean attachment, and an existing window is modified in connection with that. There is no new opening in the blind wall, some 10 metres in length, but only a square veranda, completely glassed in, at the far end, serving as a study. The details are minimal and endow this construction a linear and neutral character: the roof is flat, made of zinc, and the frames on the veranda are painted white. There is not a single piece of unpainted wood. Along the interior path, however, the levels follow the slight incline of the land, and they are articulated at three different levels. It is therefore the theme of small changes in elevation that Siza explores to give the entire residence a certain continuity: here we rediscover the sensations of the shifts and the delicate links present in the first construction; thus the ramp, a little dark and mysterious, between the kitchen and the entrance, is perceived as a very strong passage and reference. This addition was, finally, an opportunity for a new awareness of a path that had never been interrupted. For this reason, too, I think that the house in Maia is a successful project, and constitutes a very fertile area for study.
EM/AC
(Travel Notes, October 1999/April 2002)

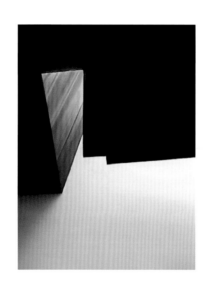

Casa Júlio Gesta

Rua de Afonso Cordeiro,
Matosinhos, Portugal

Client: Júlio Gesta

Collaborator: Beatriz Madureira

Lot area: 300 sq. m.
Built area, ground floor: 130 sq. m. + 20 sq. m.
Garage: 20 sq. m.
Portico: 55 sq. m.
Second storey: 85 sq. m.

Project Description

The house extends over two storeys, with an opening towards the east and the west; its interior spaces are organised in such a way as to avoid rigid subdivisions by zone, without compromising comfort and functionality. At the centre of the house, then, are the dining-room and the living-room, adjoining, with an opening that links the two storeys, bounded by the access corridors leading to the bedrooms (on slightly offset levels). The fireplace in the hall, or great room, with the vertical chimney and the large skylight, characterises this space destined, in particular, to family life. The service rooms, with independent access, constitute a nucleus that participates in a less direct manner than the other spaces, for normal purposes of use.

The exterior space constitutes an extension of the interior (to the east) or the entryway (to the west) in which the roof over the enclosed spaces and the garage, merging with the volume of the house, delimits a patio of carefully defined proportions, in which it has been possible to preserve a handsome existing pine tree. The construction, fairly economic – in the sense of economies in resolving the problem of maintenance – utilises stone or brick walls upon which brick attics are built, with elements of reinforced concrete where necessary. The roof is set on the lofts.

The interior and exterior walls are plastered and painted in white; the wooden window frames are painted and enamelled with a colour to be determined. Terracotta flooring (in rooms 2, 3, 4 and 11) and in ceramic tiles (for bathrooms, kitchen, pantry and rooms 6 and 9) and pine floor boards (in the other rooms). The walls of the bathrooms and of the kitchen will be covered with *azulejo* (Portuguese ceramics) tiles to a height of 2 metres.

A great deal of attention has been focused on the problems of lighting and ventilation. Efficient transverse ventilation has been assured, reinforced by the upper ventilation of the open space of the central zone; the ventilation of the bathrooms and the pantry has been resolved with spaces of natural ventilation. The kitchen was designed with openings in two opposite walls (east and west) as well as a hood over the cooking range.

The current appearance of the land, with the wall and the greenery that can be seen or glimpsed, remains almost untouched, due to the setback of the volume of the two storeys.

The lot is treated as a single construction, since it does not have the usual dead or open spaces around the house, constituting a sad caricature of a garden in most of our residential streets.

Álvaro Siza
Oporto, 8 October 1962

1. *Planning model*
(Source: Álvaro Siza Archives, undated)

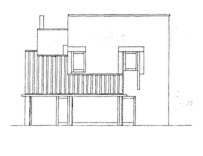

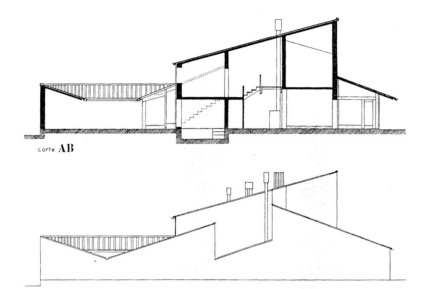

corte AB

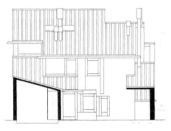

2. *Elevations and cross sections (1:250)*
(Source: Álvaro Siza Archives, August 1961,
original scale 1:100, 1:50)

3. *Ground and second storey floor plans (1:250)*
(Source: Álvaro Siza Archives, undated)

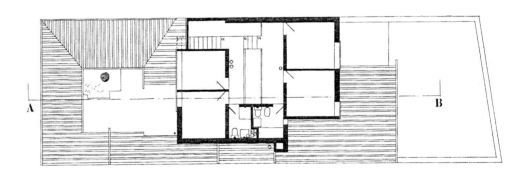

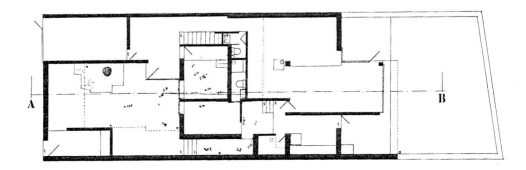

Casa Ferreira da Costa / Miranda Santos

Matosinhos, Portugal

Client: Fernando Ferreira da Costa / Miranda Santos

Collaborators first phase: António Madureira, Beatriz Madureira

Collaborators second phase: Jorge Nuno Monteiro, Tiago Faria, José Luís Carvalho Gomes

Lot area: 660 sq. m.
Built area: 185 sq. m.
Ground floor: 157 sq. m.
Second storey: 95 sq. m.
Garage: 28 sq. m. (first phase)

Project Description

The project refers to the house that Fernando Ferreira da Costa wished to build in the "Nova Urbanização da Azenha de Cima", in Matosinhos. The building in question occupies a corner lot, at the beginning of the access road to the shopping area of the zone. The placement and the study of the volumes proposed tend, on the one hand, to avoid the problems of a lot that was excessively visible and, on the other, to consider the relationship to the future adjoining buildings, and likewise the equilibrium among volumes built and free spaces. Therefore, certain inclines were established for the roofs, certain heights, and likewise the relationship between the garage designed and that of the adjoining lot, so as to obtain, in particular, a degree of equilibrium along the path towards the shopping area, a fundamental route within the urbanised area. A study of detail that, in the case of single-family homes, makes use of the design volumes indicated only as a point of departure, seems, for that matter, consistent with the spirit of the plan. The internal organisation of the lot is characterised by the lowering of the elevation of the ground floor in such a way as to obtain a volume in keeping with the dimensions of the land, and avoiding, at the same time, a problematic staircase for so small a house. The living-room occupies a large and fairly well articulated surface area

to make up for the small surface areas of the other rooms, which are however in compliance. This surface area includes zones differentiated by the articulations mentioned and the way the light hits. To the west, therefore, there is a strong relationship with the garden, so as to create an intensely lit area. To the east the wall has no opening, since this part of the hall receives light from both short sides, to the north indirectly, from the main glass door, and to the south from overhead, so as to obtain intense lighting near the fireplace, as well as an efficient ventilation. Thus, the zones most likely to be used enjoy an optimal lighting, making it possible to enjoy also the less brightly lit zones, a fundamental contrast in a house. The building, economic in nature, makes use of stone or perforated brick walls, upon which rest roof units made of perforated elements (attic loft and roof). The interior and exterior plaster is whitewashed and the window frames are made of painted wood. The floors are in terracotta, waterproof ceramic tiles and pine boards. The walls of the bathrooms and the kitchen are lined with ceramic tiles – *azulejo* – up to a height of 2 metres. The roof is made of Portuguese tiles.

Álvaro Siza, Oporto, 15 May 1963

Ferreira da Costa Residence

This last house was built after several "slightly larger" buildings. Maybe that is why it is less personal, less self-enclosed (which is not a question of fewer or more windows). What I have tried to do here is change certain preconceptions from my training, attempting to understand certain taboos. When I was designing it I determined that I was "sick of gables!" which I tried to give a broader meaning than simply being tired of roof tiles, and now I am working on a house with flat roofs, which we can now do, freed as we are from the ties of Neoplasticism, Corbu, Gropius, and many other gentlemen, Viana de Lima, Wright or… Aalto. We shall see if this is an illusion, or whether it was worthwhile for Tavora to design Ofir, at home, on a roll of paper that he then brought into the studio, and many of your writings, and reviewing Godinho, and the publication of the *Inquérito*.

Álvaro Siza, Oporto, 26 January 1967

Letter to Nuno Portas in *Siza. Writings on Architecture*, Skira, Milan 1997

1. *Overall view (1:2000)*
(Source: Camara Municipal de Matosinhos)

2. *Plan of the ground floor (1:250)*
1. Entryway / 2. Living-room / 3. Study / 4. WC
/ 5. Closet / 6. Study / 7. Kitchen / 8. Pantry /
9. Bedroom / 10. WC / 11. Garage
(Source: Álvaro Siza Archives, undated,
original scale 1:200)

3. *Plan of the second storey (1:250)*
12. Gallery / 13.-15. Bedrooms / 16. WC
(Source: Álvaro Siza Archives, undated,
original scale 1:200)

4. *Transverse cross section (1:250)*
(Source: Álvaro Siza Archives, undated,
original scale 1:200)

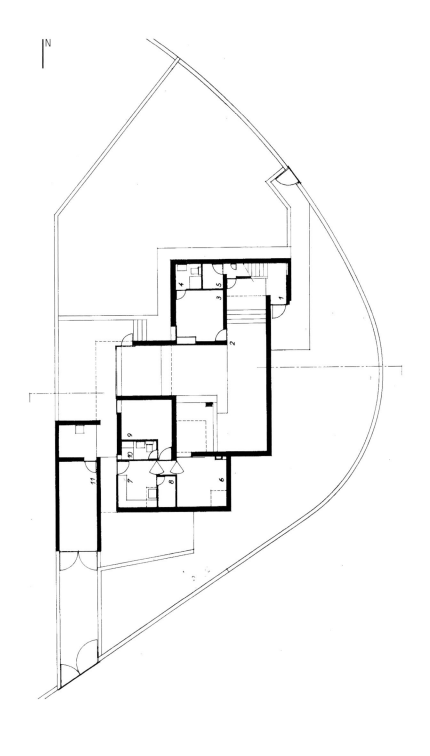

5. *Working details of the round glass table*
(Source: Álvaro Siza Archives, undated)

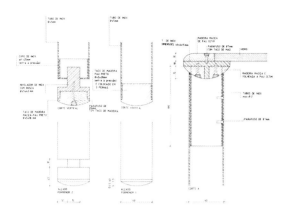

Descriptive Note

During our visit, we learned about the different phases of the construction and fine tuning of the house, following a succession of owners, even if the basic character of the house has remained unchanged. In fact, the theme of expansions has to do with the garage: the original structure was elongated, in two successive moments, until reaching all the way out to the road.

It is the originally designed furniture that over time has offered a further level of quality and interest to this project. Recently, moreover, the owner asked for a new garage for sport cars and motorcycles: this further structure is located to the north, with the opening of a second access to the road. This last volume has modified the equilibrium between the house and the garden, possibly reduced excessively. The house is today protected by dense vegetation and can barely be seen from the road. What can be perceived are the sharp lines of the volumes, the succession of the planes and inclinations that identify the complex. The residence extends over two storeys: the ground floor is much more extensive and intricate than the more compact upper floor. The articulation of the floor plan and the segmented, expanding silhouette of the volumes accompany the curving boundary line of the street in a balanced succession. The house is entirely closed towards the street, and only the main door offers a passageway. On the interior of the lot, a small, slightly sunken courtyard establishes a proportion for the space of outdoor life: this point offers the only large opening of the hall, or great room. This large space is a product of specific requests by the writer Luisa Ferreira da Costa: light is sensed in a diffuse, soft, overhead manner, and makes it easy to read and write at any moment of the day. The levels of the interior flooring are articulated into different zones: entryway,

dining-room, den, fireplace and parlour. In the middle of this generous space is set the only pillar in the complex, indicating the need for continuity and opening. Here, in contrast with other houses, this fluidity is especially resolved on the interior, to the point that we might think of this hall as an underground space. (In fact, it is slightly sunken.) The sense of protection and isolation from the outside world is an objective pursued with great clarity. The dining-room is also lit from above, without any direct openings, and functions as a connection with the service area (kitchen, pantry, service bedroom and bathroom). The single-pitch roof slopes gently down to cover the garage and laundry-room, separated by an outdoor passageway. At the far end, the entryway articulates the paths and connects the interior levels (sub-basement and upper floor) with the outdoor level of the garden. The movement that takes us from the walkway to the entryway requires a double rotation: the door is not visible from the street. The stairs lead to the bedrooms, which all look east, with distribution via a broad gallery closed at the end by the internal volume of the skylight, which lights the hall below and which, like the gallery, is lit by the opening in the western façade.

This project was part of the period of the *Inquérito* ("Arquitectura popular em Portugal", 1961), a research project that involved all of the architectural culture of Portugal and was quite influential. In this case, for instance, the wooden frames extend to cover the walls in a quest for a more abstract quality of the structure, aside from any narrow structural or functional demands. They seem to be elements of traditional origin, utilised however as continuous planes, or as fixtures that empty out corners, in a spare and abstract composition. All of the massive frames made of natural wood, meticulously finished, increase the powerful

simplicity of pure volumes. When, after twenty years, Siza took on the second phase of adjustment in response to the requests of the new owner, Miranda Santos, the requirements were quite different.

This is a project in which the principle is one of semantic densification of the work, a stratification of signs that are basically successive and easily identifiable, but at the same time, unified.

In the large hall and in the dining-room the overhead light is integrated by the opening of two new windows, both facing south, which indicate a need for more light and views to the exterior. We should note the character of the openings: as in the Maia house, wood is no longer used in its natural colour, but painted white and, especially, the openings are point-shaped – holes in the walls – with sills and features in marble. A principle that for Siza was not at the time practicable. The current owner, the son of Miranda Santos, thought this was a good time to build a "house-museum", in which all the furniture could be exhibited as an essential part of the architecture itself, and, with this view, undertook a frequent schedule of meetings with Siza. During this "persecution", he accompanied the architect from the apartment in which he lives to his studio, and sometimes took him to and picked him up from the airport, so that during the drive he could obtain a sketch, an idea, a correction or an approval. As a result, nearly all the fixed and movable furnishings are by Siza, and many of the objects are now produced on an industrial basis as well.

This enormous body of work, well documented by the magazine *Domus* (no. 759), expresses Siza's method with respect to furnishings. The design develops from the concrete nature of specific requirements, from the individual nature of each situation. It is a process that involves successive periods of reflection, reasoning, attempts,

extending to all the elements that make up the interior of a house: right down to the design of the house keys. These, conceived for both cupboards and cabinets and for doors, are small pieces of brass and stainless steel, fitting together, curved, for a specific placement in space, in relation to everything as well as to the mechanical gesture of opening. The repertoire of objects includes lamps, tables, pantries, seats, easy chairs, night tables, desks, stools, bookshelves, dressers, bathroom accessories and even keys.

There is a round table in the hall with a transparent surface: the glass is set nicely on a line with the wooden edge, which has a rounded corner to house the stainless steel structure, the legs with round cross section, establishing the four seating positions, slender and solid, with a rounded wooden insert as a small footrest, invisible to the eye. But the gaze roams, catching a small imperfection. It is one of the footrests: the leg is shorter, the piece of wood fits into a stainless steel ring that can be turned to adjust the height, to adjust for the floors of our houses, never quite level. "An exercise in design" as Pierluigi Cerri has pointed out "that takes on the smallest, most common elements of a system of objects that display no impossible technologies but rather an attention to that which is essential and accessible but shifted in direction sufficiently to reveal a certain disquiet, which is resolved in the priceless silences, the light footfalls, the precision of the surgery. A great lesson in poetics for those who show off unlikely exercises in style and excessive talent."
EM
(Travel Notes, April 2002)

Casa Rui Feijó

Moledo do Minho, Portugal

Client: Rui Feijó

Collaborator: António Madureira

Lot area: 395 sq. m.
House: 205 sq. m.

Excerpt from the Degree Thesis

… The request for an overall study is based on the wish to control personal and shared opinions, since in any case a simultaneous construction plan is not in the picture. Type of residence: with the possibility of being used on weekends and for relatively extended vacation periods, with a programme as follows: living-room with adjoining terrace, service area with kitchen, pantry, bathroom, service bedroom and an exterior annexe, three bedrooms with a bathroom (one master bedroom and the other bedrooms for two or three persons), covered space for automobiles. The choice was made to reduce the area of the bedrooms to allow for a fairly large living-room, with a focus on an internal organisation by zones. The block in which the group under study is located forms part of the first zone for which the preliminary project adopts a type of urbanisation "… with a free development of houses in the park, with the suppression of enclosure walls or other common urban characteristics [...] allowing the continuity of the National Park of Camarido towards the south" and taking into account, not a potential demographic increase, but rather the creation of a habitat that would be compatible with the dominant function of Moledo Beach [...] Deviation from the street so as to enable a superior adaptation to the ground and the insertion of the buildings into the zone at a higher lev-

el (on a line with the streets). Linear and peripheral insertion of the homes (conditioned by topography, access, prevailing winds) with inclusion of the following aspects: a) continuity between the houses with walls that enclose the exterior zones for owners and service, with evident advantages in terms of function and placement in the landscape; b) free central zone, protected from wind, preserving the extension of the land to the north and a generous transverse space between dwellings; c) different criteria in the relationship between the street and the house for the lots to the west and the east. The house on the street (only passage and parking spaces called for) is prevalently towards the interior of the block, facing west.

House set back and facing the street (with the possibility of a curtain of greenery for protection) to the east (despite the relationship with the interior – considered desirable – it should be reasonably protected for the surrounding constructions). … Finally, we would indicate the example of older local buildings on similar terrain, to the south, taken as reference as a criterion for the insertion into the landscape (there was no demand, in any case, for an integration in formal terms, nor a mimetic integration or an artificial transposition of effects).

Álvaro Siza

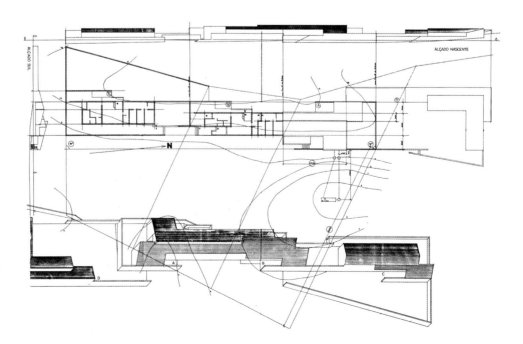

1. *Plan, elevation and overall axonometric plan*
Degree Thesis, 1965, 20 points
(Source: Álvaro Siza Archives)

2. *Floor plans, elevations and cross sections
(1:250)*
1. Hall, or great room / 2. Bathroom /
3. Bedroom / 4. Kitchen / 5. Pantry
(Source: Álvaro Siza Archives, February 1964,
original scale 1:100)

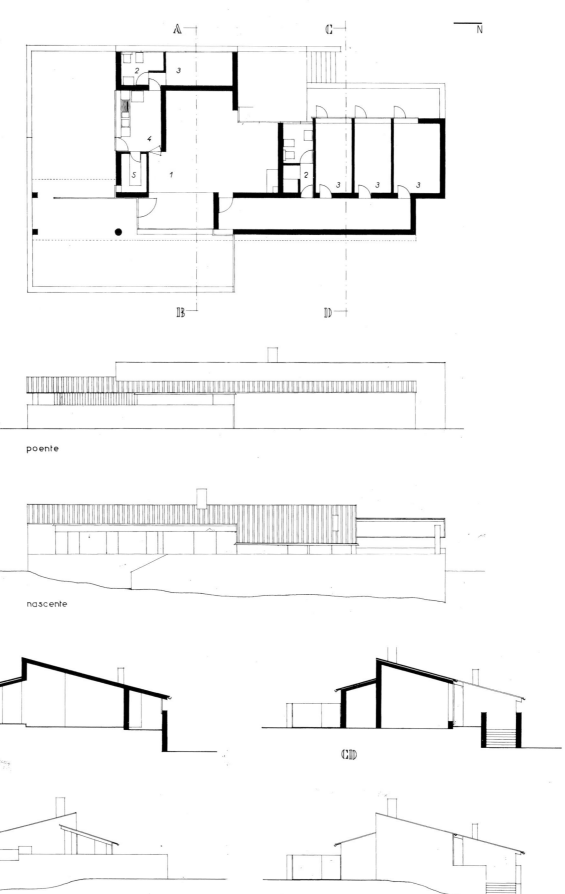

poente

nascente

AB   CD

norte   sul

Casa Alves Costa

Moledo do Minho, Portugal

Client: Henrique Fernando Alves Costa

Collaborators: António Madureira, Francisco Guedes de Carvalho, Alexandre Alves Costa

Lot area: 1310 sq. m.
Roofed area: 210 sq. m.
House: 177 sq. m.
Garage: 33 sq. m.

Project Report

The house was developed on a single storey, in a seashell shape, in relation to the topography of the land, so that the inhabited areas are turned towards the interior. The result of this principle is an exterior space, as an extension of the house, marked off by the volume of the building and the relief of the land, a space of sufficient intimacy, sheltered from the prevailing winds, that compensates the reduction to a minimum necessary of the covered area. The placement proposed is not exactly as indicated in the planimetric view of the urbanisation plan. All the same, since it is a result of a careful study of the land, it is not in any case out of keeping with the spirit of the plan, which basically calls for variations on the volumetrics indicated, as long as they are justified. The proposed built volume, which does not interfere with the silhouette of the landscape given that, without relying on excavations that would modify the terrain, it is located at the lowest elevation, seems to be the most appropriate. Special care has been devoted to respecting the topography, in the belief that altering it, on the interior of each lot, would entail the destruction of what constitutes one of the most positive aspects of the area: the landscape. The building is economic in nature: load-bearing walls in stone or brick, plastered and whitewashed, upon which rests the wooden roof structure. The window frames are made of wood, to be painted, and the floor is in waterproof ceramics.

Álvaro Siza, Oporto, 15 February 1965

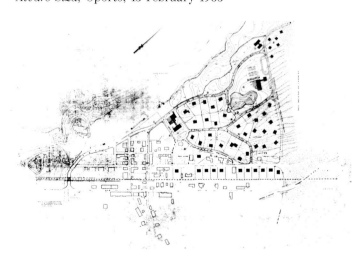

1. *Urbanisation plan for Moledo do Minho*
(Source: Álvaro Siza Archives, undated)

2. *Insertion into the urbanisation plan
(redesign, 1:2000)*
(Source: Álvaro Siza Archives, undated)

3. *Plan of the ground floor (1:250)*
1. Entryway / 2. Living-room / 3. Bedrooms /
4. Kitchen / 5. Garage
(Source: Álvaro Siza Archives, undated)

4. *Elevations (1:250)*
(Source: Álvaro Siza Archives, February 1965,
original scale 1:100)

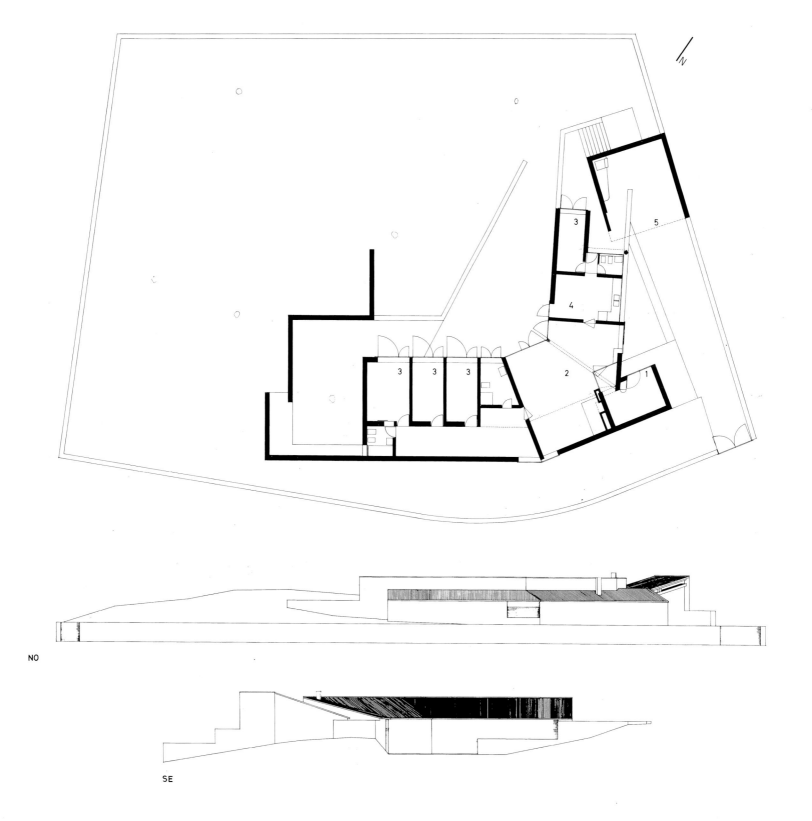

NO

SE

5. *Transverse cross sections, longitudinal cross section (1:250)*
(Source: Álvaro Siza Archives, February 1965, original scale 1:100)

6. *Detail study: vertical cross section of the southern façade, typical bedroom window*
(Source: Alves Costa Archives, undated)

CORTE CD

CORTE EF

CORTE AB

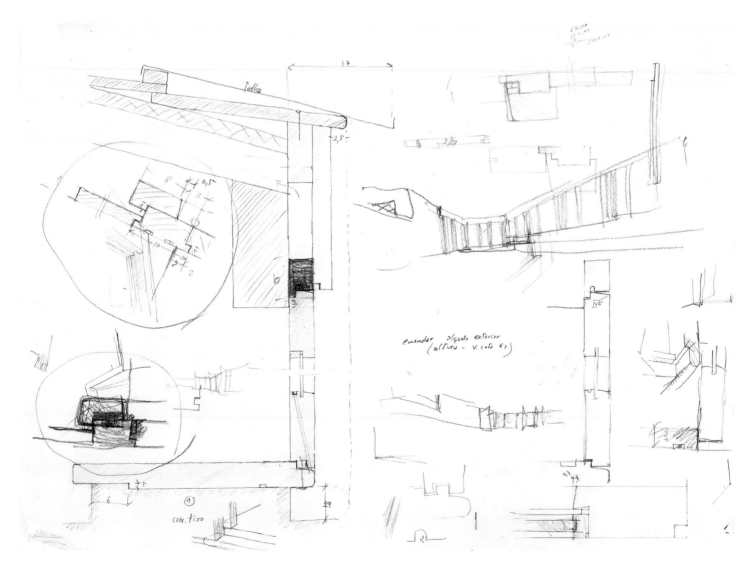

Notes from a Conversation with Alexandre Alves Costa

There was a wonderful relationship with my parents. Siza would spend a few days of vacation there and he would create an atmosphere of a certain intimacy with his clients. My father would say that people who wanted to have a house built on the beach want to see the water, this is normal. But Siza explained that it was also horrible to see the sea all day long, morning and evening: he wanted to create a different world. Now we say: "Bless the day that we decided to cut the view" and in the end it's not so surprising: the house is interior because it represents a separate world, in fact, it is a private home and it functions very nicely. Siza was seeking in that period a sort of protection from the outside world, an intimacy that was in fact very domestic and private.

But in my house everything is somewhat different. We should consider also that my parents were quite open-minded people, who always liked to have guests in their home, the door was never closed, people went in and out, and so it was necessary to reconcile this sense of extended community, and everyone could find a space of their own in the house.

The complexity of the hall is surprising. It is a reasonably open space, you can see everything, but there are also different corners, isolated, a little more private. The house has a sort of dual meaning: on the one hand it has this closed, labyrinthine aspect, and at the same time, you sense it as if it were a vacation house, a house for many people. In effect, it is a house that you need to see full, with plenty of people. It is an experience. It seems incredible that you can get thirty people in here and that everyone has a comfortable space. This point of compromise, between open and intimate, was one of my father's favourite

things. [...] There have been lots of changes during construction. At the time, it was not necessary to make complete projects, everything could be changed. Construction began with the plans submitted to the City Hall, which served to establish a flat rate. But then changes were very relaxed. In terms of method, questions were left open: "we'll see later", he used to say. Now that is certainly not possible... it was until the 1970s.

As for the construction, I believe that it was a fruitful and positive collaboration. The builder was very skilful, a man who built yachts, a refined and skilled woodworker. Siza learned a lot from him. He didn't mind not knowing something: he would ask, he wanted to know. And he did it in a very healthy way. The relationship between this woodworker and Siza was quite interesting, because he was much older and very proud. He would treat Siza badly and say to him: "you don't know a thing!" ... In reality, he considered him a genius, but without a submissive attitude. The house was built four years after it was planned, and I think it can be considered a transitional project.

It is a project made with great freedom. Construction was a fundamental moment, and Siza really liked to be in the construction yard, he would go there in the morning and stay all day. There was lots of time, lots of time to do things. Because, when we went to the construction site, it was for fun, to spend time, a whole day. To eat. Food was an important aspect. Siza likes this house, also because there is no designer furniture. My father did not have much money, neither did I, and so it is all sort of thrown together, and there is nothing to show off. [...]

My mother liked the way wood had been used in the house at Maia, but Siza managed to persuade her to paint the wood.

My mother would say: "it seems a pity to paint such nice wood". But Siza wanted it to have the same colour as the walls. The main material is space: space and not the design of details is the central theme. [...] In certain parts, it seems like a very small house, especially during the construction it seemed like a small house. My father would go to the construction site and lie down on the ground to get a sense of the space, and then they would talk and talk. I remember my father saying: "I can't sleep here." I have a great photograph: they are both there, Siza and my father, on the ground, to see whether two people could sleep in what would be a bedroom. Siza measured everything with the body... then, now not, now he already knows everything. But in effect, that is how it is. At least in his first projects.

Before this project, for instance, we took a trip to Santillana del Mar, near Santander. There is a very nice vernacular architecture there, that Siza liked very much, and which he liked to measure. In fact, the house has minimal dimensions, just the minimum to fit inside. Siza also liked a mosque in Fez very much, which has a remarkably low entrance, I think you can walk through it, but it feels as if you can't. A month ago, some Americans came, and they almost couldn't get in, they wouldn't fit. The ceiling was lowered in the bedrooms and in the passageways, to get out, where you have the feeling you need to duck down, even though you fit just fine. Even the Americans, in the end, fit through.

Oporto, 3 October 1999

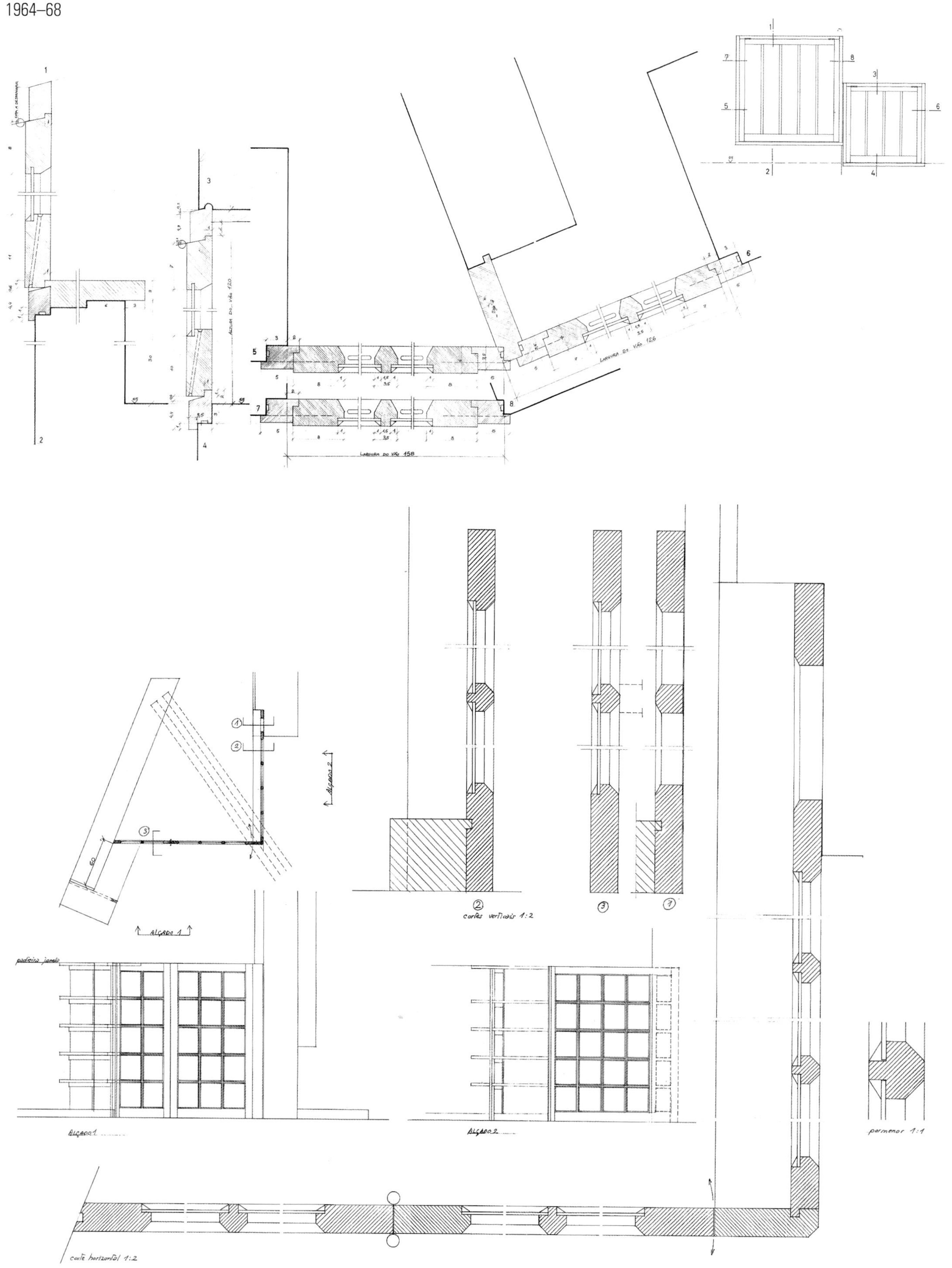

ALÇADO 1

cortes verticais 1:2

ALÇADO 2

parmenor 1:1

ALÇADO1

ALÇADO2

corte horizontal 1:2

7. *Working detail of the window frames
on the north side*
(Source: Alves Costa Archive, undated,
original scale 1:20; 1:2)

8. *Working detail of the entry screen*
(Source: Alves Costa Archive, undated,
original scale 1:20; 1:2; 1:1)

9. *Preliminary sketch. Entry and garage*
(Source: Alves Costa Archive, undated)

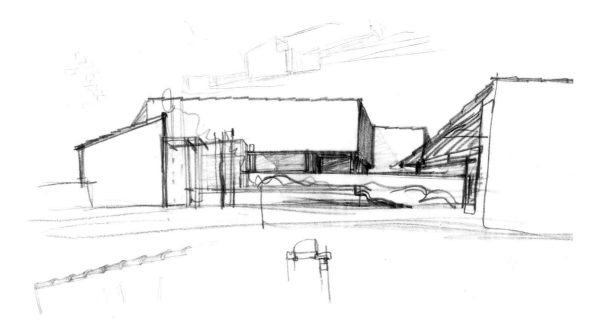

Descriptive Note

Just over an hour's drive from Oporto, along the road leading to the north of Portugal, towards Galicia and the mouth of the Minho, Moledo is an elegant vacation spot between the ocean and the hilly interior, with plenty of greenery.

We visit the house for the first time late one morning, the light is milky, someone left the door to the living-room open, the night before there was a party. We are invited to come back, to stay: two years later, accompanied by Sergio Fernandez, who worked on the construction of the house. He fleshes out details, confirms our hunches, and tells us about a particularly successful project in terms of the friendship and esteem among client, architect, collaborators and craftsmen.

The house is close to the beach, deep in a pine grove. It turns its back to the beach, to the sea, almost entirely devoid of openings onto the road. A system of blind walls prevails. It opens towards the interior, instead, towards the pines, to the southeast. An intimate, cozy dimension, at first sight anomalous for a beach house. But the presence of the ocean is in the wind, suggested by the sand among the pines. When it was built, there was no other building to protect against, no specific need for isolation: the other buildings came later. But from the very beginning this was an inward-turning, closed house. By Siza's attitude and wish in those years, by a sort of anticipatory defense and for reasons of a rational order contained in the project description. The latter is extremely significant, because of the attention paid both to the question of the scale of the landscape and that of the house's intimacy. Questions of such importance as to contradict the general plan of urbanisation. The house is configured in a "L" shape, with a light double rotation, and a single storey:

it presents itself as closed and low, well integrated among the pine trees, with a pitched roof with Portuguese tiles, uniformly towards the interior, only in part towards the street.

The covered area is distributed into three zones: on the one side, the zone with three bedrooms and two bathrooms, in the middle the hall, or great room, and the entryway, on the other side the service area, with kitchen, service bedroom and bathroom, garage and laundry-room. The openings face out over the pine grove, with the exception of the kitchen, turned towards the entrance. In this exterior space, which is separated visually from the garden, a cement podium, raised over the ground, constitutes an external extension of the house as a separation from the vehicle access point. From here, the path that leads to the pine grove is not direct, but follows a labyrinthine sequence, articulated around the intersection with the garage. The movement that must be made in order to enter the house is likewise labyrinthine, obliging a double rotation. In fact, the entry door is not even visible from the street.

The house lies languidly on the terrain, opened towards the pine grove with a continuous system of doors and windows. Patios bounded by retaining walls link the levels and define three different areas of reference. In particular, one of these cement walls, which contains on a diagonal that little bit of terrain, marks off an exterior level space upon which the space of the hall opens out. Moreover, it marks a support or bench among the pines. The hall is the principal space of the house, a linking space that can be crossed from all sides. Even in its reduced size, it has a complex configuration, composed of different and continuous environments. The two doors that link the hall to the sleeping zone and the service zone are identical, glassed in, with a double-casement movement, to ensure a certain fluidity. The hall can also be opened to the entry zone: the large square window is actually a large sliding door that connects it to the exterior entry podium. The roof is sloped and this makes it possible to differentiate the space and orient it: the area of the fireplace is perceived in fact as a more intimate and private corner, with a targeted light. The dining-room table, instead, enjoys dual, open views, with the oblique covering of the side wall, a reference to the roof, identifying its setting. A false drawer made of natural wood corresponding with the diagonal beam, the only unpainted element, is in fact the support for a specially designed lamp: it represents at the same time an element of fragility and a sophisticated and disquieting complexity of thought. In the hall, or great room, but throughout the house, one has the impression of a very strong sense of attained domesticity: in the way people assemble or sit separately, moving through the house, looking around, setting down an object. Everything has a place. An inward-looking house, which, by the character and the life style of the owners, finds in the hall a way of greeting dozens of guests in parties and meetings with a "strong sense of community."

Work on details is present but disguised, so as to allow space and the way that space is filled become the principal material. It is in this house that wood no longer appears in its natural form, but is for the first time covered with paint entirely.

The window frames are lined up with the outer surface, and the windows, whether casement or swinging, are thus turned outwards. As the only system of screening the light, curtains are used that can be rolled up on bamboo poles, a material that suggests life on the beach. It is possible to observe in the structural details that this

frame is actually designed as a covering that rises to the roof. On the opposite side of the house, on the other hand, the window frames of the kitchen and the service bathroom are located on a line with the interior wall: this is a long strip window with a swinging opening.

Alexandre Alves Costa talks to us about the slow gestation of the windows in the front facing the street, the general problems Siza encountered in those years in designing openings in elevations, of the way he made use of two possible, extreme alternatives: completely closed or completely open. In fact, in the initial design, there was no plan for any openings in the façade facing the street: the two windows were added only during construction. This is a pair of offset windows, which have a very specific dimensional relationship, and which are located exactly on the corner. On the interior, they are also very important. The window frame has an unusual design, like a *loophole*, utilised only towards the street and echoed in the glass entry door. It is a matter of hierarchies, specifying the nature of each element: wall, diaphragm and opening each find a comprehensible placement on the interior of the general strategy.

The interior-exterior duality, a constant in Siza's early houses, is in this case not only the reason for the different design of the window frames, but also a different expressive quest. In particular, we see a study design referred to the entry area that in Alves Costa's opinion inaugurates Siza's move towards a greater design independence. The first designs of the Casa Magalhães date from the same period. These are pure volumes, with hollows, slashes, intersections, which were moreover made possible only by the use of reinforced concrete: the construction system used in Moledo was still hybrid, that would

no longer be the case in Oporto.

The gutter was a significant element that expressed this tension towards a more experimental language and, at the same time, the critical abandonment of the traditional systems as a privileged vehicle of expression. Characterised by a rectangular cross section, the gutter was no longer made of copper but was painted white and was slightly separated from the roof: a minimum space to express autonomy.

The roof is composed of load-bearing beams and small secondary wooden beams. At the point of greatest span, on the diagonal convergence of the pitches of the roof, the beam is double and exposed to view, emerging from the false ceiling; it is supported by a wooden pillar. In a system of load-bearing walls, this single corner pillar opens the house towards the pine grove.

The false ceiling is a further element of quality. Taken as an interior covering, it consists of conglomerate panels that are painted: it appears as a membrane and punctuates the space, dividing it into partitions.

A slight but evident chromatic discontinuity marks the passage between the interior and the exterior. On the exterior, the colour is colder: window frames, gutters and plaster are all painted in pure white. On the interior, the space is homogeneous and extensive, and the soft and luminous tones of warm white prevail (almost a crème colour) on walls, ceilings and finishings of all the wooden parts; the ceramic of the floors is sand coloured; the curtains are in bamboo. It is possible to sense, on the interior of the house, the presence of the pine grove, of the beach, of the sea.

AC/EM
(Travel Notes, October 1999/November 2001)

Casa Adelino Sousa Felgueira

Oporto, Portugal

Client: Adelino Sousa Felgueira

1. *Preliminary studies*
(Source: Álvaro Siza Archives, undated)

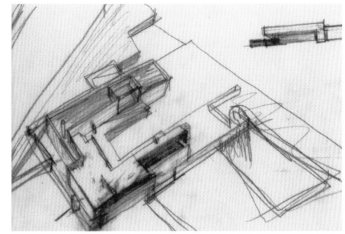

Casa Alves Santos

Rua Padre Afonso Soares,
Póvoa de Varzim, Portugal

Client: Manuel Alves dos Santos

Collaborators: António Madureira, Francisco Guedes
de Carvalho

Lot area: 1150 sq. m.
Roofed area: 215 sq. m.
Ground floor: 170 sq. m.
Second storey: 80 sq. m.
Porticoed areas: 45 sq. m.

Project Description

Developing in an "L", the floor plan of the house defines an exterior space, sheltered from the dominant winds that blow from the two respective sides (north and west), and bounded to the south and east by the enclosure wall of the lot.

This space entails an exterior extension of the principal spaces of the ground floor (living-room and dining-room, study and work-room).

The service zone extends to the east with a partially roofed patio. The zone of the bedrooms develops on the upper storey, looking south.

The construction is based on traditional methods and materials: load-bearing walls and partition walls made of stone and brick, lofts on the second storey and the roof in perforated elements, with reinforced concrete structures where indicated in the design.

The roof is covered with tiles and the walls are plastered and painted white both on the exterior and interior, with coverings of ceramic tiles to a height of 2 metres in the kitchen and the bathrooms.

The floors are made of terracotta (ground floor), pine boards (second storey) and waterproof ceramic tiles (kitchen, pantry and bathrooms). Window frames, interior and exterior, made of wood, to be painted.

Álvaro Siza
Oporto, 7 February 1966

1. *Setting (1:2000)*
(Source: Camara Municipal do Póvoa de
Varzim, April 2002, original scale 1:2000)

N

2. *Plans of the floor, cross sections, elevations (1:250)*
1. Atrium / 2. Hall, or great room / 3. Service / 4. Study / 5. Kitchen / 6. Pantry / 7. Bedroom / 8. Service / 9. Work-room / 10. Portico / 11. Portico / 12. Garage / 13. Access-room / 14. Service / 15.-18. Bedrooms / 19. Service / 20. Terrace
(Source: Álvaro Siza Archives, May 1966, original scale 1:100)

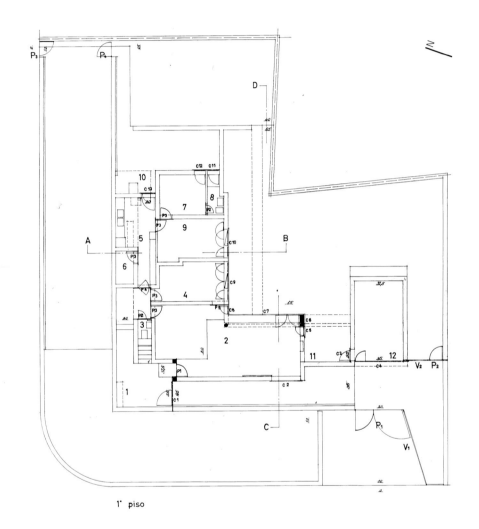

1° piso

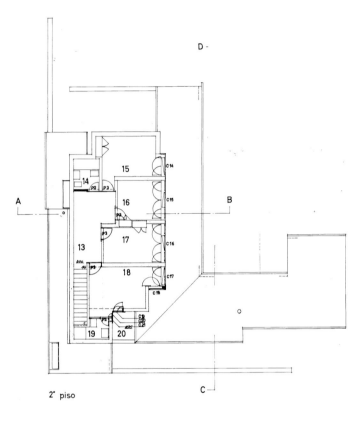

2° piso

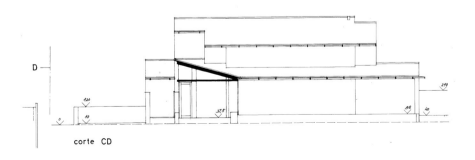

corte CD

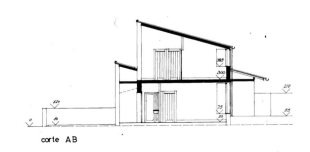

corte AB

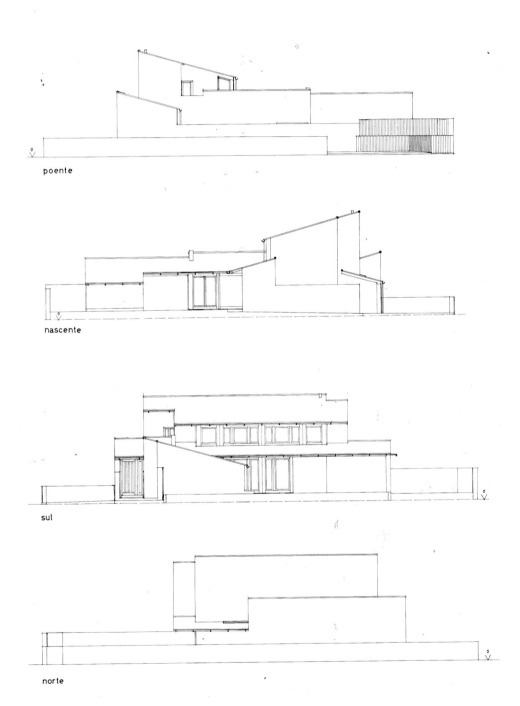

poente

nascente

sul

norte

3. *Detail of the skylights*
(Source: Álvaro Siza Archives, December 1967,
original scale 1:20; 1:2)

4. *Detail of the flashings and gutters*
(Source: Álvaro Siza Archives, February 1968,
original scale 1:5; 1:100)

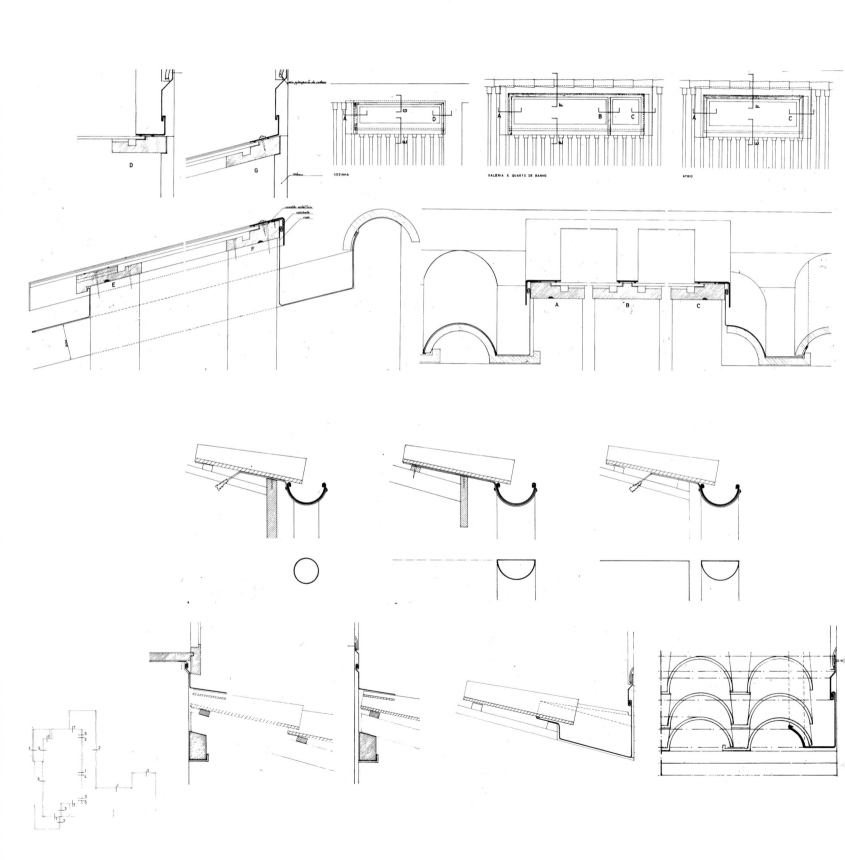

Descriptive Note

The commission for the house came through a common acquaintance who told the clients about the talent of the young Siza. During the construction which went on longer than expected, a solid relationship developed between client and architect: Siza went often to the house for meetings and dinners. The relationship remained a close one. Our tour took place in the company of the owner, and was filled with feelings of sadness and affection, rich in anecdotes. She is alone now, and she showed us every space and detail of the house in which she lived for forty years, which coincide day by day more and more with the memories of her life. The house is situated on a small regularly shaped corner lot, like many others, along a residential street in Póvoa. The nature of the house is inward-looking, as it is completely closed to the exterior (the neighbours spoke of the *wall of shame*, of a *warehouse*). The blind walls of the two fronts facing the road are load-bearing walls upon which the roof rests directly, with a single pitch, extending to shelter the interior fronts, totally open and characterised by a continuous window frame. The composition of the structure is therefore mainly entrusted to the counterpoint between a completely closed part and a completely open one, resolved in contrasting ways.

The entry route has a strongly architectural character, obtained with walls that extend the building limit of the lot, subdividing the exterior spaces and directing the movements.

A blank door, blind as the walls, leads into the house. In effect, the house is above all gathered into a dimension of intimacy, sought in the interior space. The rigour of the layout and the consistency of the constructive system adopted can be seen in a construction in which the "L"-shaped floor plan divides two worlds: the exterior world and the rich and comfortable domestic space. And so, on one hand everything is constrained to the most radical abstraction, exceedingly refined in its lines and the succession of vertical planes, in which even the sole opening of the great room towards the street – the square window – fits into the blind wall with a window painted white and flush with the wall. On the other hand, on the interior, we witness instead the creation of its opposite, a world made for sensations, in which expressivity is based on tactile and optical perception. This world is made up both of the vegetation in the garden and the construction materials. The garden is rich in plants and colourful flowers arranged around a small lawn.

The structure envelops it with planes of natural wood and glass, zinc and tiles. If there is a downspout, it is painted red. The possibility of a total closure of the glass parts by means of wooden panels, internal and on both storeys, constitutes a sumptuous sheathing for the entire façade. (Particularly noteworthy are the ten book-folding panels that are stored in the corner of the hall).

This membrane of wood and glass envelops the patio and allows the rooms to expand in continuity with the garden.

The interior-exterior continuity is marked by the emptying of the corner in the hall, obtained by the use of a point of support in reinforced concrete, as a sole exception to the structural system of load-bearing stone walls. On the interior, the window frames with fixtures in natural wood (red Kambala) are covered, in part by pink curtains. A diffuse pinkish, warm hue, extends to the colour of the sofa and the bedcovers, and to the floors in "Spanish ceramics", blending with the southern light that enters from the garden, mediated by the porticoed space and the vegetation. This tone contrasts with the colder tone that characterises the service spaces, all arranged to the north. Here a few points of entry for overhead light, small and well postioned, resolve the illumination of the blind zones of the house in a very efficient manner. The contrast of the chromatic tones of the interior spaces, cold on one side and warm on the other, underscores and emphasises the dual character of the construction. The roof gutters in the back, on the kitchen side, painted white. There is also a contrast in the way that the roof gutters are coloured: white towards the street, red towards the garden. Everything converges.

Another constant theme is that of the substantial work on the ground. Small shifts in the ground floor introduce variations in elevation. On the one hand they resolve the vertical connection in the two-storey structure: as previously in the Casa Ferreira da Costa, the ground floor is slightly sunken, so that the staircase that leads to the upper floor is shorter and more appropriate for a smaller house. These differences in elevation are, moreover, a way to find the correct relationship in scale between interior space and garden. All of the rooms are at a lower elevation that renders much closer and more intimate the perception of the garden: seating upon an easy chair in the great room it is possible to appreciate the precision of the measurements. The horizontal ceiling emerges in continuity and the height of the portico thus appears lower than that of the great room: these variations in height are fundamental in controlling the succession of spaces.

The work on construction details is exhaustive and intelligent. If you look carefully at the working sketches, the blueprints of the roof feature a plan with the indications of the various fastenings and gutters, resolved as well in cross section one by one in the appropriate scale; the blueprint of the skylights, with the glass laid over the frame and the theme of zinc flashings, completes the indications for the roof. These are two simple blueprints, with clear, fine lines, precise texts, which testify to the pleasure of the profession, the delight of resolving the construction and with it the character of the work.

The Casa Alves Santos is in some ways a work of closure, the point of arrival in a path that is upheld as well by the artisanal quality of the builders, who were still available at the time: a path that began with the Boa Nova restaurant and carried on for nearly a decade, in a Portuguese setting in which – as Siza wrote – "from the tension between Regionalism and Internationalism, a possible identity was being designed, made up of continuity and contrast".

"A house is like an outfit, it is like a shawl in which we wrap ourselves", says the owner. Then, remembering a conversation, she repeats a typical answer of Siza's: "… it's not much, but it's enough": these simple words are fixed in our minds as an absolute truth.

EM
(Travel Notes, November 2001/April 2002)

Casa Manuel Magalhães

Avenida dos Combatentes, Oporto, Portugal

Client: Manuel A.C. Magalhães

Collaborators: António Madureira, Francisco Guedes de Carvalho

Lot area: 485 sq. m.
Roofed area: 152 sq. m.
House: 115 sq. m.
Portico: 18 sq. m.
Garage: 37 sq. m.

Manuel Magalhães Residence
This project reflects a moment of interruption in a slow development in two directions: that of a quest for a more open language referred, though in a limited sense, to certain influences, and that of a greater, less selective and also more detached involvement in the conditions of the place.

Álvaro Siza
Oporto, May 1979

From an Interview
"On this street, where the houses are large, it is possible to live in bedrooms overlooking the street, or else close up and look out over the garden. In effect, when you walk down a well-to-do street of Oporto like this, you never see people at the window, their life goes on without any contact with the outside world. Windows and balconies that overlook the street are used only for religious processions. When it is necessary to go open the door, it is a servant who actually moves. It was not possible to build a mansion, it would have been too expensive, and so we built a house overlooking the garden. This house in Oporto reflects this fundamental characteristic of bourgeois life which intends to preserve the intimacy of the family."

Interview with Álvaro Siza, Oporto, 8 September 1977, published in *AMC*, no. 44, 1978

1. *Setting (1:2000)*
(Source: Camara Municipal do Porto)

N

2. *First version of the project*
(Magalhães Family Archives, March 1968,
original scale 1:100; 1:50, design approved,
13 February 1969)

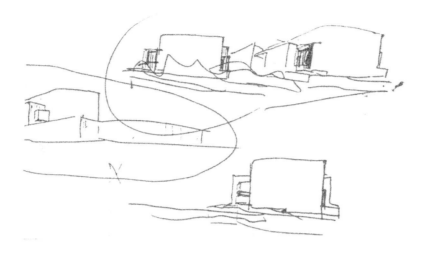

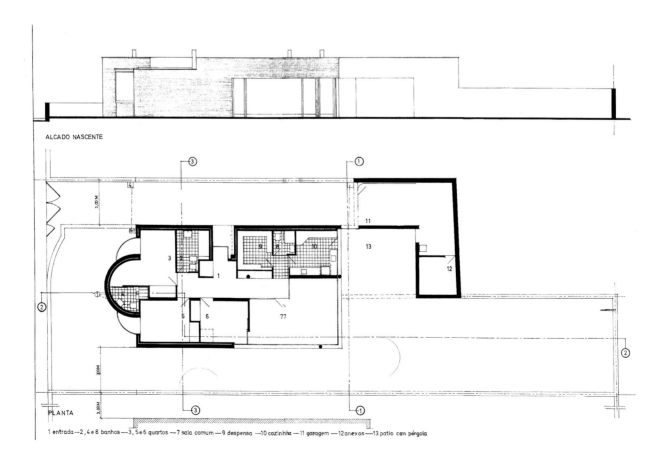

ALCADO NASCENTE

PLANTA

1 entrada — 2 , 4 e 8 banhos — 3 , 5 e 6 quartos — 7 sala comum — 9 despensa — 10 cozinhha — 11 garagem — 12 anexos — 13 patio com pérgola

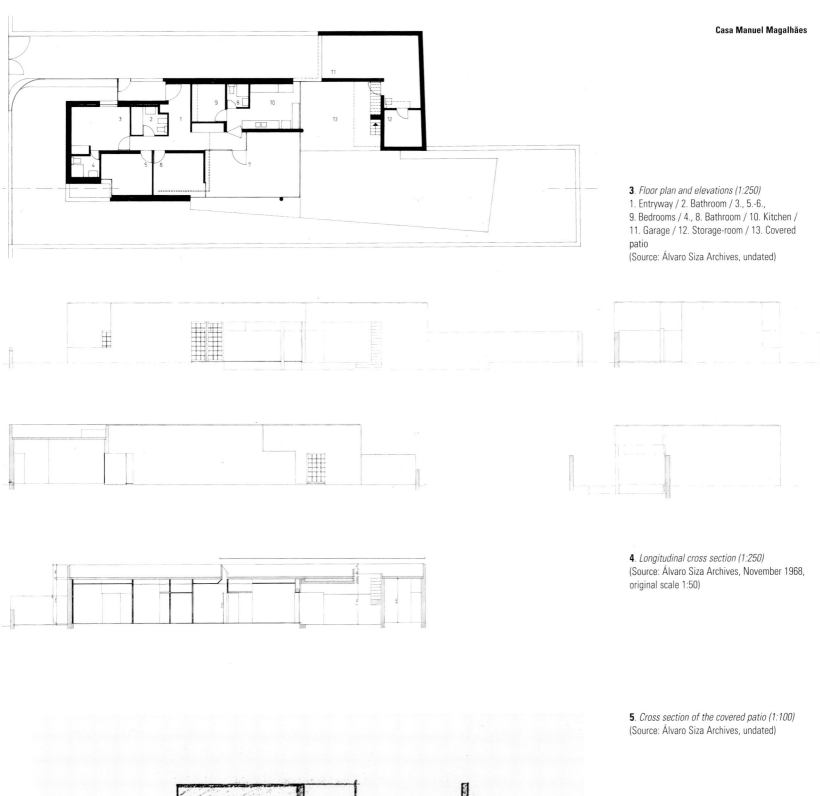

3. *Floor plan and elevations (1:250)*
1. Entryway / 2. Bathroom / 3., 5.-6.,
9. Bedrooms / 4., 8. Bathroom / 10. Kitchen /
11. Garage / 12. Storage-room / 13. Covered
patio
(Source: Álvaro Siza Archives, undated)

4. *Longitudinal cross section (1:250)*
(Source: Álvaro Siza Archives, November 1968,
original scale 1:50)

5. *Cross section of the covered patio (1:100)*
(Source: Álvaro Siza Archives, undated)

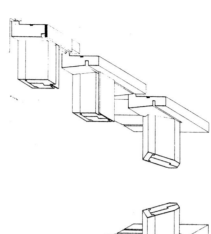

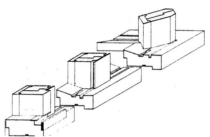

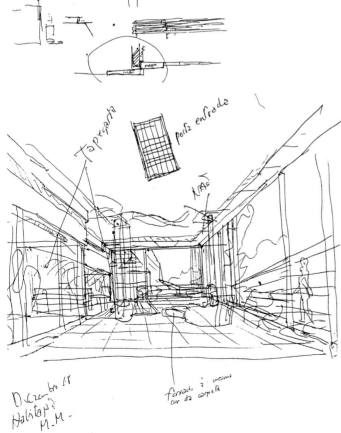

Descriptive Note

This project is the product of the wish, on the part of the client, a lawyer in Oporto, to build a small rental residence in a lot adjoining a house he owns. From a real estate investment, the house is soon transformed into the family residence. Today, a grand daughter of Manuel Magalhães lives here. This is Antas, a residential quarter to the north of Oporto, along a silent, tree-lined street, characterised by middle-class, generally two-storey houses, surrounded by a garden. In general terms, this house has a number of innovative and singular aspects, since it was the first house with a flat roof and the only with visible reinforced concrete. It was Siza himself who later expressed with oblique bluntness the broader meaning of this project, in the context of his body of work. The lot is a narrow, deep rectangle. The placement of the two volumes – residence and garage – in relation to the form of the lot produces two well-defined exterior spaces, one in the back and one on the road, linked by a portico but visually separate.

The first thing that you notice, clearly, from the street, is the long line of the enclosure wall: a wall standing 1 metre tall, made of rough cement, crowned by sheet metal painted white, which runs, curving, towards the entrance of the house. Behind this double line of grey and white, the house appears as a prismatic volume made of cement with the principal elevation almost devoid of openings. The design of the gate, of the fixtures on the ground and the street address, are elements that express the quality of the residence from the outside. The enclosure wall is in fact this house's true façade.

The rough and horizontal volume is eroded, worked on, carved out: the joints between cement and metal, cement and glass and the corner hollow points are manipulations controlled with a sculptural sensibility. The house is characterised by the visible cement planes, punctuated only by the marks of the moulds and, on high, the green line of the copper flashing. The casting of the wall was shaped with a hollow a few inches deep, so that the flashing fits in without overlying the level of the façade, slightly inset. The green of the copper folds onto the grey cement. A first version of the project involved, in the main façade, in relation to the bay window of the neighbouring house, a central semicircular volume with two symmetrical openings. In the built project, instead, you will note the total absence of elements with a single opening on the street, but in the corner, through a process of subtraction. At the same point, the prismatic volume is then recomposed by the wall of the balcony, an element that marks the continuity of the plan. The bedrooms have point openings, always mediated or screened, of limited size.

The service-room is instead lighted only directly from above, in order to avoid an opening on the entry area. The house opens entirely towards the interior of the lot, facing northeast; the largest opening, entirely glassed-in, occurs on a line with the living-room and the kitchen. This large framework is composed in part with sliding doors, in part with fixed glass, on a line with the interior.

The space of the living-room is strongly characterised by the presence of a system of internal shutters made of natural wood with narrow laths, and with a visible guide rail hooked to a special metal structure, operated with free poles. A false ceiling allows it to disappear flush.

This system of shutters transcends its own role as an instrument for the modulation and filtering of light to take on another significance: it allows the recomposition of

the void into a solid, and as a sumptuous covering, confers a marked sense of quality to the hall, or great room.

On the interior, the space is articulated and subdivided into sequences: access takes place through an indirect path of entry, made up of shifts and punctuated by mechanisms of filtering and spatial partition such as glassed-in partitions, sliding or hinged, on a line with the atrium and between the kitchen and the living-room (here two thin wooden slats, hinged fanlike at a single point, attach the glassed partition to the wall). Similar mechanisms are found in the almost contemporary Casa Alves Costa.

All of the window frames, interior and exterior, are to Siza a fundamental moment of structural and spatial definition. The raceways, the little socles, the vertical coverings in the points of passage, the bookshelves, the upholstery, all offer continuity and resolve all the intersections of wood and masonry; from the upper cornices of the doors there extends, in some cases, a thin wooden stick, which runs horizontally along the wall and is used to hang paintings, photographs, and small objects. This is the continuity of the wood, enamelled white, which turns and links everything as a continual covering, leading us through the house in the succession of rooms.

The skimpiness of the space is underscored, almost emphasised, and it becomes an occasion for poetry. The heights vary from a minimum of 2 metres in the corridors, to a maximum of 2.9 metres in the service-rooms, and 2.6 metres in the other rooms. The vertical height is compressed, the passageways are narrowed, a tiny door was designed, as if to focus attention on space, as a datum that should not be taken for granted, or considered gratuitously, but to be rediscovered and appreciated in all its

variations. In this house, everything is millimetric.

The false ceiling, separeted by a small shutter, is also used to place, for instance, the handsome corner lamp in the entry area. This, like the conjunction of levels between the hall and the den, is resolved with a curving design. These are moments of expressive density, as concrete solutions to a precise necessity, with delicate lines, suggesting the latent singularity of every corner of the construction.

They tell us that the narrow opening (about 35 centimetres) linking the kitchen with the entry area, which we could not guess the reason of (door? ventilation port?) also allowed for the morning delivery of fresh milk, while still keeping the house practically closed.

The house is raised with respect to the garden, characterised by a trapezoidal excavation, about 30 centimetres in depth, which reveals the ground, sloping slightly downward, towards the end of the lot. From the living-room, you can see this garden in negative as a patio, in continuity with the construction.

The work on the levels is determined by an obsessive attention to the terrain, the decision not to destroy the existing topography, but rather to make use of it, imposing on the area slight changes in elevation.

In structural terms, the house consists of a membrane in reinforced concrete, with 20-centimetre walls. The horizontal loft is set directly on the perimeter walls and the interior walls.

In this house as well we find a pillar: it is circular in cross section, made of cement, to empty the mass of the wall where needed in order to allow the continuity of the corner window frame. The flat roof, sheathed in elements of prefabricated cement, is accessible

from an exterior staircase corresponding with the garage.

The design of the details and the construction of custom pieces is especially present in this house; the handsome stainless steel lamp in the hall, with adjustable reflector dishes and a flexible shaft, was later developed for mass production (*Flamingo* lamps, 1972, and *Fil* lamps, 1992).

The chromatic juxtapositions clearly point to a sharp distinction between a heavy, harsh exterior and sweet and harmonious interior: cement in plain sight, copper and panels painted white on the exterior, towards the street. On the garden side, the grey of the cement is brightened by the orange of the window frames and the copper of the rain spouts.

The interiors are dominated by bright and modulated hues: a warm white for the smooth plaster walls, for the wooden elements, and for the furniture – only the son's bookshelf is made of natural wood – and cork for the floors. A cooler tone for all the bathrooms and for the kitchen, where the floor is made of grey linoleum. The guide rails for the shutters are made of brass. Wood, glass, cork, brass, all modulate the interior of the "box", defining a space of sensation, enveloping, epidermal. Tactile as well as optical. Small and extremely dense, this house remains one of the most ingenious and complete creations by Siza.

EM/AC
(Travel Notes, October 1999/April 2002)

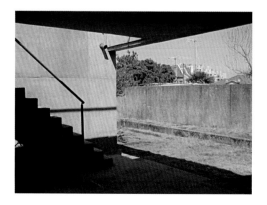

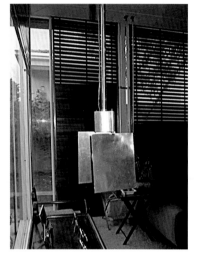

Casa Carlos Vale Guimarães

Aveiro, Portugal

Client: Carlos Vale Guimarães

Casa Alcino Cardoso

Engusto, Moledo do Minho, Portugal

Client: Alcino Cardoso

Collaborators first phase: Francisco Guedes
de Carvalho, Adalberto Dias
Collaborator second phase: José Luís Carvalho Gomes

Lot area: 1780 sq. m.
Roofed area: 235 sq. m.
Two-storey house: 90 sq. m. (55 + 35)
One-storey house: 80 sq. m., existing
Expansion: 100 sq. m.

Casa Alcino Cardoso at Moledo do Minho
Adaptation of two small agricultural buildings, including an expansion in compliance with the programme. There is an attempt to recover the character of the buildings and the landscape. The existing and new elements are clearly in contrast, and interpenetrate with a certain violence.

The swimming pool, planned later, was designed as a ruin, invented in correspondence with the memory of the many things that belong to the landscape of the Minho as well as other landscapes. It is oriented to the path of the sun and is meant to have a relationship to everything that surrounds it – new or old – as if it were an intermediary or an (im)possible synthesis.

Álvaro Siza
Oporto, 1979

1. *Map*
(Source: Álvaro Siza Archives, undated)

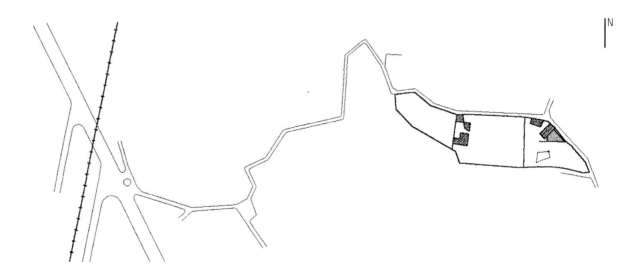

N

2. *Planimetric view, existing state (1:1000)*
(Source: Álvaro Siza Archives, undated)

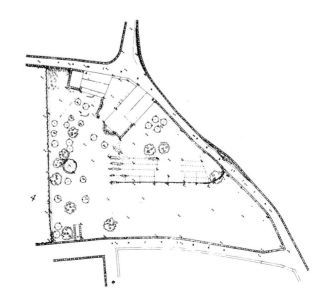

3. *Elevations and cross sections (1:250)*
(Source: Álvaro Siza Archives, October 1971,
original scale 1:100)

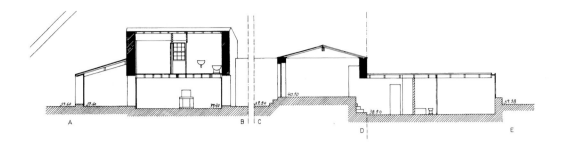

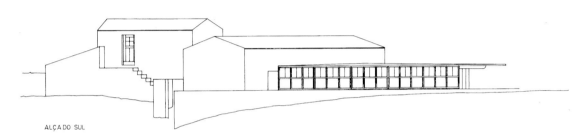

ALÇADO SUL

4. *Pan of the ground floor (1:500)*
1. Hall, or great room / 2. Bathroom /
3. Kitchen / 4. Bedroom / 5. Portico /
6. Swimming pool
(Source: Álvaro Siza Archives, October 1971,
original scale 1:100)

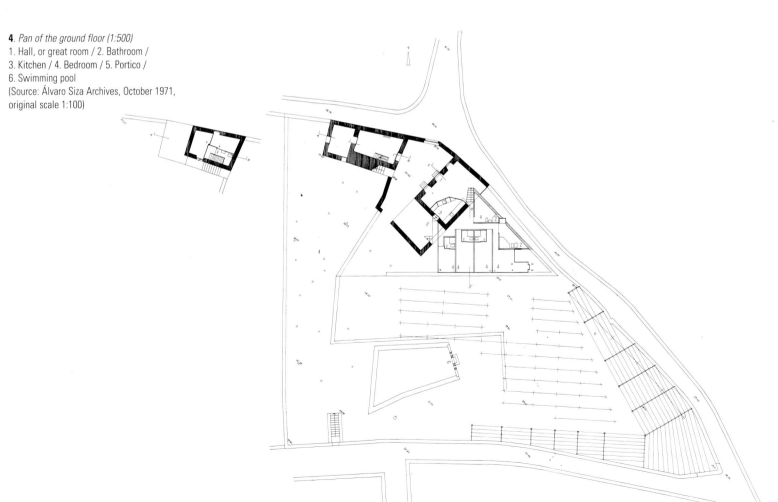

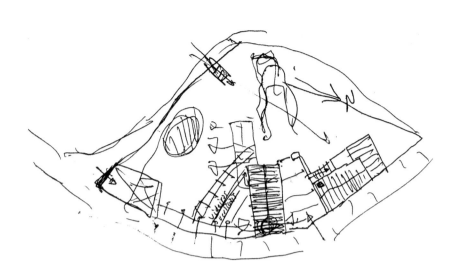

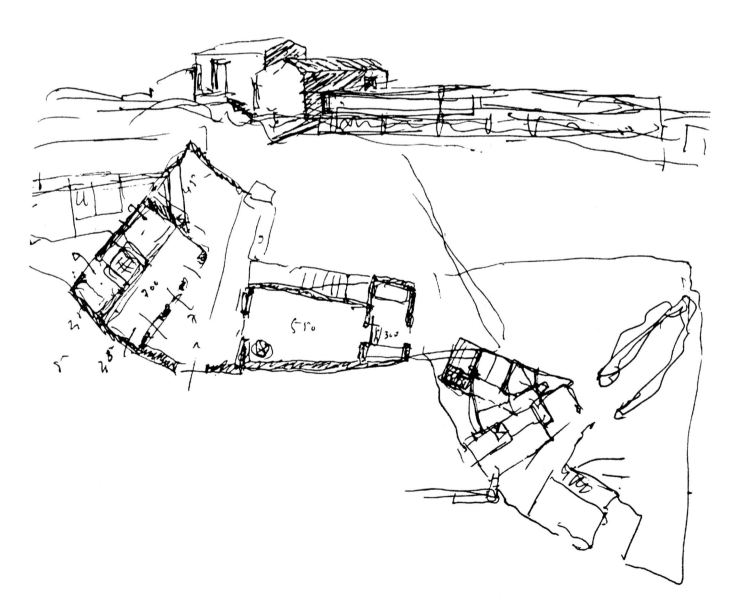

5. *Planimetric view of the addition, southern
prospect and cross section (1:100)*
(Source: Álvaro Siza Archives, December 1971,
original scale 1:20)

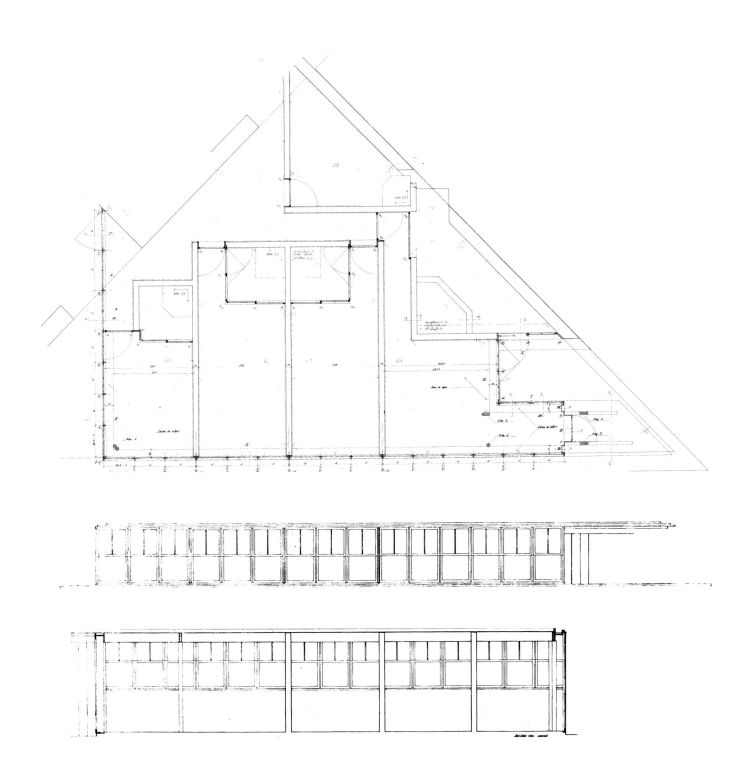

6. *Vertical cross sections, phase 1 (1:50)*
(Source: Álvaro Siza Archives, December 1971,
original scale 1:20)

7. *Vertical cross sections of the roof, phase 1*
(Source: Álvaro Siza Archives, December 1971,
original scale 1:2)

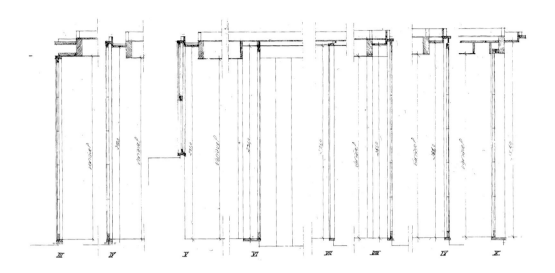

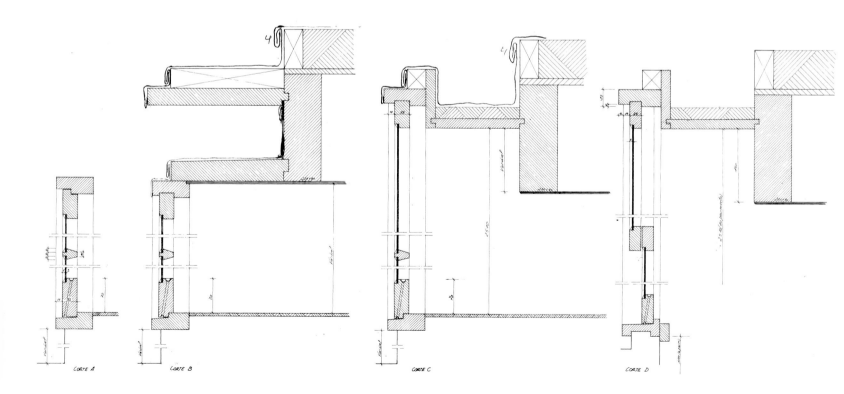

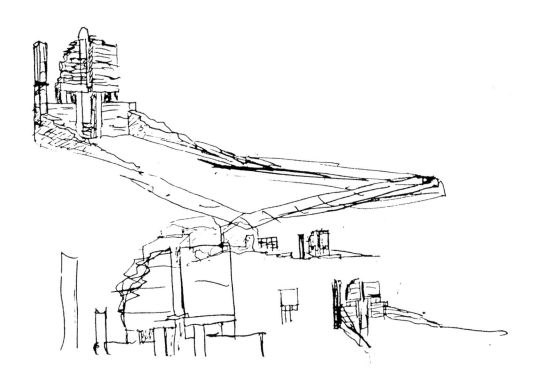

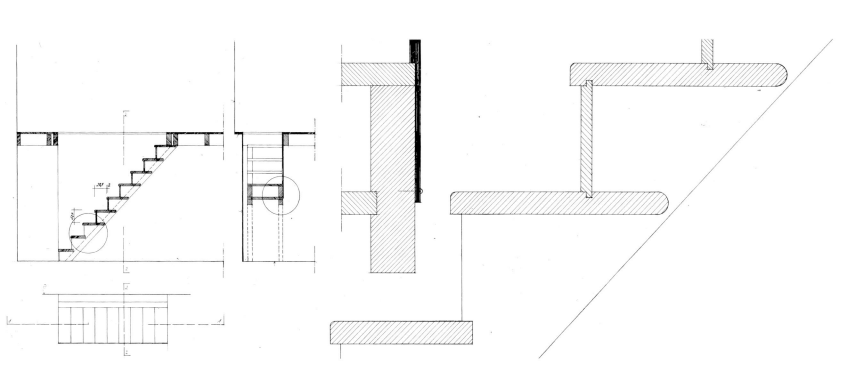

1988 - phase 2
Lot area: 2765 sq. m.

House A
Built area, ground floor: 90 sq. m.
Built area, second floor: 90 sq. m.

House B
Built area, ground floor: 40 sq. m.
Built area, second floor: 25 sq. m.

House C
Built area, second floor: 30 sq. m.

9. *Plans of the ground floor and second floor, phase 2 (1:250)*
1. Portico / 2. Hall, or great room / 3. Fireplace / 4. Service / 5. Bedroom / 6. Armoire / 7. Bathroom / 8. Small kitchen
(Source: Álvaro Siza Archives, January 1988, original scale 1:50)

10. *Elevations and cross sections, phase 2 (1:250)*
(Source: Álvaro Siza Archives, January 1988, original scale 1:50)

Project Report

The project consists of a preservation of the morphological characteristics of the houses (named A, B and C). The work calls for the transformation of the ground floors, which were originally used as stables, and are now integrated into small residential units. House A, on the ground floor, possesses two bedrooms with private bathrooms and two small kitchens; on the upper floor, two great rooms, a small fireplace and a bathroom adjoining the loggia. House B has a great room, a bedroom and a bathroom while house C, given its small size (29 square metres), has only a bedroom and a bathroom. For the roofing, both existing structure and tiles will be restored. The exterior walls will maintain their visible stone structure; on the interior, the finishing will be in tinted plaster, and, in the service zones, ceramic wall covering to a height of 1.5 metres. The floors will be made of wooden boards with a wooden understructure and with waterproof ceramics in the service areas. The interior and exterior window frames will be made of wood and enamelled.

Álvaro Siza, Oporto, 4 February 1988

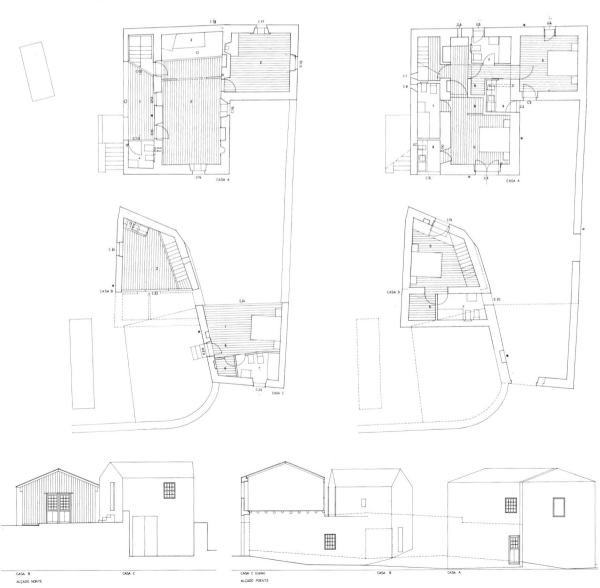

Descriptive Note

The complex is located in an intact rural area, above Moledo do Minho.

The initial intervention consisted of the restoration of two abandoned buildings and their expansion as a vacation home for a banker from Oporto, on the interior of a lot that was planted with grapevines, enclosed by walls. In an adjoining lot, a few years later, other rural buildings were restored, which made it possible to house a comfortable agritourism operation. This project is especially significant because, first of all, it explores the delicate theme of the relationship between the old and the new in architecture, and resolves it in an exemplary manner. The character of the existing structures was preserved, with the stone walls and the two-pitch roof in Portuguese tiles. In the dimensions, the existing volume dominates the added volume of the extension that is partially buried, establishing a very clear relationship of scale. The height of the new pavilion coincides, in particular, with the height of the supports under the grapevines; furthermore, there is a strong significance in terms of plan as well, echoing the disposition along the principal front: the result is an addition that contrasts with the character of the existing buildings but at the same time well integrated into the landscape.

The piece of furniture designed to hold clothing, semicircular in form, expresses on the scale of furnishings the geometric principle followed to resolve the different parts of the project.

Like a hinge, it unites and opposes different things: all the new pieces – the pavilion of the bedrooms, the kitchen, the piece of corner furniture – are all related to a dominant element in keeping with the same geometric principle. In the floor plan, the new triangular structure, with five

bedrooms, is organised in a rigorous way in keeping with the scansion of the façade and the structural module. All of the rooms are subdivided according to this structural layout. There are no intermediary structures between the two buildings. A small staircase resolves the interior change in elevation between the two parts and marks the point of transition. The hall, or great room, and the kitchen are placed in the existing house. The new structure consists of a stone base and continual series of frames above it. The base is presented as a retaining wall which emerges from the slightly sloping terrain which shapes the horizontal support of the entire line of windows. We are told that a window frame found on the site was taken to the workshop and used as a model. This traditional design is utilised in the same years as well in the houses of Oporto and Caxinas. In this case, however, it takes on a different constructive role: the window frame is understood as a continuous façade, as a curtain wall, and not as a single window in a wall.

The façade comes to an end in such a way as to conceal both the gutter and the thickness of the roof, resolving with inset wooden boards both the channel and the attachment to the façade framework. This detail, light and genial, certainly not simple to resolve, is a fundamental point of the project. In cross section, moreover, there is clearly a sharp difference between the thickness of the base and the fragile ribbon-like window frames, lined up with the interior wall. The system of sliding windows makes it possible to open almost completely the entire pavilion, as if it were a veranda. The wooden structure is arranged in parallel to the principal façade and supported against the thinner interior walls – which are at the same time partitions and load-bearing walls – and at the corners on pairs

of circular wooden pillars. The flat roof is in zinc. The ceiling is faced with plywood panels, like the doors and sliding panels; the partition walls are plastered and satin-finished; the floors are in cork.

The system utilised to subdivide the rooms is especially significant. The division between bedroom and bathroom takes the form of entirely movable wooden panels or, even, just plastic curtains. These are elements in keeping with the character of the new buildings, fragile, almost provisional, which speak of a light and sensory form of construction.

The material and structural aesthetics employed finds a possible reference in naval architecture, confirmed if only by Siza's close and fertile collaboration with a local ship builder.

The interiors of this vacation house are especially impressive for their chromatic quality and lightness. It is surprising, for instance, to note the use of pure colour in the plastic shower curtains, green and orange, and in the fabrics used for the beds, yellow. But the most original aspect, perhaps, is constituted by the curtains that cover the entire plate-glass window: the fabrics, the mechanisms for moving the curtains, their efficacy and domestic nature. They are used with the same lucidity with which the floor plan is organised. The shadows of the leaves and the colour of the strong afternoon light filtering through the red and orange fabric create in the bedrooms a magical, exotic atmosphere. The relationship between the height of the new construction and the vineyards becomes in this sense an even more significant aspect of the project. A project in which it is possible to detect a strong degree of experimentation, in terms of construction as well.

The smaller of the two existing buildings has been transformed into an independent

living unit. On the interior of the structure, fully emptied, wood is the material adopted both in terms of structure and covering – vertical and horizontal. A wooden staircase, slightly separate from the wall, connects the two levels.

The exterior spaces present a series of elements whose provenance we are unable to decipher: existing or new presences, they – low walls, benches, floors, ledges, vases – constitute a sort of undated archaeological field.

In this sense, the pool is the dominant element: designed as an agricultural cistern, it is deformed and its lines are bent to emphasise certain sharp corners, those of the house and the lot. The geometry issues forth as a synthesis of diverse presences and the movement of the sun. An "archaic" portal of stone blocks, designed as a ruin, fragmented and unstable, now completely enveloped by vegetation, is the sober and ritual invitation to the act of bathing.

EM

(Travel Notes, November 2001)

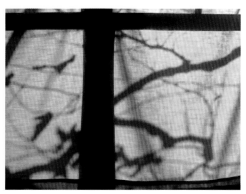

Casa Marques Pinto

Oporto, Portugal

Client: Marques Pinto

Collaborators: Francisco Guedes de Carvalho

Lot area: 1140 sq. m.
Roofed area, ground floor : 390 sq. m.

1. *Floor plan of the ground floor and the
sub-basement (1:500)*
(Source: Álvaro Siza Archives, 1972)

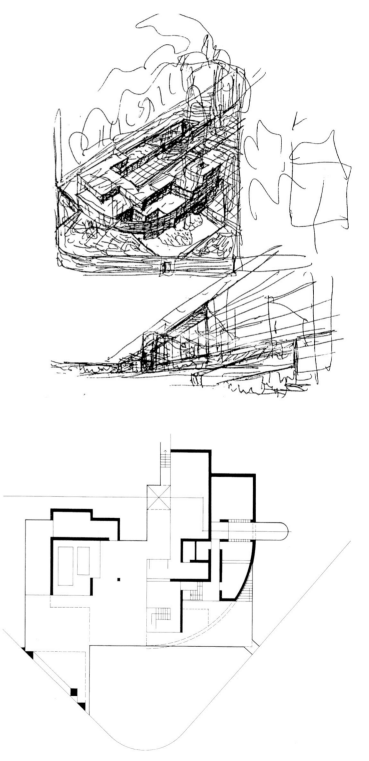

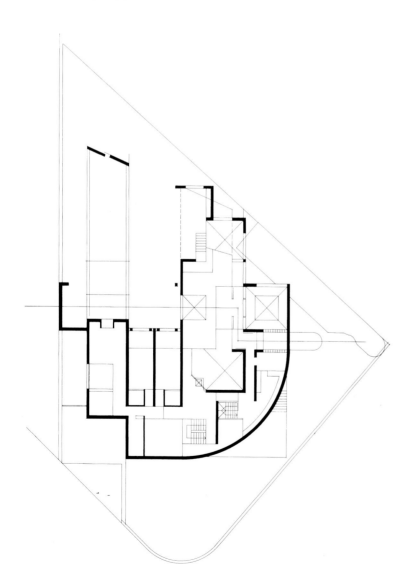

House at Azeitão

Azeitão, Setúbal, Portugal

Client: Fernando Silveira Ramos

Collaborators: António Madureira, Francisco Guedes de Carvalho, Adalberto Dias, Nuno Ribeiro Lopes, Edgar Castro

Lot area: 17,500 sq. m.
Roofed area, ground floor: 650 sq. m.
Garage and storage: 100 sq. m.

Project Description

The summer house being designed is located at the far southwest corner of the property, while the rest of the lot remains unencumbered, with no modifications of its topographic configuration and its vegetation. The programme, composed of five bedrooms with antechamber and bathroom, shared living-room, dining-room, kitchen, game-room, swimming pool, tennis court and portico for cars, is developed on a single storey with slight changes in elevation following the line of the land.

Points of access are found at the most favourable elevations, reducing to the lowest possible level the shifts of earth; the portico for cars is at the sub-basement level.

The construction is resolved with pillars, beams and low roof lofts made of reinforced concrete, and with divider walls in brick, and will be plastered and painted.

Exterior window frames made of iron sections, protected and painted, and interior window frames in enamelled wood.

All of the interior floors will be covered with waterproof ceramics and the walls of the kitchen and the bathrooms will be entirely lined with ceramics.

All of the rooms have natural lighting and ventilation, and in the bathrooms, a supplementary forced ventilation will be installed.

The sanitary system as shown in the outlines attached to the general design, in keeping with the obligatory minimum distance of thirty metres from the location of the water cistern.

The structural plans will be presented in compliance with deadlines.

Álvaro Siza
Oporto, 2 April 1974

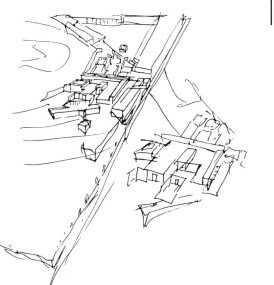

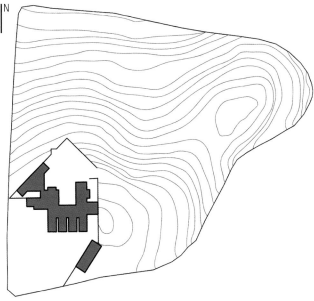

1. *Overall view (1:2000)*
(Source: Álvaro Siza Archives, undated, redesign)

2. *Floor plan, elevations and cross sections*
(1:500)
1. Entryway / 2. Hall / 3. Gallery /
4. Dining-room / 5. Kitchen / 6. Bedrooms /
7. Game-room / 8. Swimming pool /
9. Storage-room / 10. Garage / 11. Tennis
(Source: Álvaro Siza Archives, March 1974,
original scale 1:100)

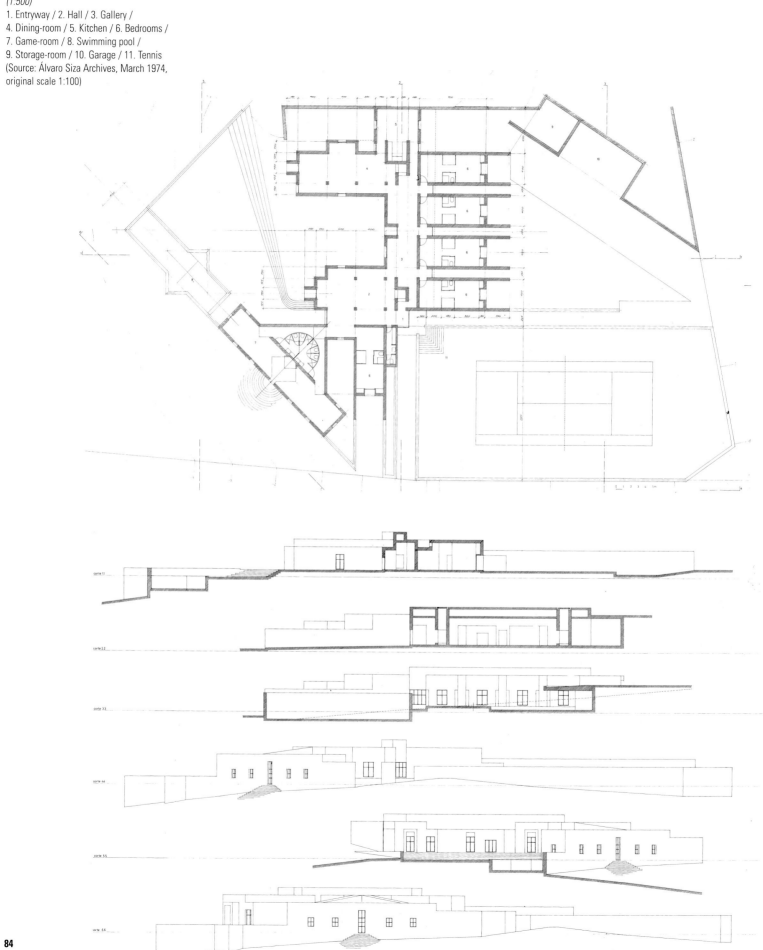

Casa Carlos Beires

Rua Dr. Antero Pimentel,
Póvoa de Varzim, Portugal

Client: Carlos Machado de Beires

Collaborators: António Madureira, Nuno Ribeiro
Lopes, Adalberto Dias

Lot area: 530 sq. m.
Roofed area: 225 sq. m.
Ground floor: 145 sq. m.
Portico: 80 sq. m.
Second storey: 135 sq. m.
Terrace: 17 sq. m.

Project Description

This residence occupies a lot of 17 × 30 metres and its volume is conditioned by the zone regulation in which it fits, by the unique characteristics of both the programme and the site. Given the intention of orienting the main rooms to the southwest, as well as opening them towards an exterior space that was properly sized and planted, the programme was then distributed over two storeys, beginning with a rectangular plan, with entries on the east side, since the rectangle was "broken" to the southwest. Living-room, dining-room and study (on the ground floor) and two bedrooms, the anteroom to the master bedroom and the master bedroom (on the second floor) open out like an amphitheatre towards this external space, since the intimacy of the spaces – exterior and interior – is ensured by a pergola and the vertical roller shutters which close off to the southwest the continuous veranda of the second floor. The service-rooms, to the north, communicate with the interior zone of the garden, articulating the space of the laundry-room and the garage.

The minimum required distances are respected, to the south and the east; on the west side, where at this moment the property borders with a road with right of way, the distance is 2.5 metres to ensure in any case a distance from the future construction of more than the required 6 metres. When the urbanisation of the area makes it possible, the strip that corresponds to the road with right of way will be annexed to the house lot.

The exterior walls are double, made of stone and perforated brick, while the interior walls are made of stone (load-bearing) and perforated brick, 7 or else 15 centimetres. The lofts on the second storey and the roof are made of elements of perforated brick set upon the stone walls or else on beams and pillars made of reinforced concrete, in keeping with the plans for the structures already submitted. The roof will be sheathed in zinc and the outer and inner walls will be plastered and painted, with a ceramic covering up to a height of 2 metres in the kitchen and bathrooms, pantry and garage. Flooring waterproof ceramic on the ground floor and in the bathrooms on the second floor. Interior and exterior window frames in wood, to be painted.

Álvaro Siza
Oporto, 3 September 1973

Casa Beires

At a time when no projects were being built, corresponding to a period of rapidly climbing construction costs in Portugal, a commission arrived for a small house, in one of the characteristic subdivisions included in the urbanisation plans.

In the first, disappointed visit to the terrain, a sketch emerged with a suggestion to accept the reality of the street, adding another volume, with meaningless spaces around it, since there was no possibility of intentional relations with the surrounding buildings.

This volume was destroyed on one of the sides, remaining as a ruin, abstractly depicted.

From the resulting rupture there emerged a glass membrane that contained the distribution of the programme requested by the client, with plan on checkered paper in hand.

Mysteriously, this house was built, and to the client's satisfaction.

Álvaro Siza
Oporto, May 1979

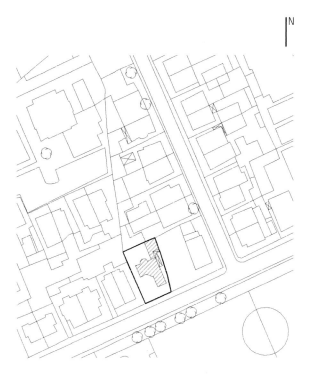

1. *Overall view (1:2000)*
(Source: Camara Municipal do Póvoa
de Varzim, April 2002, original scale 1:2000)

From an Interview

A common feature of your houses in the 1960s is the determination to enclose them around the patio, turning their backs on the road.

"Right up to the end of the 1960s, practically all the houses that I built were conceived around a patio, closed off towards the exterior, without windows or doors, opening only onto the patio. It was an attitude that now, in an act of self-criticism, I reject. This choice sprang from a response to the task of building on a street in which I disliked intensely the neighbouring buildings; so, I closed myself off and tried to create a small, impossible paradise, impossible like all paradises. Later houses no longer have this attitude and the relationship with the street is much more direct. This determination to turn inward was not a product of an analysis of traditional architecture, instead it was a personal preference, a little odd and rather moralistic with respect to the surrounding architecture."

The flip side of the coin is Casa Beires.

"Casa Beires, then, would be the product of this self-criticism. As such, it is a little exuberant, a little exotic, though perhaps not as much as it looks in the photographs. I took into consideration the context, a street with isolated houses, in a different way, even if it is not certain that I conceived it in this way for this reason alone, since I continued to dislike the houses around it. All the same, I did not believe that the correct response was close up around a patio. Quite simply, I designed a block, like the other houses, which all follow the same rules."

In the Casa Beires it is important, perhaps to an excessive degree, that there be a great many mechanisms, inventions for closing off or placing in communication the spaces, to protect or open the gallery, and so on.

"I would say that it was subconscious. But now I interpret it as something of a farewell to this capacity for invention, for craftsmanship. I hope that it is a temporary farewell. It might even be the product of an encounter with types of architecture that were absolutely unknown at the time. I don't know; I could talk about the Maison de Verre or the Soane House or other things still."

Interview with Álvaro Siza in *Quaderns d'Arquitectura i Urbanisme*, no. 159, 1983

"When I was commissioned to design Casa Beires I said to myself: another horrible lot! The clients wanted a patio-home, because they liked the house that I had designed in the late 1950s, Casa Rocha Ribeiro in Maia, which is built in a large garden around a magnificent tree. I said that would be impossible, there was no space, there were no trees, there was nothing.

At the time I didn't have much to do. The houses that I had designed hadn't been built. Even though I didn't think that I would ever build anything – the family was not even rich – I did the design all the same. It reflected precisely the organisation of space supplied by my client on a sheet of checkered note paper. I said to myself, here I can only make another block, nothing more, but then I broke it to organise that series of rooms around an inner courtyard; I must confess, I wasn't sure I could build it. But then the family came into an inheritance and decided to build the house. I had to keep the idea, I couldn't say no.

It is a project with very complex details. In northern Portugal, and to an even greater degree in Galicia, there are galleries, consisting of a sort of wall-window curtain. From the street you see the house, the main walls, the entry door, etc., and then you see a sort of enclosed veranda. It is an intermediate space that controls the variation in temperature between interior and exterior. It can be found in some houses from the eighteenth and nineteenth centuries, both in the city and in the countryside. That is why these 'guillotine-style' windows are used, to create a certain type of ventilation.

For me, it was a sort of exercise with different 'languages' on the interior of the same little house. In the back, the window frames are made of steel, where you find those 'rationalist' volumes, while in the front it is much more organic – that's what I wanted at the time. It all derives from the project of Caxinas – to establish the relationship between different formal languages, develop the environment making use of the same materials, and the same language, control complexity, which does not mean to 'close off' a house, but rather to design it so that it reflects the various elements of its own context."

Interview with Álvaro Siza in *Bauwelt*, no. 29/30, 1990

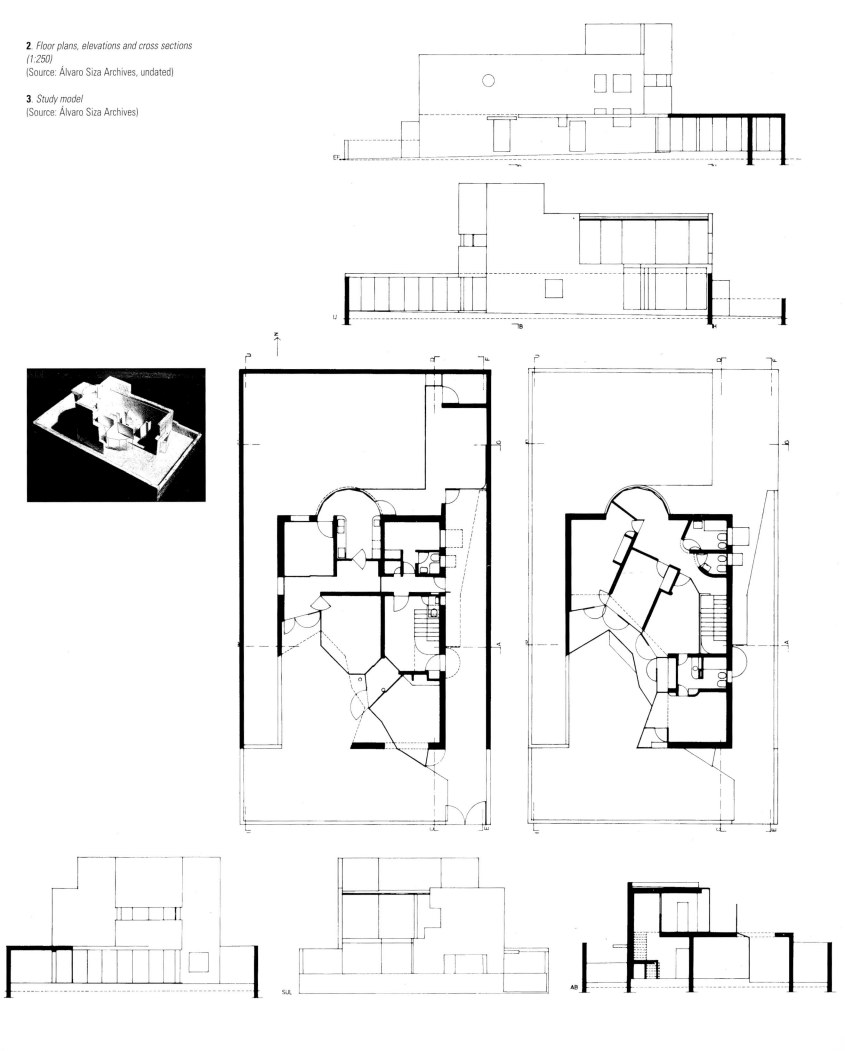

2. *Floor plans, elevations and cross sections*
(1:250)
(Source: Álvaro Siza Archives, undated)

3. *Study model*
(Source: Álvaro Siza Archives)

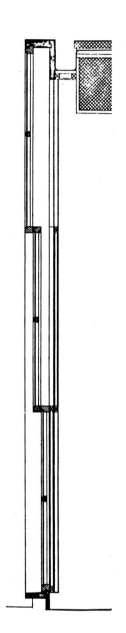

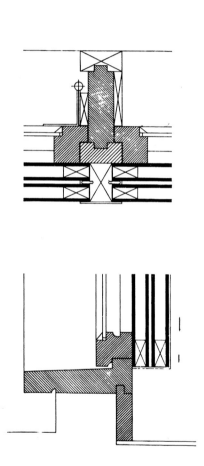

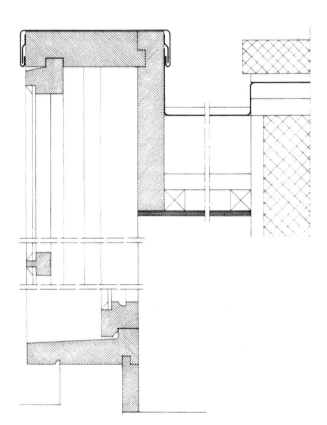

4. *Window frame of the bedrooms on the second floor* (Source: Álvaro Siza Archives, original scale 1:2)

5. *Vertical cross section of the façade* (Source: Álvaro Siza Archives, original scale 1:2)

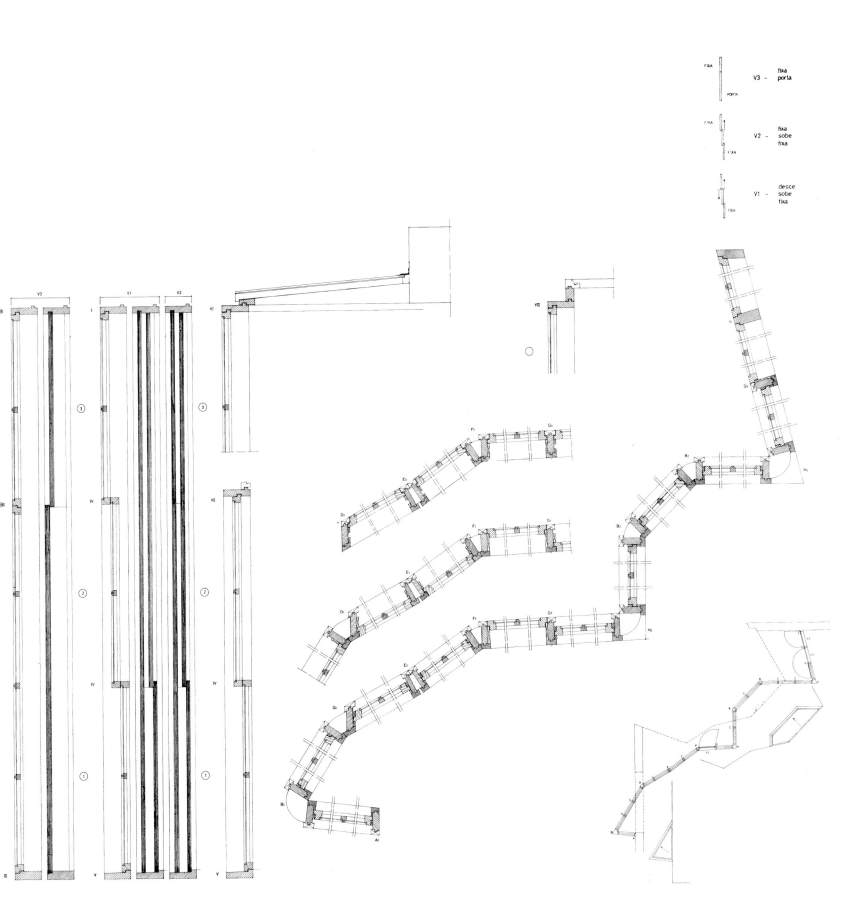

6. *Horizontal and vertical cross sections of the continuous window frame on the ground floor* (Source: Álvaro Siza Archives, undated)

7. *Axonometric plan and design sketches*
(Source: Álvaro Siza Archives, undated)

8. *Iron bow window frame*
(Source: Álvaro Siza Archives, undated)

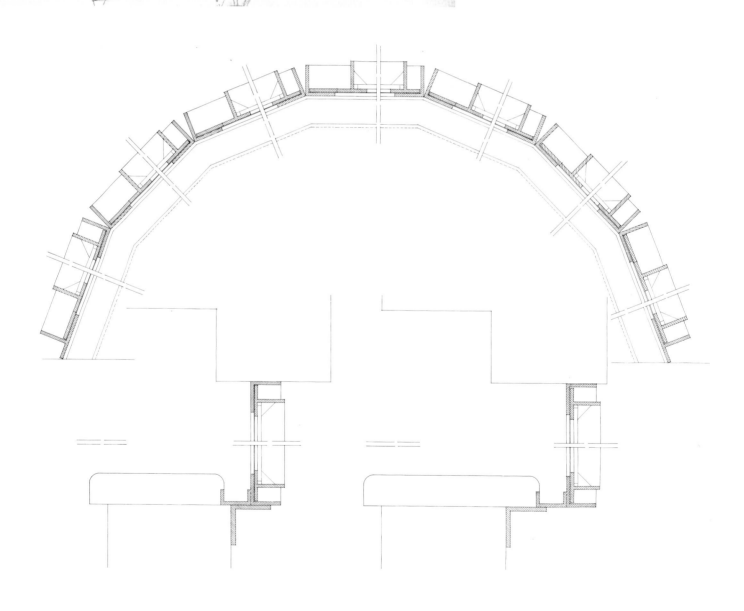

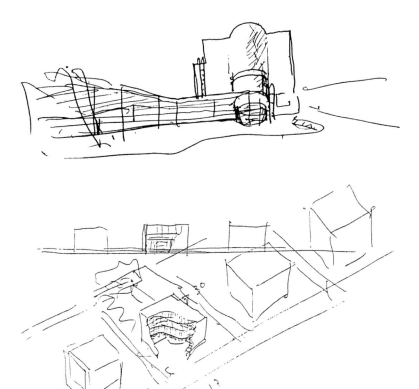

Descriptive Note

The visit to the Casa Beires was only possible after numerous attempts, allowing us to see from within the world that we had imagined so long through the designs and photographs published. The house had recently been repainted and the owners were preparing to undertake the first maintenance of the interior, after thirty years. The yellow of the plaster, the black and red of the window frames and the downspouts are once again very strong colours, immersed among the trees in the intense luminosity that saturates all the tones. In fact, the first impression, (perhaps) unexpected, is that of a "journey" in a tropical garden that invaded the space of the patio and the whole house.

Given its oddities, the *bomb house*, as it was called, a "sign of my alienation", immediately prompted a variety of enthusiastic comments (see references to Mendelsohn, Aalto, Van Eyck, Venturi… to indicate its flamboyant complexity). This project was especially dense with meaning, in which the living function does not seem to be entirely dominant. It also expresses a political and personal disquiet, a critical discourse on architecture, the quest for a language and many other things that the architect himself recalled in short essays and interviews.

What was most urgent to describe at the beginning was the procedure whereby the project was to find its bizarre configuration precisely through what, in that period, the operation meant in terms of idiom: "in the common model of Rationalistic domestic architecture, almost literally transcribed, the main façade was destroyed, as if it had been bombarded," Alexandre Alves Costa explained.

While in previous houses the design emerged from the singular aspects of the terrain with a radical interiorisation of the domestic space, here one senses an instinctive and creative approach that burst into the neutral world of the lot: "a violent expression of rupture" – as Siza recalls – induced by a "practical impossibility". Today the perception of the house is finally conditioned by the vegetation, as well, just as the plan called for.

It results in an comprehensibility that is supported precisely by those sensations that were at first only imaginable.

This is a block more or less like the others, as we can observe from the axonometric drawing in pencil, a two-storey volume with a rectangular floor plan in which a sort of patio is inserted: full and empty, a void that is however only provisional and finally occupied by vegetation, re-compose the volume of the house.

This void has a very expressive geometric configuration that lacerates the continuity of the rectangle. The placement of the main volume and the adjoining service spaces, like the placement of the patio, introduce, while still within their direct compliance with regulations, an imbalance within the regular terrain, along a diagonal line.

From the street, the segmented profile of the façade is no longer perceptible and it is possible only to glimpse the side elevation, where a lot is still unoccupied. The house and the garage define a hard entry space, similar to the one at Casa Magalhães. Between the boundary walls and the higher wall of the house are articulated a series of awnings that cover the paths and unify the various access points to the portico, situated at the far end.

In the back, the circular bay window characterises the entire front (a reference to the first version of Casa Magalhães) and closes off the garden. These two contiguous fronts are characterised by point openings and small sizes; they are blind walls that protect the living space and the patio, entirely turned to the southwest. The patio, an element that characterises all the early houses, is in this case facing the street, and not enclosed on the interior of the lot; but it is not the relationship with the street that determines its position, but rather its relationship with the sun. The patio opens towards the sun and shows that the house is effectively configured as a solitary and vigorously self-sufficient object. In keeping with the same dual principle as the nearby Casa Alves Santos, apparently so different, the construction is marked by the counterpoint configuration of the façades: completely open (continuous window frames) and completely closed (blank walls). A composition that relies upon the use of floors. The glassed floor identifies the privileged space around which the house lives its life, a space that is in any case private, tactile and sensorial, separate from the rest of the world; rich in vegetation, colours and light, bounded by a metal pergola and fragments of walls. The façade is conceived as a continuous, transparent membrane upon which this natural world is reflected, amplifying itself, and through which it penetrates, invading the domestic spaces.

The richness of the façade is a quality of the design that emerges from the stratification of segmented lines – space, structure, covering.

This contrast between two parts, two worlds, is manifested here right down to the design and selection of fixtures: those set in the walls are made of steel and painted red, while the continuous window and door frames are made of wood painted black. An important aspect of the visit is offered by the possibility of moving and using the mechanisms developed to open and close off the façade. It is Nuno, the violinist/grandson, who shows us the numerous methods of transforming the

spaces, with all the enthusiasm of a game. On the ground floor the window frame is darkened with the use of an interior curtain, no longer needed given the dense greenery. The guillotine-style windows can all be raised vertically and, at certain points, the lower part of the frame opens like a gate. On the upper floor, the window frame is divided into three parts, and opens in the same way, but is also composed on blind interior panels, to completely darken the bedrooms.

The system glass/curtains/shutters is a complex structural element that is a screen, at once transparent and opaque.

These fixtures are painted in two different colours: glossy black on the exterior, cream-yellow on the interior, in keeping with the shade of the walls and floors in red ceramics.

The contrast between the pure tones used on the exterior – yellow, red, black – and the more modulated and soft colours on the interior reappears as a constant attitude in the houses by Siza.

In looking at the floor plan, the comprehensibility of the distribution, the singularity of all the rooms, the partial structural coincidences, can be explained in part by imagining that we see, beneath the plan that we know today, the design the Beires family brought to Siza.

On the ground floor, the sequence of living-room, dining-room and study along the façade is a fluid space, quite luminous, and in direct contact with the vegetation. The continuous glass doors along the façade, the lightness of the fixtures and the curved guide rails, the little skylight of the hall, or great room, which brings the emptiness indoors as well, punching a hole in the attic, indicate the complexity of the reasoning and the space. The service-rooms and the entry hall with the staircase follow the orthogonal nature of the base rectangle, in contrast,

and have a very delicate luminosity. The landing of the staircase is curved and the railing is red… The kitchen is nicely situated in correspondence with the bow window: the exit links it to the laundry-room and the garage.

On the upper floor, the bedrooms are arranged in keeping with the façade, according to the rotations that do not coincide with the partitions of the ground floor.

All of the rooms possess a special shape all their own and are freely placed on the interior of the perimeter. The geometries are hybrid, the paths are not always immediate, everything possesses a sort of enthusiastic spontaneity. The result is a living space in which nothing is taken for granted, repetitive, conventional. Only two examples: the dressing-room space, set on the façade, which separates the master bedroom from the antechamber, intentionally generous; the ceiling designed by the double curve of the little bathrooms.

Certainly, the house, at the time of our visit, was too full, certain spaces were jammed with objects and furniture, it was all fairly chaotic, turned upside-down, with furniture of Asian origin, from India and other far-off lands. A very unusual, singular house, in its use as well, after so many years. On the interior, the sensory richness is almost excessive and the perceptions proliferate in a continual ricochet of vibrations: the glass reflects fragments of a world in movement, the rustling of leaves, the shadows, the inhabitants of the house… In total agreement with the luxuriant garden, the atmosphere evokes the interior of a colonial house or, perhaps, that of a greenhouse in a slightly overgrown botanical garden. Immersed in this emotional state, the exterior world, a few yards away, seems in fact very distant.

Leaving the house, almost stunned, we wander among the surrounding constructions, we observe how repugnant they are, then we look at one another with the amazement of someone who has suddenly opened their eyes again.
EM
(Travel Notes, April 2002)

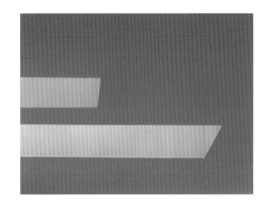

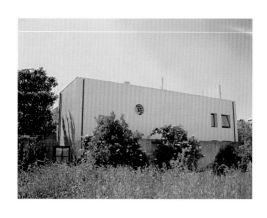

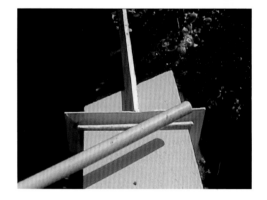

House at Francelos

Francelos, Vila Nova de Gaia, Portugal

Collaborator: Nuno Ribeiro Lopes

Lot area: 685 sq. m.
Roofed area: 210 sq. m. (house, 180 sq. m.)

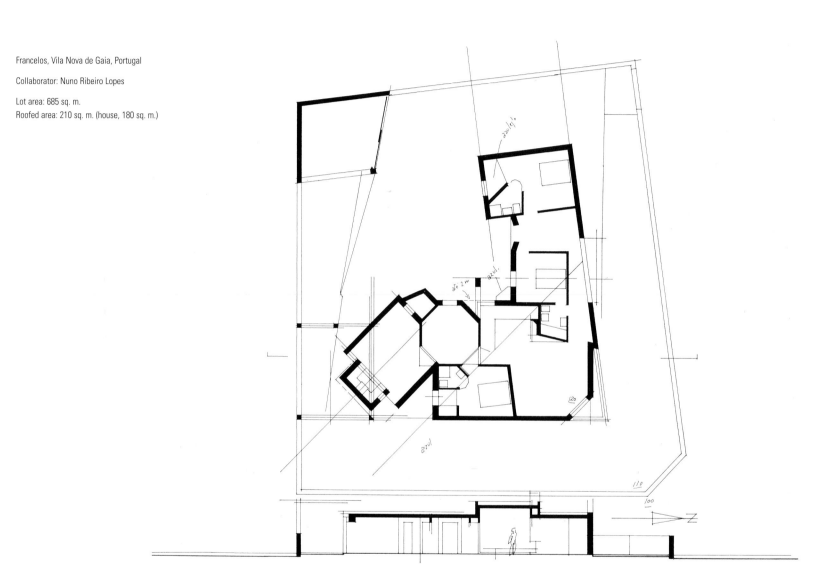

1. *Floor plan and cross section (1:250)*
(Source: Álvaro Siza Archives, undated)

Casa António Carlos Siza

Rua S. João de Deus,
Santo Tirso, Portugal

Client: António Carlos Melo Siza Vieira

Collaborators: Nuno Ribeiro Lopes, António Madureira

Lot area: 465 sq. m.
Roofed area: 180 sq. m.
House: 150 sq. m.
Garage: 25 sq. m.
Portico: 5 sq. m.

Project Description

The programme considered (living-room and dining-room, kitchen, pantry, service-room, four bedrooms, two baths) occupies a single storey, with access to the various rooms that extend around the central patio. The form of this residence is the product of a compromise between intentions of internal organisation and adaptation to an existing topography and occupation of the land. The materials and the processes of construction utilised correspond to the requirements of durability, affordability and quality. The load-bearing walls will be made of cement blocks upon which will be set the lofts of the roof. Finishing in tinted plaster, in the service-rooms ceramic wall coverings to a height of 1.5 metres. Flooring in waterproof ceramics and window frames, interior and exterior, made of enamelled wood. The design, the structures and systems will be presented within an appropriate time frame.

Álvaro Siza
Oporto, 23 November 1976

António Carlos Siza Residence

A single-storey residence of 150 square metres, built on a very strict budget. The project was conditioned by the difficulties caused by the shape and size of the land, and by the invasion caused by the unbridled growth of the city. The programme develops around a small patio and starting from the intersection of two axes implied by the twisting of the terrain, so as to ensure the respect of the alignment imposed and the apparent expansion of the free space. The limited amount of space inside is compensated for by the existence of visual axes that cross the built area lengthwise and transversely.

Álvaro Siza
Oporto, May 1979

From an Interview

"This house has relationships, for instance, with Baroque architecture, but that's not what matters. It is an exercise that I like and that my brother likes. It is something different, a project that gave me a chance to do some research, outside of the conflicts, the other problems, the other more important jobs. And that is always useful."

Interview with Álvaro Siza in *AMC*, no. 44, Paris 1978

"I must say that it was a very complicated project, but also a very stimulating one. First of all, because of the terrain, because the lot was small and quite irregular, and then because it was for my brother. I also had problems with the authorisation with respect to the layout of the house's floor plan. Since the majority of the lot extends diagonally to the street, in my first project I had positioned the house on the long side and not parallel to the street. There was, in that case as well, an interior courtyard, inasmuch as I wanted to create an intimate open space because in the summer it is hot, and I knew that my brother likes to eat outside, but sheltered from his neighbours. The project was not approved, the authorities wanted the façade to be parallel to the street. And so I had to change everything just when I was already bubbling over with ideas for this house. But I did not want to change the project completely, on the contrary: there was a sort of struggle between the first idea and the second. Finally, I succeeded in maintaining the interior courtyard but, in order to obtain a harmonious relationship with the available garden, I introduced diagonal lines and a repeated variation of axes. The terrain is small, it was not easy to insert an interior courtyard there, even if the rooms are small. And so I linked the interior spaces, cutting them with openings arranged along a line, so that it is possible to perceive in every point of the house, according to my idea, a sort of spatial continuity. Through the dining-room you can see the courtyard, but also – in the opposite direction – through the courtyard, you can see the rooms and the open area. I believe that in this house I created a dynamic space, though in a very limited context: an expansion of the space, but at the same time a sensation of intimacy. I believe first of all that I want to define the spaces in which people will live, and at the same time give a sensation of protection and openness. In this house, this was possible through the control of all the elements on an appropriate scale. When I see the house in published form, I no longer recognise it. The sensory impressions are created with the movement, it is not possible to reproduce the sensation of finding oneself in a space. Perhaps only with a video could something of this sort be achieved."

Interview with Álvaro Siza in *Bauwelt*, no. 29/30, 1990

1. *Aerial photograph, 2001*
(Source: Camara Municipal do Santo Tirso)

2. *Model*
(Source: Álvaro Siza Archives, undated)

3. *Design study*
(Source: Álvaro Siza Archives, undated)

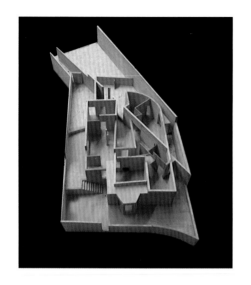

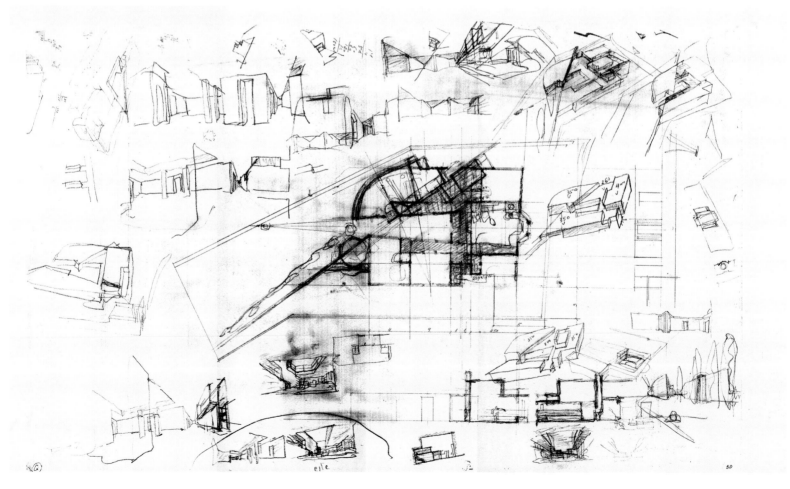

4. *Floor plan with lot (1:250)*
1. Portico / 2. Entryway / 3. Closet / 4. Dining
area / 5. Kitchen / 6. Services / 7. Living-
room / 8.-11. Bedrooms
(Source: Álvaro Siza Archives, undated)

5. *Elevations and cross sections (1:250)*
(Source: Álvaro Siza Archives, undated)

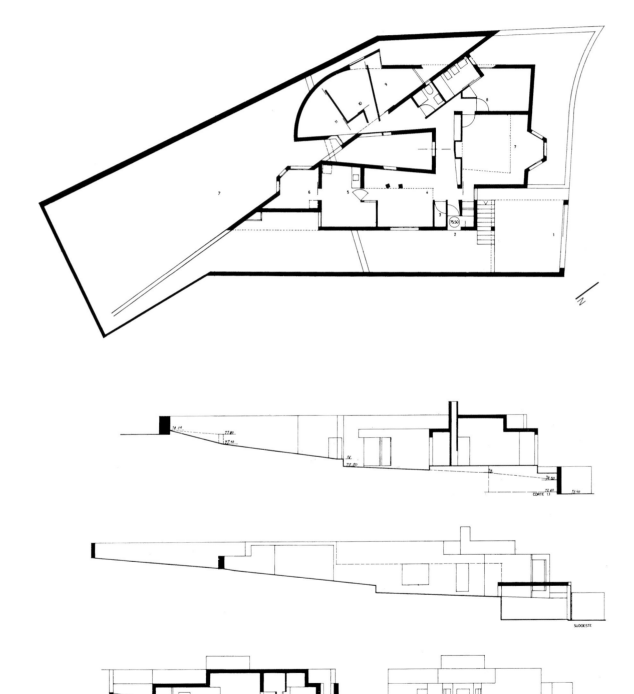

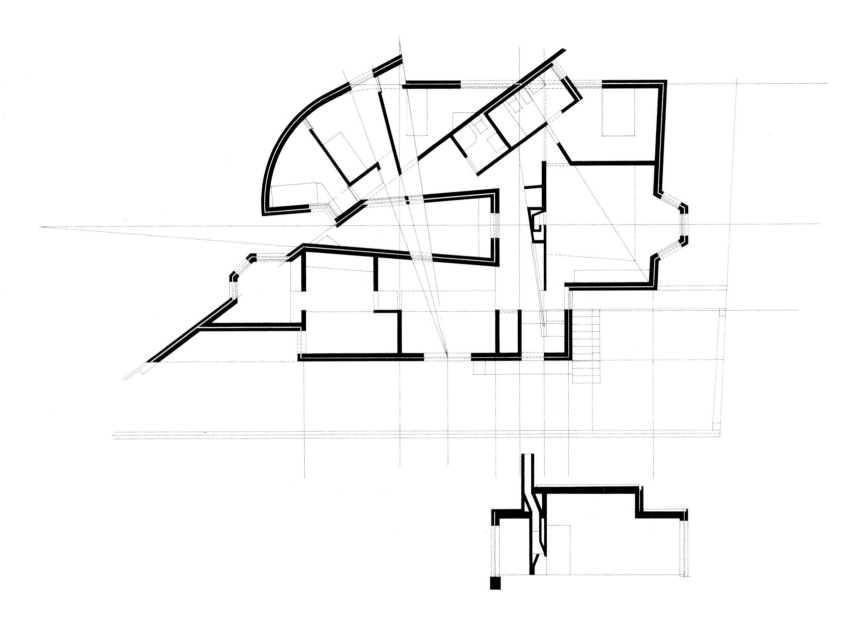

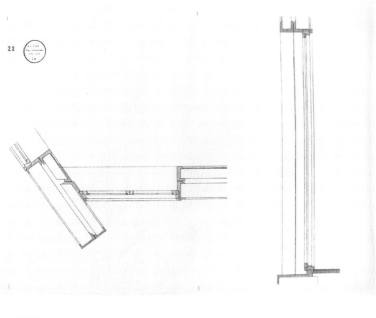

7. *Details of the window frames:*
vertical and horizontal cross sections
(Source: Álvaro Siza Archives, undated)

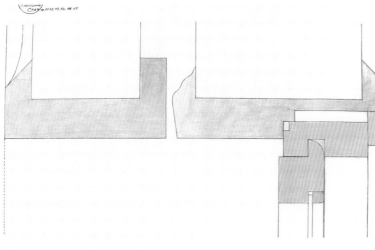

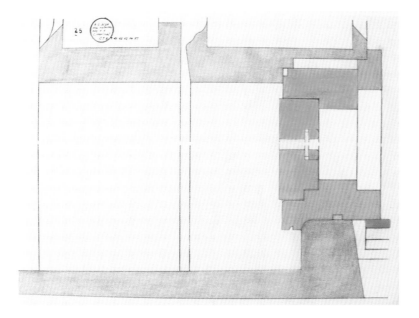

Descriptive Note

We tour the house on a sunny autumn
afternoon. We are in Santo Tirso, a small
centre in the metropolitan area of Oporto,
an urban environment without qualities,
chaotically developing, hostile. The house is
situated on a secondary street, surrounded
by single-family residences; not far away,
two ugly, violent buildings blight the view.
The project was conceived and developed,
at least in part, in reaction to this context,
in an obstinate attempt to protect and
create an intimate and welcoming space.
The extreme difficulties, intrinsic to the lot,
are the only certain base for a project
that constantly overcomes itself. This is,
certainly, the terrain on which Siza feels
especially at his ease and expresses
his talent most completely. A creative
moment of extreme sensitivity in a small
"unforgettable" house. This project was
undertaken on a very tight budget,
short resources, and extreme lucidity.
The architecture is made up of just
a few elements, always the same: walls,
windows, elevations and measurements, the
continual relationship with the world and
with people. Without separating the
technical aspect from the representative
one, with essential, never pompous modes.
The floor plan has a complex geometry,
curves, angles, twists, outlines: a design
that emerges empirically from a manual
effort, at the drawing board, made up of
stabs, intuitions, and continually checked
against sketches and the architectural
model, in keeping with an established
method.
Everything is sought out from square one,
tested, until a path is patiently created.
(The exploratory sketch, in pencil though
still provisional, is covered with work.)
The construction is very simple and,
in a certain sense, tends to coincide with
the balsa-wood model: devoid of covering

and without flashings, all the connections round without any mediation. A construction that was in fact reduced to a minimum level, there is only one material: all ochre-yellow plaster. This reduction of media is also, but not only, the necessary response to limited economic resources. The house, like the model, like a unique artwork, like a sculpture, clearly shows that the essence of the design is its form. But here, as in other houses, we are not considering just a strictly personal discourse: the entire project is directed generously towards the inhabitant, the final protagonist of the built space.

The house develops according to a closed "U" configuration that would be used again and again in later projects. In this case it is interesting to note its articulation, induced by the subdivision of the programme into three parts: kitchen and dining-room, hall and main bedroom, children's bedrooms. These programmatic zones are marked by three taller volumes, separated one from another but linked by a low structure that ensures continuity to the entire plan.

From the exterior the house has a simple, modest appearance, now completely enveloped by the vegetation of the garden. A series of steps resolves the difference in elevation and leads from the street (and from the garage) to the entrance, set on the side. On the interior, you experience a continual interplay of shifts and correspondences between walls, openings, full walls and glassed walls. The living-room is marked by the presence of a central bay-window and is turned towards the street. Along the southwest side, dining-room, kitchen and a service-room succeed one another with a second bay-window opening towards the end of the lot. The kitchen is a little dark, the table and the benches are custom designed, alongside a high interior window that illuminates them.

On the opposite side, to the northeast, there is a line of little bedrooms and the bathrooms.

Each room seems to possess its own autonomy, a certain something that distinguishes and identifies it: nothing is taken for granted, nothing is repetitive. The interior circulation is articulated around the conical patio, which serves as an element to expand the space, as if it were an optical device for crossing and referencing: many of the openings are concentrated there, the views extend and invade the house. The patio is the most important space in the house.

It squeezes to allow a narrow walkway to the garden. The colour contrast between yellow and light blue marks the boundary. This is a space that astounds us with its form and colour, the shadows (and the violet and pink petals, fallen on the pavement from a twisted tree).

The light, coloured pale-blue, ethereal and weightless, invades the interior as well. Each of the rooms absorbs some aspect of this generous presence, and one has the sensation that the house is alive ("the little impossible paradise"?).

All of the construction is marked by the tension of the lines and the visual axes, in a coherent design that extends all the way to the scale of the construction detail. Each element is resolved in accordance, and it is the profundity of Siza's reasoning that makes it all credible. The interior is minute and sweet, and even the sharper corners or the most unlikely solutions seem natural, domestic and evocative. The pair of pillars in the dining-room: one pillar is twisted, the other is crowned by a sort of capital, also slightly twisted. These are precise, if minimal rotations, which fill the space and deform it. As one approaches, their size and configuration, their reciprocal distance, attract the gaze. They seem like bodies,

tactile presences, petrified inhabitants (who support the construction). You perceive, here and at other points, a sort of intimate and accessible monumentality, sharply dissimulated but still present on the interior of the little house.

In this project, Siza abandoned the composition by planes, in keeping with the two extreme possibilities of total closure and total opening. In fact, it seems that the theme of transitional spaces took on here a decisive importance in the development of his architecture. Not only the patio, but such other elements as the bay window (utilised not once but twice), the gallery, small-scale hollowings out, minimal courtyards enclosed by walls, all make up the built volume. Thus, the complex geometry also emerges from the articulation of the interior-exterior relationship, always mediated by these spaces in which the openings are concentrated, resolved meticulously as moments of expressive density in a continuous control of passages of scale.

The theme of the variation of heights is fundamental in this sense.

These continual variations are not obtained with plaster false ceilings, rather it is the structure itself that is articulated in false planes. The scheme of the roof allows it to include all the heights and geometries of the ceilings.

The structural elements are reduced to the bare essentials. The guttering is set within the roof, resolved however without metal flashing thanks to a system of waterproofing, at the time an innovation, and much cheaper than zinc, which consisted of a waterproof paint that was the same colour as the façade. Where the wall meets the ground it turns directly into the cement flooring with no protective covering.

A double-wall system was adopted, with

perforated bricks and load-bearing blocks, in keeping as well with the form of the plan: the interior wall is continuous and bends, marking off the rooms, a central space separates it from the exterior wall. This system, which makes it possible to execute with considerable ease the fair number of acute angles and twists, is also an expressive choice: for instance, in the entrance, where the exterior and interior walls are painted different colours.

As can be seen in the structural details, all the window frames are fixed directly on a line with the interior masonry; the fillings are in plaster and the threshold in cement. Of all the construction solutions, it is the cheapest, extremely spare.

The interior materials are the ones that we find in the houses built in those years: cork for the floors, enamelled wood for the fixtures and for much of the custom-designed furniture (such as the bookshelves in the living-room and kitchen). The windows are screened by curtains. On the interior the walls are plastered and polished smooth, with a warm white hue. The interior fixtures are painted a glossy yellow, slightly different from the colour of the façades.

Closely tied to this house, Siza is keen to play a role in even the smallest changes. It no longer belongs to his brother. When it was sold, a few years ago, the current owners received a notebook with indications of the colours of the plaster, the window frames, as well as the architect's complete availability to help on all elements of maintenance. As if to say, it is necessary to preserve, starting immediately, the works which will one day belong to posterity at large.
EM/AC
(Travel Notes, October 1999)

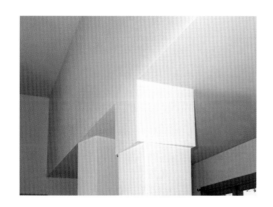

Casa Maria Margarida

Arcozelo, Vila Nova de Gaia, Portugal

Client: Maria Margarida da Rocha Pinto Pinheiro
Sousa Machado

Collaborators: Miguel Guedes de Carvalho, Eduardo
Souto de Moura

Lot area: 380 sq. m.
Total built surface area: 135 sq. m.
(house 115 sq. m. + second storey, 20 sq. m.

Project Description

The ground floor, with a surface area of 115 square metres, consists of entrance kitchen, living-room, two bedrooms, a complete bathroom and a closet. On the
planned lane, a garage is proposed.

The choice was made for a flat roof because of the windy
nature of the site, with the resulting construction of an
appropriately sheltered terrace, overlooking the sea.

The structure of the entry is subdivided in height, making it possible to use the upper floor, with a surface area
of 20 square metres, occupied by a bedroom with bathroom.

The construction materials and processes correspond
to economic and quality-related criteria. The load-bearing walls are double, built with blocks of cement upon which are set the lofts of the roof. The finishings
are made of painted plaster and in the service-rooms
is planned a ceramic lining to a height of 1.5 metres.
Cork floors and interior and exterior window frames
made of enamelled wood.

The structural and system plans will be submitted in
due time.

Álvaro Siza
Oporto, 14 August 1979

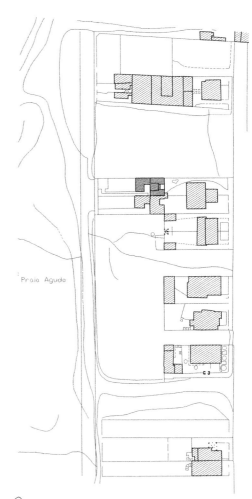

1. *Overall view (1:2000)*
(Source: Camara Municipal de Vila Nova
de Gaia, original scale 1:2000)

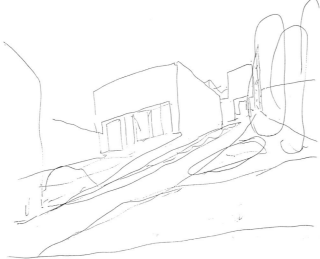

2. *Floor plans, elevations and cross sections, preliminary study (1:250)*
(Source: Álvaro Siza Archives, undated)

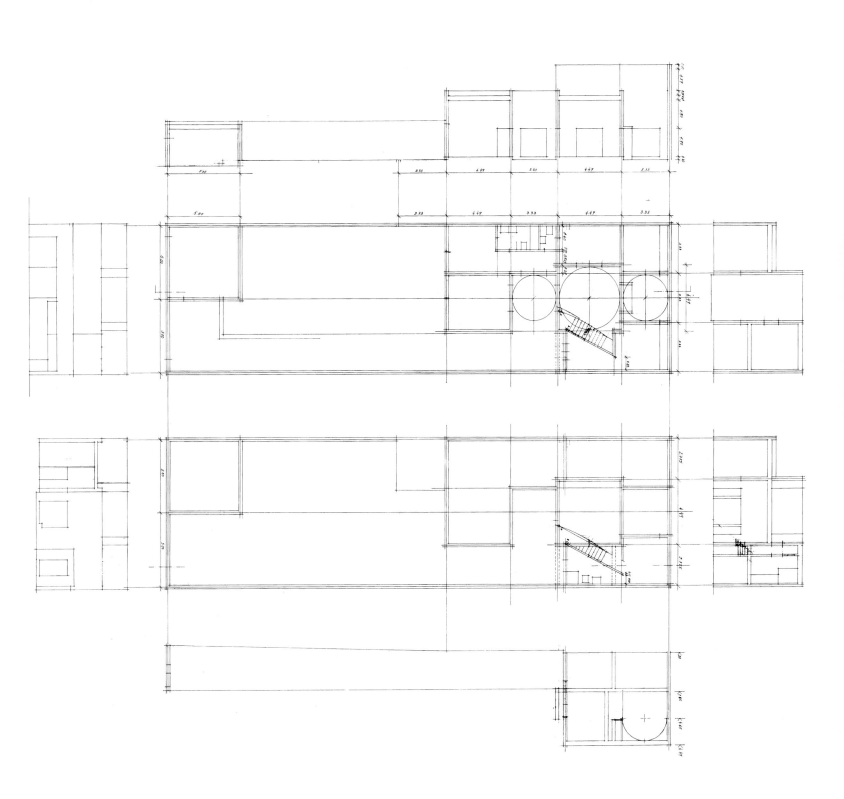

alçado norte

Alçado poente

planta piso 1

planta piso 2

planta piso cobertura

Corte 1.1

Corte 2.2

3. *Floor plans, elevations and cross sections (1:250)*
(Source: Álvaro Siza Archives, undated)

4. *Geometric layout of the diagonal axes, fireplace, staircase and pillars* (Source: Enrico Molteni, 2002)

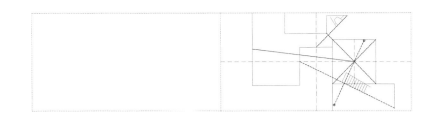

Descriptive Note

This is the smallest of Siza's houses to have been built. A complex and successful project, it has received little attention from the critics, with a few rare exceptions (Juan António Cortes): it constitutes a point of completion and synthesis.

A few kilometres to the south of Oporto, Arcozelo has the appearance of a sleepy vacation spot on the oceanside. Along the sand dunes shaped by the wind runs a road characterised by recent construction, on the whole mediocre, chaotic buildings, which leads to the house. The small building, designed for a couple with a child, occupies an elongated rectangular lot, oriented towards the ocean. The structure has a greyish, almost banal appearance, and from the exterior there is nothing particularly attractive about it. In fact, in the design intentions, the structure of the garage, unfortunately never built, was meant to hide the sight of the house entirely.

The project is radically inward-turning towards the interior of the walled enclosure of the small lot, in which a masterful design of the space is implemented. The form of the plan substantially echoes that of the patio-hosue for the quarter of the Malagueira, established in May 1978, in which, as at Arcozelo, the lot has only a single free front. The terrain is understood as a metric field organised as a whole in keeping with precise principles. If we examine the early sketches that Siza made, we find numbers which are more abstract measurements than real ones (non-constructive) such as 3.33, 2.755, etc. We see primary figures, such as circle and square, perfect volumes (a 4-metre cube), axes of symmetry, rhythms and successions, which permeate the design with ideal tension and rigour. The project is based upon proportion and clearly believes that in geometric relationships it is possible to find the essence of space, the harmony of space.

From this first project, there emerges a distributive scheme of a closed "L". Superimposed upon this distributive scheme is a principle of transformation that operates punctually, focused on the perception of space and tied to the movement, the visual axes, the light. Each environment thus assumes an identity all its own in a sequence of continual references and relationships. It is the more familiar elements of the house that are utilised as singular moments of expression, in the definition of a comforting and natural domesticity. The fireplace and the staircase are the eloquent presences of this complexity of the work, stretched between rigour and exception – here in the precarious equilibrium of a tightrope walker.

In the cubic hall, or great room, a central representative space for the house at large, you can sense at the same time the presence of axes and symmetries and the presence of diagonal tensions and movements. At the entrance, the pillar that is slightly off kilter from the wall above is certainly not an error of execution nor an exuberant formalism, but the first tangible signal of this second oblique layout, made up of slight shifts, inclinations and freely manipulated elements.

In cross section, on the other hand, you can appreciate the sequence of the proportions of the rooms and the patios, following the enfilade of square-plan spaces. It is a succession of growing volumes by the same margin (2 metres), from the street to the end of the lot, following the incline of the land. The terrace is treated as an open volume, set as a roof over the hall: this "volume" is symmetrical to the two-storey structure of the entryway, in which the low space is on the ground floor, alternating the overlap of high and low. On the interior, the diaphragms of separation and the passages are set at 2 metres, while the net heights are exactly double – 4 metres – and give a certain

nobility to the small rooms. All the spaces in effect have very nice proportions.

In plan, the distribution is organised by separating the bedrooms by means of the central patio, which one reaches from any side and which, since it is open to the south, distributes light to the whole house. The strong midday light hits the square patio with the oblique aspect of sharp, strong shadows. A second patio, smaller and darker, brings light to the rooms set at the end of the lot (kitchen and hall).

The exterior and interior paths always follow a route on the perimeter or a transverse route with respect to the axial arrangement of structures and voids – and the relative openings, and are marked by the series of "architectural accidents". These elements are also evocative in a two-fold sense: domestic and monumental. The marble column between hall and fireplace, for instance. Such a refined equilibrium of spaces, between the ideal and the singular, rigour and exception, between the representative and the intimate, does not emerge however from an entirely autonomous abstract process: it is inserted, indeed, it emerges also from concrete circumstances, in a specific context. As can be seen in the planimetrics, the volume of the house is in fact totally constrained, in form and size, by that of the adjoining house, already in existence, of which it can be seen to be an "almost" exact copy. But all the distance between the two structures can be noted in the line of shadow that just separates the volumes of the two houses. The patio and the garden are designed with different surfaces and materials: slabs of white stone, low dark green shrubs, earth for the climbing vines in the patio and lawn. The design and the arrangement of the exterior reiterate, in their cunning and sophisticated architectural construction, that this is a unitary and fully controlled lot.

On the exterior the walls are plastered and painted with a light-blue/greyish colour, with the horizontal lines of the white ceramics, with a round cross section (it reappears in the Carlos Ramos pavilion, in black) for the ground line and the thin upper line of the cover of the walls, in white stone. These are two important elements, reused later on numerous occasions.

A colder, more neutral exterior is balanced by an interior characterised by a delicate tone, and by the successful design of each detail, meeting point, exception. The tone of the interiors, says Siza, comforts and rests the body from the aggressive pounding of the ocean beach.

The window frames are made of wood and open outwards, painted white, like the interior doors and all the shutters. The staircase in natural wood, the impressive fireplace made of ceramics with marble inserts, the vertical coverings in ceramics, it all confers a rarefied elegance to the house. The glistening surface of the ceramics, the natural brass of the hardware, the measured richness of the marble, the white wood, hand enamelled.

The vibrations of white prevail: shiny, opaque, pure, soft.

The current owner, a painter and collector (in one of the bedrooms is *The Angel of Malagueira*, a drawing by Siza), has arranged paintings and objects in a measured way; the furniture, too, is well chosen and carefully placed. She likes, she says, the luminosity of the interiors, the thorough views, the sense of calm and tranquillity. You can perceive a strong sense of affection and awareness: a complicity between architecture and inhabitant is rarely found in such a clear and complete form as in this small, marvellous house.

EM/AC
(Travel Notes, October 1999)

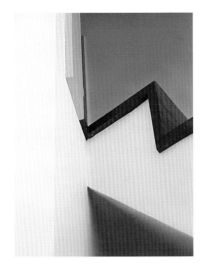

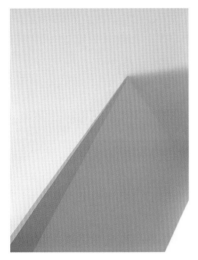

Casa José Manuel Teixeira

Taipas, Guimarães, Portugal

Client: José Manuel Teixeira

Collaborator: José Luis Carvalho Gomes

Lot area: 10,200 sq. m.
Roofed area: 925 sq. m.
Renovation of the existing structure:
290 sq. m.
New addition: 380 sq. m.
Garage: 150 sq. m.
Pergola: 100 sq. m.

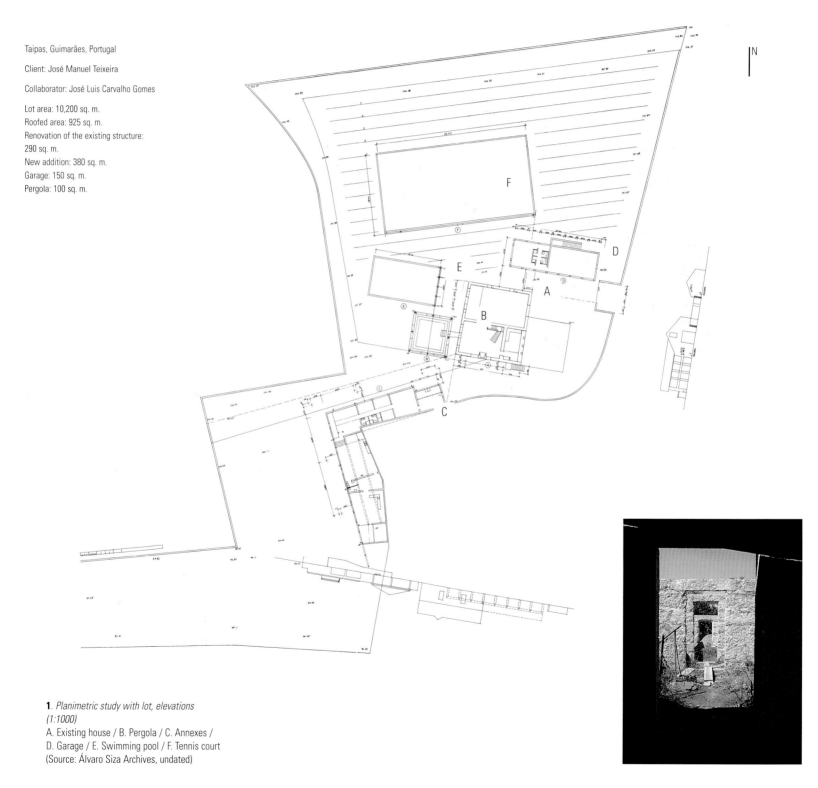

1. Planimetric study with lot, elevations
(1:1000)
A. Existing house / B. Pergola / C. Annexes /
D. Garage / E. Swimming pool / F. Tennis court
(Source: Álvaro Siza Archives, undated)

Descriptive Note

The intervention consists of the renovation of an old rural building and a granary. This first intervention was joined by a series of subsequent expansions, at the owner's request. The new construction, in magnificent blocks of granite, has a low, horizontal configuration which balances the mass of the existing farmhouse. Granite, employed in various ways, is the material that ensures unity to the composition, conferring a natural quality that fits in well with the surrounding landscape. Alongside this volume with a new plan, situated in the interior corner of the lot, there is added a swimming pool, a fountain and a series of architectural elements, situated in various points around the garden.
It is exactly these elements which enclose and surround the house that give this work a grandeur and an urban dimension, making this an exemplary enclosure.
AC/EM

The property is partly abandoned and the lush vegetation has grown wildly, which is why we were unable to tour it.
The photographs are by Roberto Collovà.

Casa Avelino Duarte

Ovar, Portugal

Client: Avelino Valente de Oliveira Duarte

Collaborators: Miguel Guedes de Carvalho, Ramiro Gonçalves

Lot area: 830 sq. m.
Roofed area: 182 sq. m.
Garage: 50 sq. m.
Total built area: 319 sq. m.

Project Description

The ground floor, with a surface area of 132 square metres, consists of an atrium protected by an awning, a kitchen with laundry-room, living-room, bedroom, a bathroom and a guest bathroom. At the end of the courtyard is a garage and a storage-room.

The second storey, with a surface area of 113 square metres, consists of four bedrooms, two bathrooms (one of which is a full bath) and a balcony. A staircase leads to an attic of 74 square metres. This space also has a terrace.

The roof is horizontal and vaulted, because of the windy nature of the place. The horizontal parts will be equipped with thermal protection and waterproofed with tarred coverings. The curved part will be coated with zinc.

The materials and processes of construction correspond to criteria of economics and quality. The exterior walls will be double, with the load-bearing walls made of concrete, supporting the roof lofts.

Tinted plaster finishings, in the service-rooms ceramic wall covering to a height of 1.5 metres.

Cork floors and interior and exterior frames in enamelled wood.

The structural and system plans will be presented at an appropriate time.

Álvaro Siza
Oporto, 24 March 1981

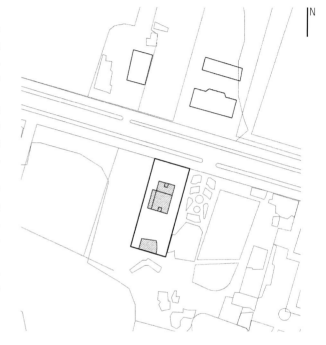

1. *Overall view (1:2000)*
(Source: Camara Municipal de Ovar-DPEP Divisão de Planeamento, Estudos e projectos, undated)

2. *Photos of the model*
(Source: Centre Georges Pompidou, © Photo CNAC/MNAM/Dist RMN Jean-Claude Planchet)

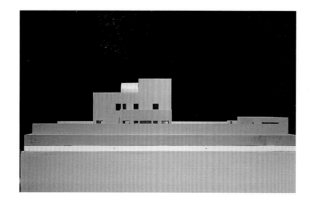

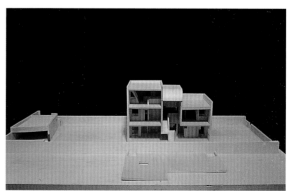

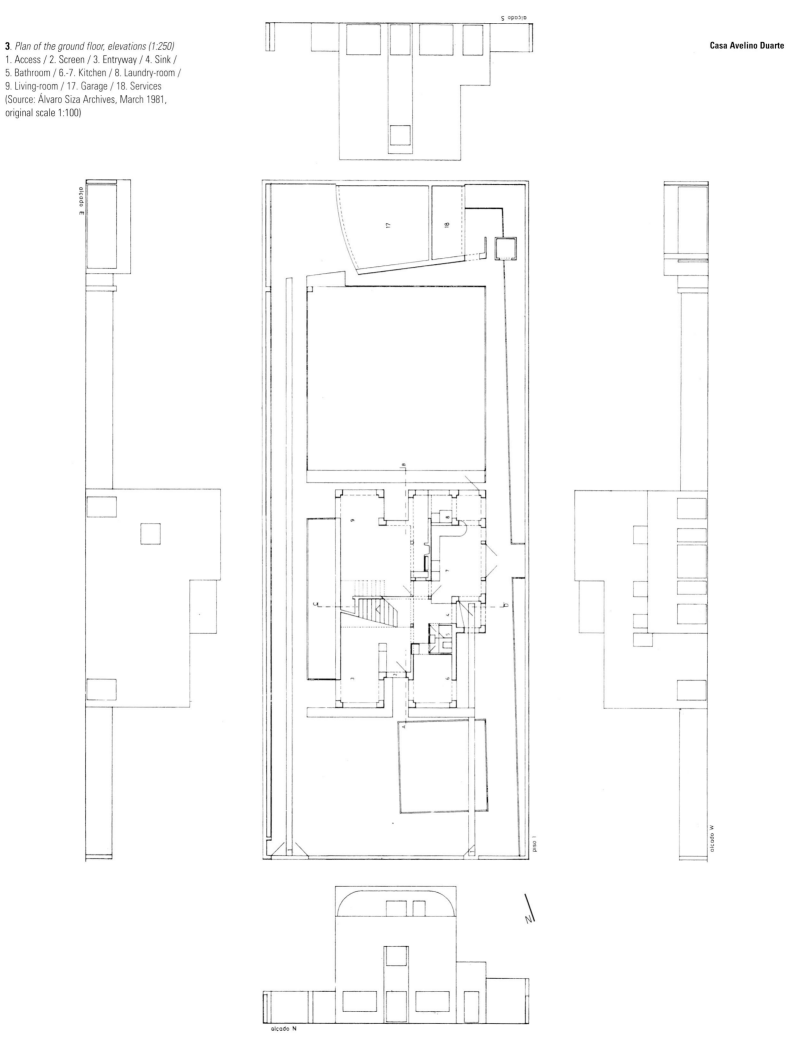

3. *Plan of the ground floor, elevations (1:250)*
1. Access / 2. Screen / 3. Entryway / 4. Sink /
5. Bathroom / 6.-7. Kitchen / 8. Laundry-room /
9. Living-room / 17. Garage / 18. Services
(Source: Álvaro Siza Archives, March 1981,
original scale 1:100)

Casa Avelino Duarte

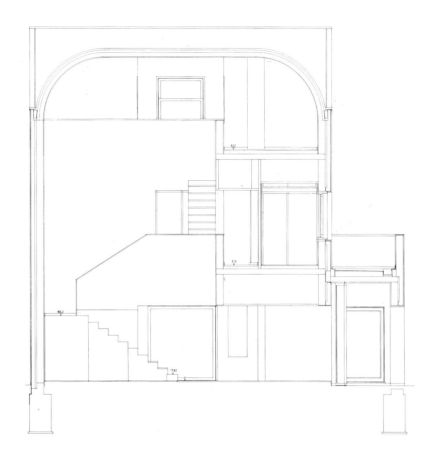

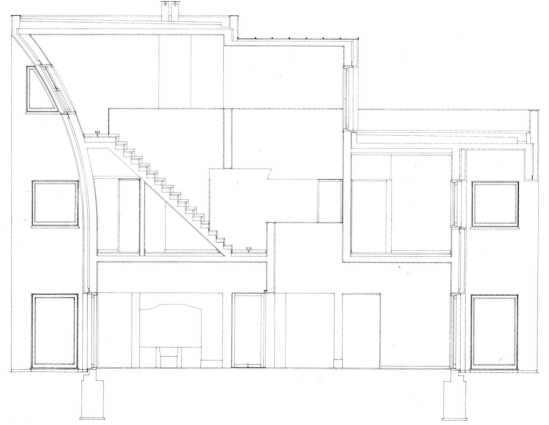

5. *Plan of the ground floor and second storey (1:200)*
(Source: Álvaro Siza Archives, May–June 1983, original scale 1:20)

6. *Plan of the attic and roof (1:200)*
(Source: Álvaro Siza Archives, January 1983, original scale 1:20; 1:50)

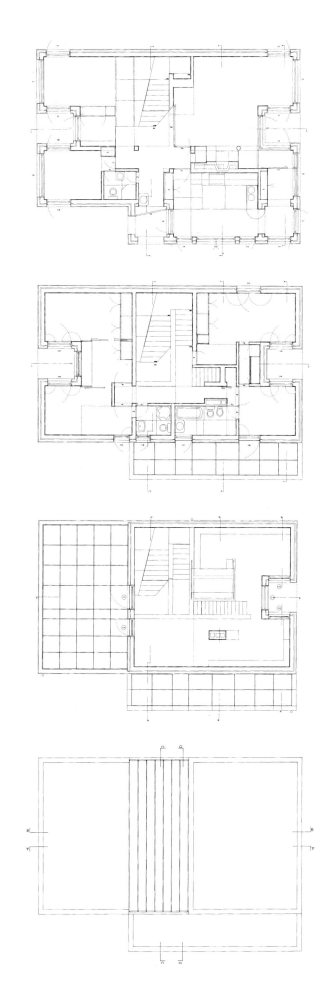

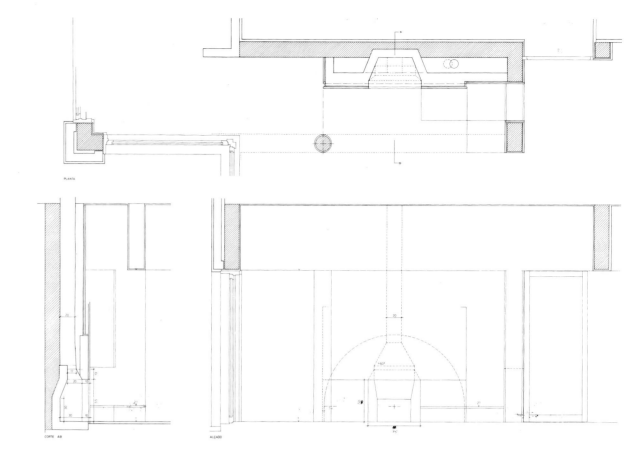

7. *Plan, elevation and cross section of the fireplace*
(Source: Álvaro Siza Archives, July 1983, original scale 1:10)

8. *Detail: horizontal cross section, vertical cross section and elevation of the window frames*
(Source: Álvaro Siza Archives, January 1982, original scale 1:1; 1:10)

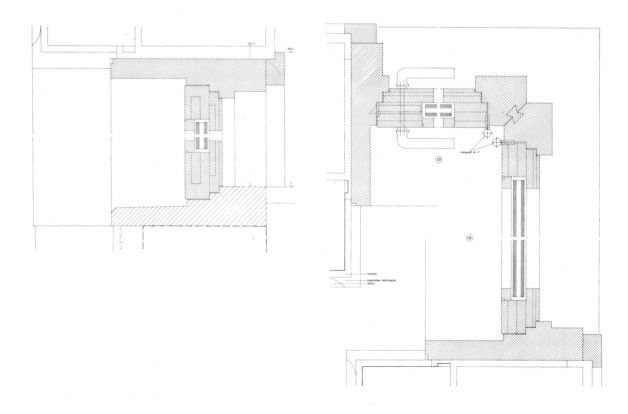

Descriptive Note

To the south of Oporto, the landscape is gentle: the ocean is not very far away. The house stands on a road lined with eucalyptus, disorderly, dotted with new middle-class single-family houses. With its crystalline geometry it stands out immediately for its tile roofs, its postmodern virtuosity and the Palladian colonnades in cement. The house, seen from the street, is smaller than one might expect, less imposing than it appears in photographs.

The tour of the interior leaves us a little uneasy, but this is certainly a personal reaction. We imagine that it was not Siza, of course, who selected the flowery curtains in the bedrooms, the ivy that is a little too green and dangling, massively present in its vase of shiny brass, the abundance of knick-knacks amidst the whites and pinks of the marble of the staircase. On the whole, there is a sense of lack or excess.

Certainly, a house is not only its design. If we think back for a moment to the rarefied delicacy of Arcozelo, a house is in the end the result of the equilibrium between architecture and inhabitant, and if this subtle equilibrium is lost because the occupant is a victim or an idol worshipper, or lacks sensibility or affinity, then nothing is left of that indispensable stratum of spontaneity, but, instead, a series of clear contradictions and inadequacies. There is a false note: will the architecture survive?

The Ovar house, with the Carlos Ramos pavilion and the Vila do Conde bank, is one of the emblematic works of the 1980s and one of Siza's most published houses. In Portugal, that was a period of social transformation and growing openness. A different type of client began to emerge, with different resources and ambitions, in a new context. For Siza, an architect climbing rapidly on the international stage, it was a time for travel and major recognitions. In 1980 he won the

Berlin IBA competition and built his first works outside of the country. This, and many other factors, led to the Casa Duarte project. The house is an object understood as an initially neutral mass in which the principles of transformation are triggered, dictated not only by contextual reasons, but also freer, broader thinking. The design takes its life gradually from a simple volume that by successive reasonings takes on a singular and composite configuration. Composed through additions and subtractions of masses, symmetries and unbalancings, hollowings out or densifications. Articulated over three storeys, the house occupies the front section of an elongated rectangular lot, the end of which is set aside for a service area.

The floor plan is characterised by a central and symmetrical excavation, featured on the two fronts. This subtraction is counterbalanced by the volume stepped roof of the attic and a low structure, limited to the ground floor, as an asymmetrical expansion of the initial rectangle: it is a sort of gallery, a transitional space along the southwest angle opening onto the garden. On the upper floors, the rooms overlook the void produced by the central excavation of the façade: this is also a transitional space, 1.6 x 2 metres deep. The light is controlled, the views are interior, the thickness proves unusual.

It is certainly true that the use of the Palladian partitions – ABABA – later abandoned, is an incisive and greatly appreciated theme in the composition of the house. It is also true that Loos is certainly a reference.

In Loos, the mass dominates over the openings in a very specific relationship of reciprocal dimensions, and the asymmetries are produced by the number and location of the openings in the walls. At Ovar, the mass dominates because the openings are substantially eliminated, and the design of the fronts – symmetrical or asymmetrical –

proves to be first and foremost a product of the manipulation of the volume. It is a sculptural work, three-dimensional and unified. The design of the openings passes into second rank. This work focuses on balancings and imbalances, references: for instance, between the curve of the roof and the curve of the southern excavation. (This curve, like a giraffe's neck, extends over the three storeys of the construction.) But from both interior and exterior, the house is an enigmatic mass, in which the façades are rarely direct and each room is inevitably mediate: the loggias, the terraces, the perimeter gallery and the enclosure wall all define the set of the house's transitional spaces with the exterior (the openings on the ground floor have the same height as the enclosure walls). It is a total introversion towards the interior of the lot – in an intentionally private and protected world. The interior space pulsates. The staircase is the volumetric nucleus of the house, its location allows an unhindered view from the entrance to the study on the upper floor.

The space is strongly characterised by an ascensional movement. The first flight of stairs is a block of marble that narrows as it descends, as if by a perspective effect, and it presents itself as soon as one enters by the main door, set in the central loggia. The kitchen is lovely: an intermediate space between the inside and outside, almost an internal projection of the garden, without marble. The floor with the bedrooms, arranged at the four corners, is quite well articulated in terms of paths and in the hybrid utilisation of the service spaces, bathrooms and wardrobe, all with double access points. The system of hinged doors is resolved perfectly, and the apparent complexity of the floor plan is not perceived. In fact, the internal organisation, resolved around the void of the staircase offers – as Frampton has pointed out – "not only ease and comfort, but also the

idea of an erotic labyrinth that you will never tire of exploring". But the interior as a whole has a quality that is rarely found in a contemporary house: this modest suburban house completely embodies the traits of an aristocratic residence of the high bourgeoisie. Every element offers an opportunity to show off the luxurious surface of the Portuguese marble, richly veined and an intense pink in colour which, with the dark wood of the floors and the doors, spreads a very intense tone to all the rooms. Though with elegance, the house shows itself off. And it is an intentional ostentation in which the shell possesses a richness that is in some cases hedonistic. The fireplace in the hall, with the panels of bevelled mirrors crowning the marble slab, is one indication of this, but not the only one. The floors and interior doors are made of natural wood. The window frames are painted a light yellow and the hardware is made of brass. The walls are plastered and painted, the flashings are made of zinc or stone, the connection to the ground is resolved with a dark-blue ceramic tile. The design of the garden identifies green areas and paths. The interior garden is well cared for, with fruit trees and swings; with a southern exposure and nicely proportioned to the dimensions of the three-storey structure. There are two entrances which, arranged along the sides, lead along the lot to the garage at the end or towards the side entrance.

To enter through the main door, you must make an "L"-shaped movement: in this way, the symmetrical volume of the house is never perceived frontally, and approximation, certainly more domestic, introduces from the very beginning to the compositional complexity of the structure.

AC/EM
(Travel Notes, October 1999)

Casa Fernando Machado

Oporto, Portugal

Client: Fernando Machado

Collaborator: Luísa Penha

Lot area: 820 sq. m.
Roofed area: house, 110 sq. m. + garage,
52 sq. m.
Gross built surface area: 280 sq. m. (sub-basement,
90 sq. m. + ground floor, 95 sq. m. + second storey,
95 sq. m.)

To Build a House

To build a house has become an adventure.

It requires patience, courage and enthusiasm.

Designing a house develops in various ways. In some cases, it is immediate. At times, it is slow and painful. Everything depends upon the possibility and the capability to find stimuli – the difficult and decisive support of the architect.

Designing a house is almost the same as designing anything else: walls, windows, doors, roof. And yet it is unique. Each element transforms itself in relation with the others.

At certain points, the design takes on a life of its own. That is when it turns into a fickle animal, with restless paws and uncertain eyes.

If its metamorphoses are not understood, or if its needs are satisfied more than the essential, it becomes a monster. If everything that in it appears evident and beautiful is captured and fixed, it becomes ridiculous. If it is excessively constrained, it stops breathing and dies. The design is to the architect as a character from a novel is to the author: it constantly outdoes him or her. It is necessary to avoid losing it. The design presses. But design is a character with many authors, and it becomes intelligent only when it is understood on those terms, otherwise it becomes obsessive and impertinent. Design is the desire for intelligence.

Álvaro Siza
Oporto, 1982

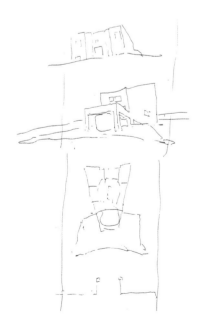

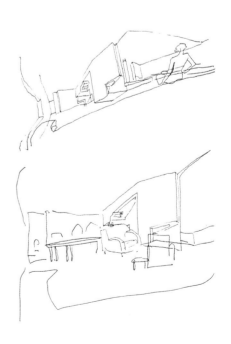

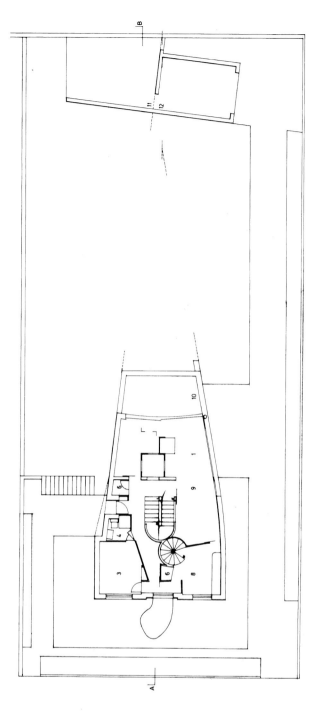

1. *Floor plans, elevations and cross sections (1:250)*
1. Hall, or great room / 2. Study / 3. Bedroom / 4. Bathroom / 5. Patio / 6. Closet / 7. Laundry-room / 8. Kitchen / 9. Dining-room / 10. Veranda / 11. Hall, or great room / 12. Garage (Source: Álvaro Siza Archives, September 1981, original scale 1:100)

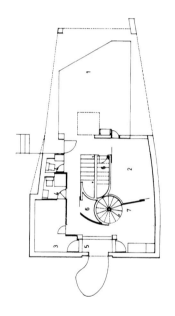
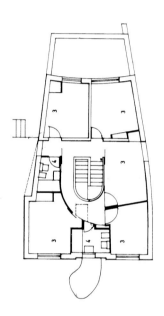

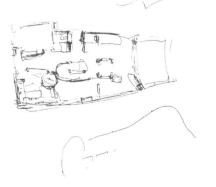

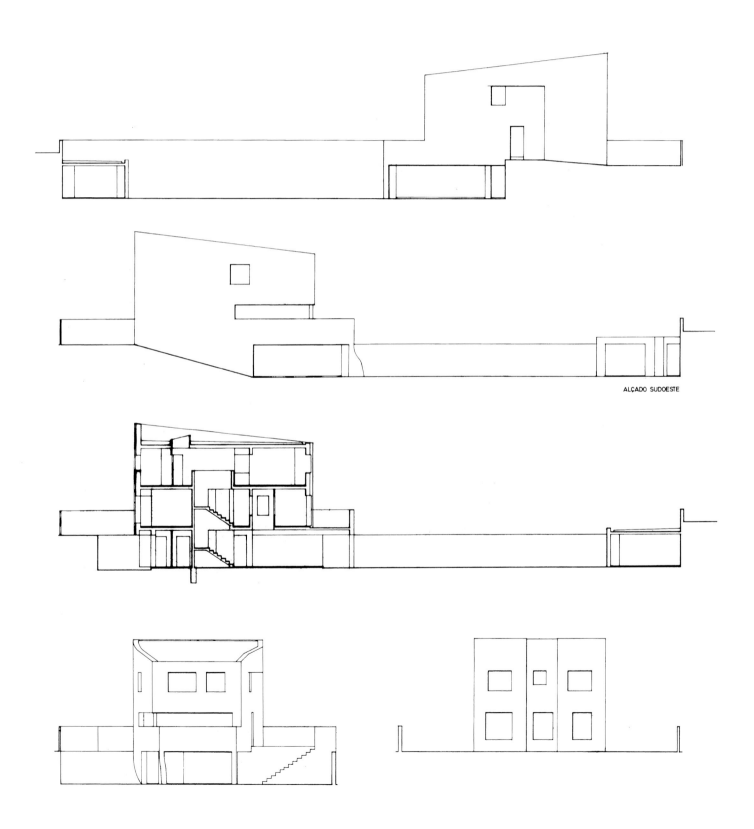

ALÇADO SUDOESTE

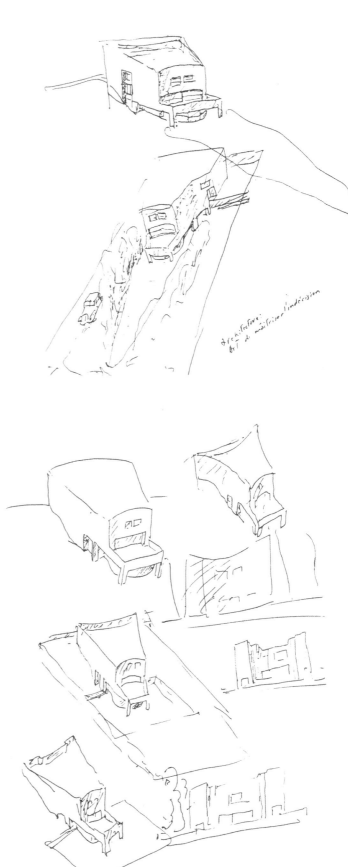

Casa Aníbal Guimarães da Costa

Trofa, Portugal

Client: Aníbal Guimarães da Costa

Collaborator: Zahra Dolati

Lot area: 1,670 sq. m.
Roofed area: 345 sq. m.

1. *Plan of the ground floor (1:250)*
1. Entryway / 2. Gallery / 3. Living-room /
4. Dining-room / 5. Patio / 6. Kitchen /
7. Laundry-room / 8. Pantry / 9. Bedroom /
10. Bathroom / 11. Garage
(Source: Álvaro Siza Archives, October 1982,
original scale 1:100)

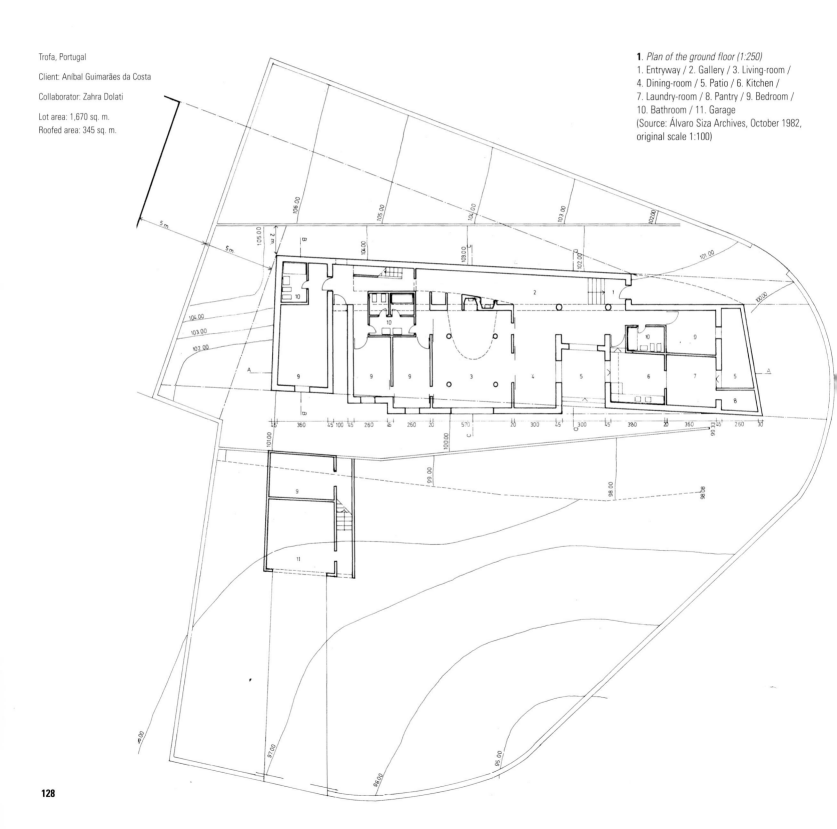

Casa Mário Bahia

Gondomar, Portugal

Client: Mario Bahia

Collaborators: Zahra Dolati, João Pedro Xavier, Clemente Menéres Senude, Miguel Nery

Lot area: 1,450 sq. m.
Planned roofed area: 390 sq. m.

Casa Bahia

I have been asked to offer some thoughts on the project of Casa Bahia, dealing with the theme of inspiration. This problem has no longer bothered me since my first two or three projects, when a growing disquiet and anxiety did plague me. It seems to me that the idea of design springs neither from inspiration nor imagination. I begin by supporting it, and then allow myself to be persuaded. Casa Bahia is designed along the slope of the river Douro, near Oporto: a few platforms (terracings of abandoned vineyards), the constraint of building just a few metres from the axis of the road, an asphyxiating landscape. Thus its design grew as a tower (the garage), the tower stood off from the slope, there appeared a patio dotted with little windows. By me: nothing. Certainly, this tower developed gradually, the elevator stretched out like a neck. The patio-house, handily arranged on the only terracing possible, extended its legs to the river, the staircases like fingers, the staircases like respiration, the windows like eyes, a round opening, a memory of a trip to China. My attention focused on all this. In teaching, all that is needed is to help this animal (each one's project). And the learning begins when you learn to see, something that never ends, when it is not forbidden, and which allows each one to design a house or a bridge or your own model of Ferrari, as long as you have the determination to listen to the others and think together, also things that you must learn. Unfortunately all my animals were annihilated. Some survive with the help of this or that, and also because the time of school is short. That is why students who fall behind are lost and at the same time the "professor-hunters" learn many things, vaguely heard and always resurfacing. It can be deduced that it is best to be neither an excellent nor a terrible student. In the Casa Bahia project, like any other, there was a client, a structure, alignments to be respected, the skills of the craftsmen, the budget, and more besides, but no one should allow themselves to be swept away by external conditions as if on a flying carpet. Perhaps that is why projects are never as good as they could be nor as bad as their restrictions might promise.

Álvaro Siza
Oporto, 1984

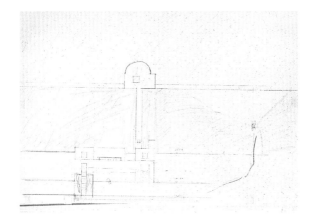

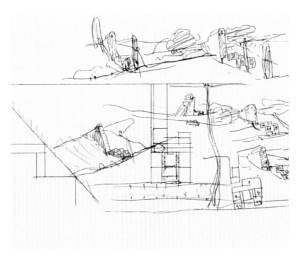

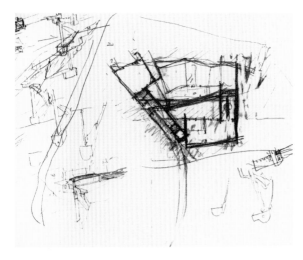

1. *Overall view*
(Source: redesign from the original)

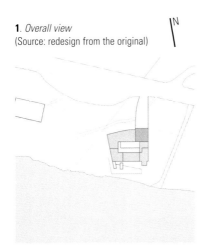

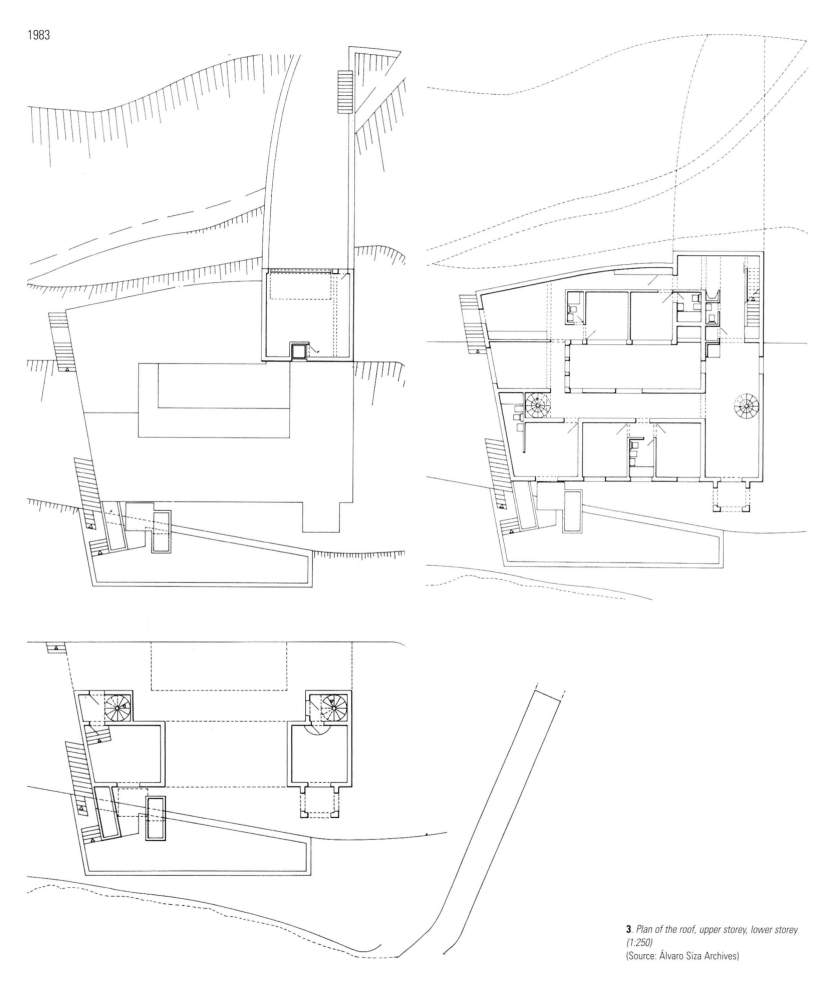

3. *Plan of the roof, upper storey, lower storey*
(1:250)
(Source: Álvaro Siza Archives)

4. *Photos of the model*
(Source: Centre Georges Pompidou, © photo CNAC/MNAM/Dist RMN Jean-Claude Planchet)

5. *Elevations and cross sections (1:250)*
(Source: Álvaro Siza Archives)

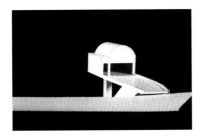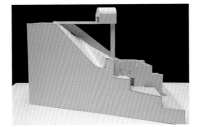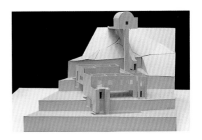

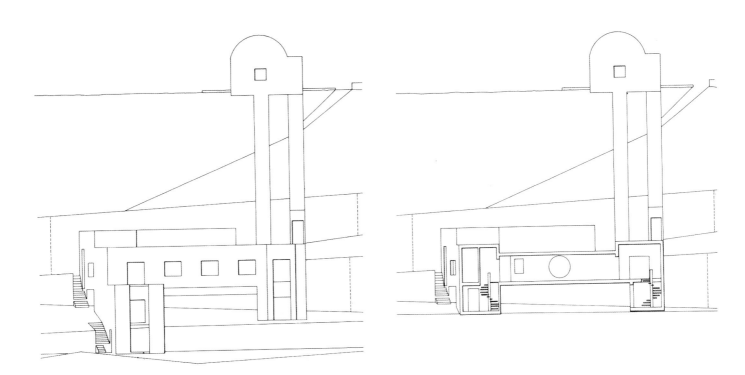

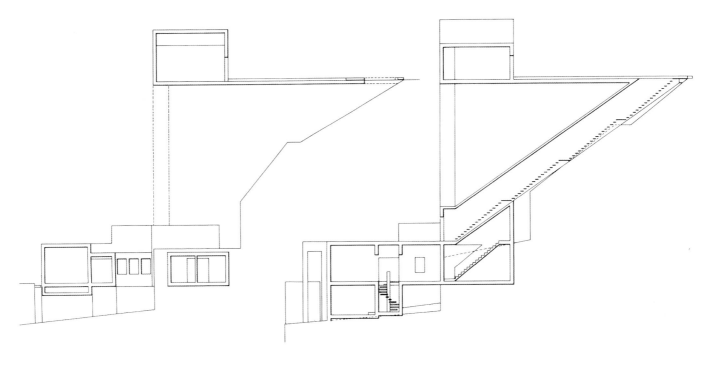

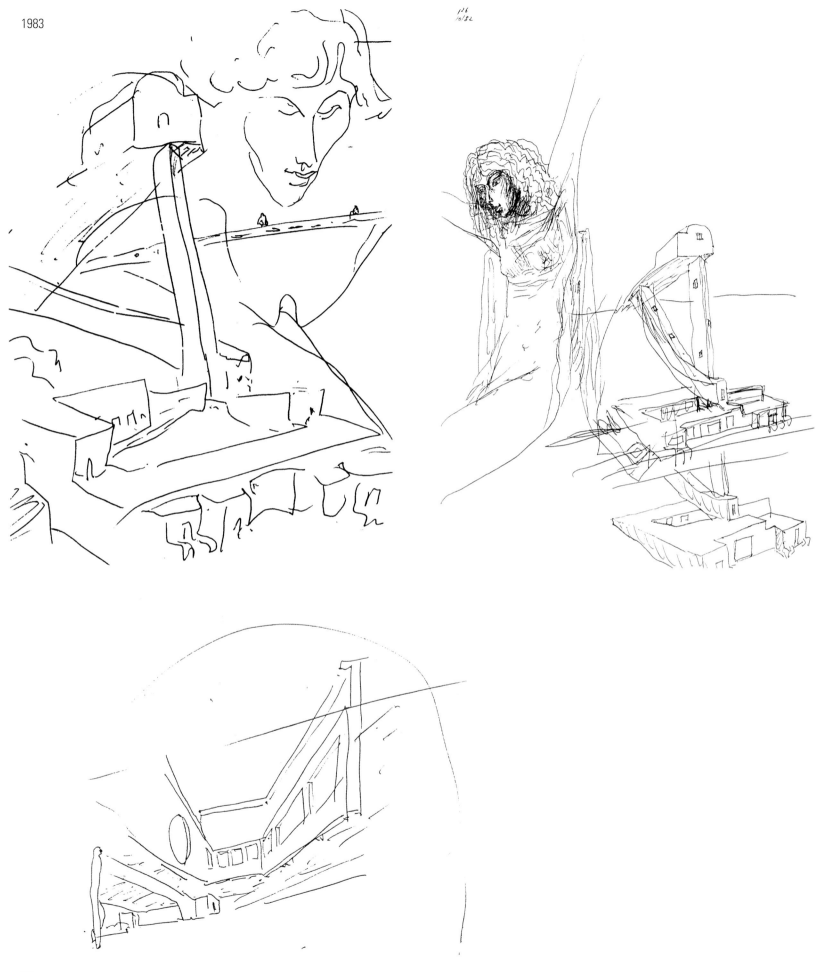

Sintra, Portugal

Client: Erhard Adolf Josef Pascher,
Brigitte Ilse Pascher

Collaborator: Miguel Guedes de Carvalho

Planned covered area: 530 sq. m. (main house)
Land area: 12,300 sq. m.

1. *Overall view*
(Source: Enrico Molteni, redesign from the
original)

2. *Floor plans, cross sections, elevations
(1:500)*
1. Entryway loggia / 2. Vestibule / 3. Access to
the library and the ground floor / 4. Library /
5. Access to the patio on the ground floor /
6. Swimming pool / 7. Hall / 8. Bathroom /
9. Service-room / 10. Vestibule / 11. Bedroom /
12. Terrace / 13. Sauna / 14. Wine cellar /
15. WC / 16. Kitchen / 17. Laundry-room /
18. Service patio / 19. Patio / 20. WC /
21. Pantry / 22. Living-room / 23. Solarium /
24. Pantry / 25. Patio / 26 Fireplace /
27. Access to the patio
(Source: Álvaro Siza Archives, February 1985,
original scale 1:100)

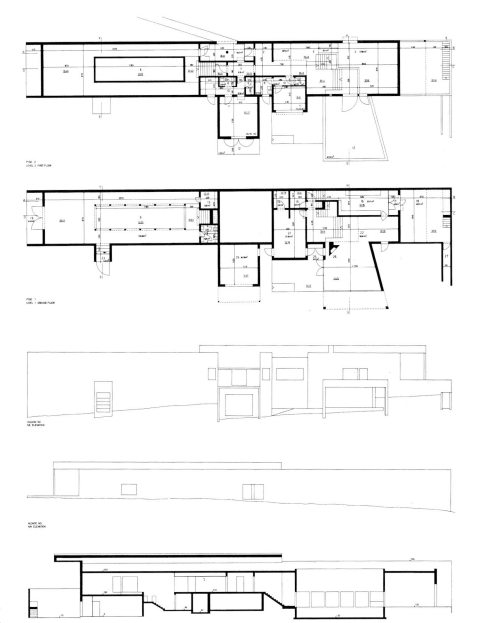

Casa Álvaro Siza

Malagueira, Évora, Portugal

Client: Álvaro Jaoquim de Melo Siza Vieira

Collaborator: Nuno Ribeiro Lopes

Lot area: 96 sq. m.
Total built area: 84 sq. m.
(42 sq. m. per floor)

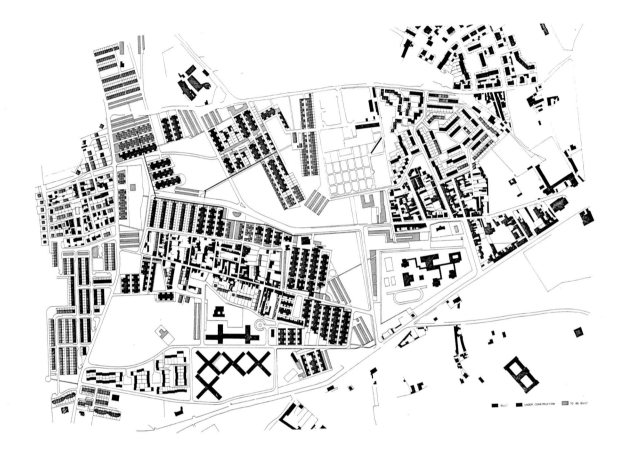

1. *Plan of the Malagueira district*
(second published version)
(Source: Álvaro Siza Archives, undated)

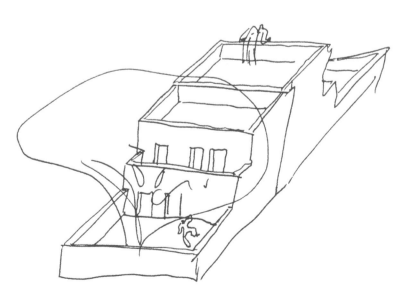

2. *Floor plan, cross sections and elevations (1:200)*
(Source: Álvaro Siza Archives, March 1984, original scale 1:50)

3. *Type A-T2 (1:200)*
(Source: Álvaro Siza Archives, June 1980, original scale 1:50)

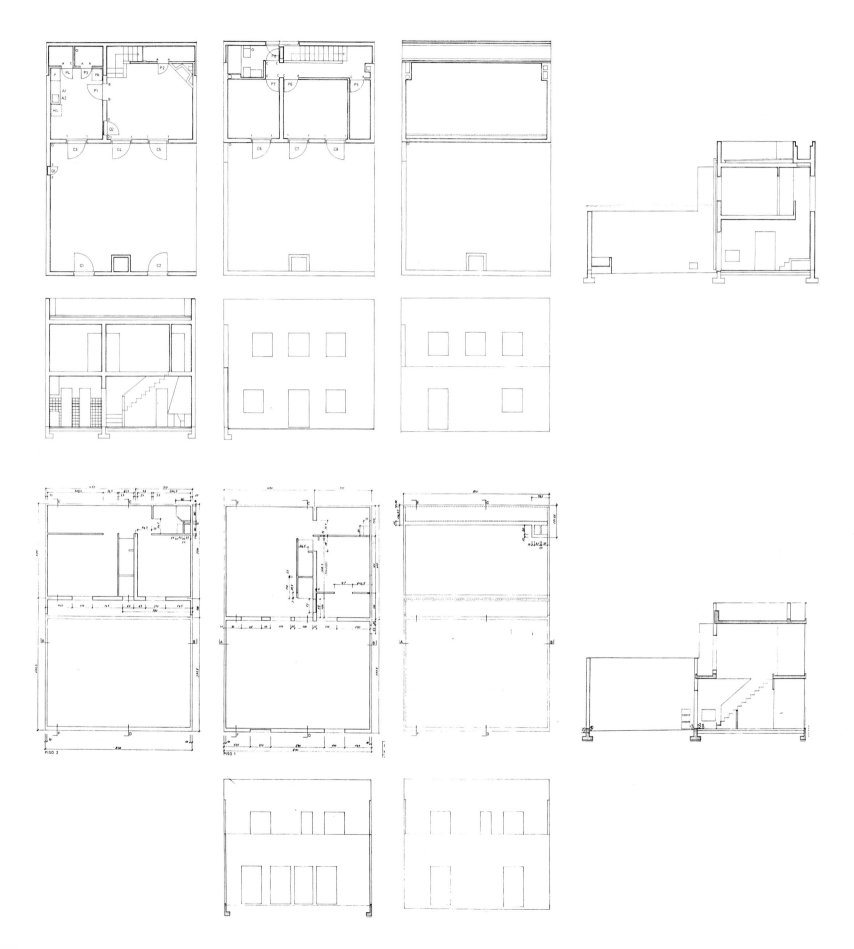

PISO 2

PISO 1

4. *Longitudinal cross section (1:50)*
(Source: Álvaro Siza Archives, March 1984,
original scale 1:20)

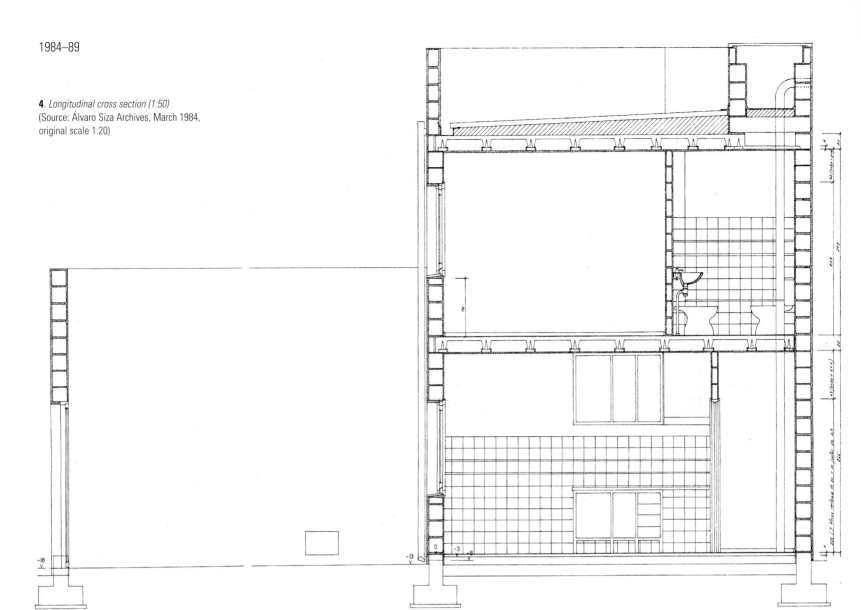

Descriptive Note

The house that Siza designed for himself is an extra house and, perhaps, the ideal house of the Malagueira neighbourhood. The design of the neighbourhood dates back to 1977. The basic lot is a 12 x 8 metre rectangle, in which different development typologies can be built with countless variants, and for 1200 residences. Several of the lots are left free for privately owned houses, outside of the sectors built by the various cooperatives. The first houses were characterised by the presence of the large transverse fireplace on the street side and by the "L" movement of the floor plan, two choices that were abandoned shortly thereafter. The reasons were clear: on the one hand, the construction costs needed to be reduced, and on the other hand the result of the first houses built triggered some

thinking about the overall design. The loveliest streets in the neighbourhood are in fact the simplest, purest ones, in which the only variation of the profile is caused by the slight slope of the land. These streets have continuous walls with doors (which are in some cases also windows) that are all the same. This tendency towards an extreme reduction of the design leads to the house that Siza built for himself, a few years later. The project was based on the typical house A-T2, defined in June 1980, upon which he impressed a further simplification. The balcony on the second floor was eliminated, bringing the façade entirely into a single plane; the design of the interior front was regularised, with the establishment of three windows per floor at the same distance, and almost symmetrical; the size of the patio was increased and the size of the house

was reduced to a minimum; the interior staircase moved to the far wall; a fireplace was located in the centre of the hall or great room; a fountain was placed in the patio. The interior distribution called for a kitchen with annexes (pantry, laundry-room) and a great room on the ground floor, while on the upper floor, a bathroom with exterior access, two bedrooms and a wardrobe. The construction design is based on the systems utilised in the neighbourhood, but with a few detailed exceptions that bring the house a discreet quality. But as we walk through the streets of the neighbourhood, we cannot detect any distinctive sign: this is one of the many houses of Malagueira, anonymous and modest.

We should note the difference between this house and the one that Nuno Ribeiro Lopes – Siza's chief collaborator for

Malagueira – designed for himself and completed at the beginning of the 1980s (see *Lotus International*, no. 37, 1982, pp. 86–87). The alterations introduced to the base of the typical house A-T4, defined in May 1978, have an entirely different principle, intended, by means of the design, to characterise powerfully that house with respect to the others. In this sense, Nuno's exercise (quite typical in the period), made up of rotations, deformations and formal exceptions, confers an entirely evident singularity to the structure.

Siza has the opposite attitude, which in this small and very simple house coincides with one of his most secret ambitions: dissolution, or the unsettling disappearance of the author.

EM

Casa David Vieira de Castro

Vila Nova de Famalicão, Portugal

Client: David Vieira de Castro

Collaborators: Luisa Penha, João Pedro Xavier
Landscape architect: João Gomes da Silva

Land area: 2550 sq. m.
Built area: 525 sq. m.
Ground floor: 300 sq. m. + porticoes, 30 sq. m.
Second storey: 225 sq. m. + balconies, 25 sq. m.

A House

The Casa Vieira de Castro, at Vila Nova de Famalicão, in Northern Portugal, is the extension of previous proposals and research, which are here compared with an unusual context. For the first time, I believe, this is a house that possesses a great deal of outdoor space. Naturally, it is very distant from the urban fabric, as is shown by the considerable size of the lot and the topographic characteristics of the terrain. The position is superb: the house overlooks the valley all along the silhouette of the landscape. The characteristics of the lot, consisting of a hill covered by a pine grove, lead to search for a different kind of intimacy with respect to the preceding houses. Here, quite simply, distance and space are the essential instruments. This solution determines a much freer relationship of the house with the exterior space, more open and extensive. Moreover, the possibility of operating on the garden as well allowed me to extend the scope of the architectural intervention to the landscape. A system of walls makes that very uneven land practicable, to the point of defining a platform, at the elevation of the house, where the swimming pool is also inset. In this context, it is possible, and necessary, to define different poles of activity, the length of the garden, which in the end prove to be interconnected. I therefore think that it is safe to be able to state that this house preserves at the same time a sufficient distance from the limits of the lot and a very strong link with the ground. It seems to me that the special character of this project lies precisely in this aspect.

The project of a single-family house, in a study of a certain dimension, requires considerable effort, since it is necessary to analyse in depth the habits, needs and aspirations of the family that will come to live there. It is necessary to conduct an especially precise analysis so that the design response will be very detailed, in respect to the programme, the functions and the aesthetic appearance. All the same, the design of a single-family house continues to be fertile because it constitutes the ideal moment for experimentation. Indeed, precisely because of the reduced complexity of the system of construction, it is not necessary to impose a rigorous and suffocating control and it is therefore still possible, during construction, to make modifications. These can also be requested by the owner, who can ask for changes in the programme, thus increasing the difficulty of the project. In a country like Portugal, where there exists a lively body of artisans undergoing sweeping transformations, which is not to say on the road to extinction, it is still possible to make prototypes that I often utilise as well in other more general circumstances. Many items of furniture, for instance, which are now mass-produced, take their origin from the furniture conceived for a certain house. For this reason as well, I continue to design single-family houses, despite the economic disadvantages of doing so.

This house was basically designed for a couple, and so it is not very big. There are a few large spaces, even if the bedrooms are not that expansive. After all, they would only be occupied provisionally by the children who, once they grew up, would go away. On the second floor, then, was a master bedroom, two individual bedrooms and a guest-room. The latter room has a degree of autonomy, with a separate bathroom, a loggia, and access to the roof of part of the house, for a direct and privileged contact with the garden.

The construction of the house has a long history, which began in 1984 and which has not yet come to an end. So long a period of time certainly entails a couple of advantages, but at the same time it transforms the project into a nightmare. The owner, from the very beginning, wanted to be involved in the construction and the choice of the companies. As almost always happens, building with several companies entails numerous problems, since there is poor coordination among them, and work tends to drag out. Quite often, there are long pauses when one phase comes to another, due to the time spent waiting for estimates for the next step. I believe that, despite the endless delays and annoyances, the owner had a lot of fun building his own house. For that matter, it is normal for this to be a fairly intense experience, just as it is common to be influenced by the opinions of friends and family. As a result, the discussions don't come to an end with the delivery of the design, but continue on the construction site as well. Precisely the continuity of the dialogue makes this sort of project more intensely participatory and more human in comparison with institutional projects, where a bureaucratic management dominates. The process, then, becomes extremely rich and concrete, and therefore particularly interesting. Moreover, the experimentation, which begins with the construction, encounters in the psychological aspect an important complementary element. Throughout the process of construction, there are crises and successes: the visit of a person who does not appreciate how things are going may discourage the owner, while the visit of a group of students may fill him with enthusiasm.

The construction of one's own house is a dream and a reality, and this reality is difficult to bring to fruition, it is not an easy process. Over the course of time, I have nonetheless noted that a privileged relationship between client and architect is no longer very common, it is beginning to disappear; the very meaning of family, in our society, is probably undergoing a profound evolution. When this relationship, intense and continuous, does occur, it appears very interesting and invites us to consider the necessity that even in the construction of collective dwellings there should be the conditions for participation, in order to make possible the slow taking possession on the part of the person who will go to live there. It seems important to me that even in the construction of lower-cost housing there should be created a dimension of belonging and ownership in order to manifest a collective, and not merely individual, appropriation.

As a child, I was sick for a long time. And so I was sent to rest to Vila Nova de Famalicão. I lived in an old house that had a large veranda overlooking the city. This was a marvellous time, intimate and harmonious, inasmuch as the fragmentation and splintering that is so visible today had not yet happened. I remember a perfect equilibrium between construction and nature. At the end of my first month's stay in that house, since I could go no further than the veranda, I began to hate that landscape, which had become obsessive.

And so I felt an increasingly strong need for a link between the interior and exterior that was not immediate and total, as it had been, instead, at first, in the ambition and practice of the architecture of the Modern Movement. This desire for absolute continuity encounters, or should encounter, in the comfort or control of thermal insulation for instance, reasons for reconsideration.

In passing from the indoors to the outdoors, we always need a mediation, a transition. We have a very rich tradition, of Arabic origin which, especially in the south of Portugal, renders visible the transitional spaces, where light changes until it loses itself in the intimacy of the interior. But this depth, this profundity is rapidly be-

ing lost, both because of the necessity of building for a great number of people (so as to reduce the areas), and because of the passion for new materials (glass or insulating panels).

And yet this transition, which basically constitutes a decompression chamber, allows one to avoid the immediate, unpleasant passage from an interior environment with air conditioning to the rigours of the exterior. Thus, these spaces, loggias or porticoes, serve the precise function that the patio has in the designs of the preceding houses, which were faced with a more or less consolidated urban setting. These transparencies can be found to a truly remarkable degree in the designs of the Venetian architect Andrea Palladio, in which on the interior of the construction of a *universe*, all the rooms communicate precisely by means of voids, arranged along the same axis, which then finds its extension in the treatment of the garden or the fields, vanishing into the distance. From here, then, comes the necessity of those pauses that, in some way, dematerialise the house and create a sensation of continuity and even of a gentle passage between the dimension of the interior and the complexity of the exterior.

The most delicate part of the project is now taking place through the domestication of that topography. That entire system of walls, ramps and stairs in the garden must develop with a constant conservation of the continuity with the core of the house, which will manifest itself not only in the correlation of spaces, but also in the use of materials and in the very treatment of construction materials.

This project, in other words, is an attempt to recover that instinctive wisdom, now lost, that has always governed the study of dimensions, proportions and spatial relations. The material utilised for the exterior is fundamentally granite, which allows a thousand finishings and is very generous in its possibilities of application. There will also be a continuity with the treatment of the vegetation but there, naturally, with the collaboration of a landscape architect.

Álvaro Siza
Oporto, September 1983
(in Álvaro Siza, *Immaginare l'evidenza*, Laterza, 1999)

2. *Plan of the ground floor (1:250)*
1. Entryway / 2. Wardrobe / 3. Service /
4. Wood-room / 5. Garage / 6. Office /
7. Wine cellar / 8. Corridor / 9. Laundry-room /
10. Bedroom / 11. Bathroom / 12. Pantry /
13. Kitchen / 14. Dining-room / 15. Living-room
(Source: Álvaro Siza Archives, March 1988,
original scale 1:40)

3. *Plan of the second storey (1:250)*
18, 20., 22., 24. Bedrooms /
19., 21., 23., 25. Bathrooms
(Source: Álvaro Siza Archives, March 1988,
original scale 1:40)

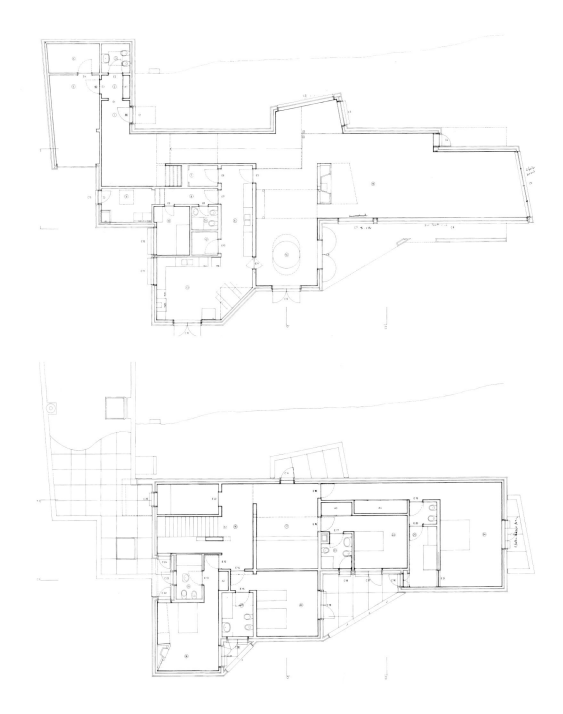

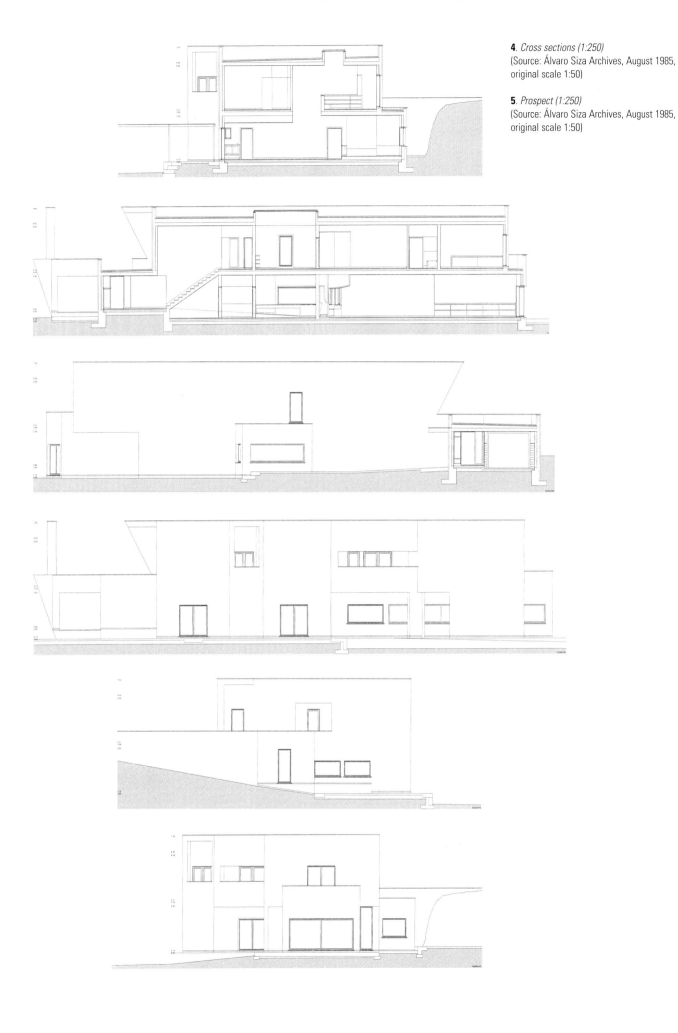

4. *Cross sections (1:250)*
(Source: Álvaro Siza Archives, August 1985,
original scale 1:50)

5. *Prospect (1:250)*
(Source: Álvaro Siza Archives, August 1985,
original scale 1:50)

6. *Details of the window frames*
(Source: Álvaro Siza Archives, undated)

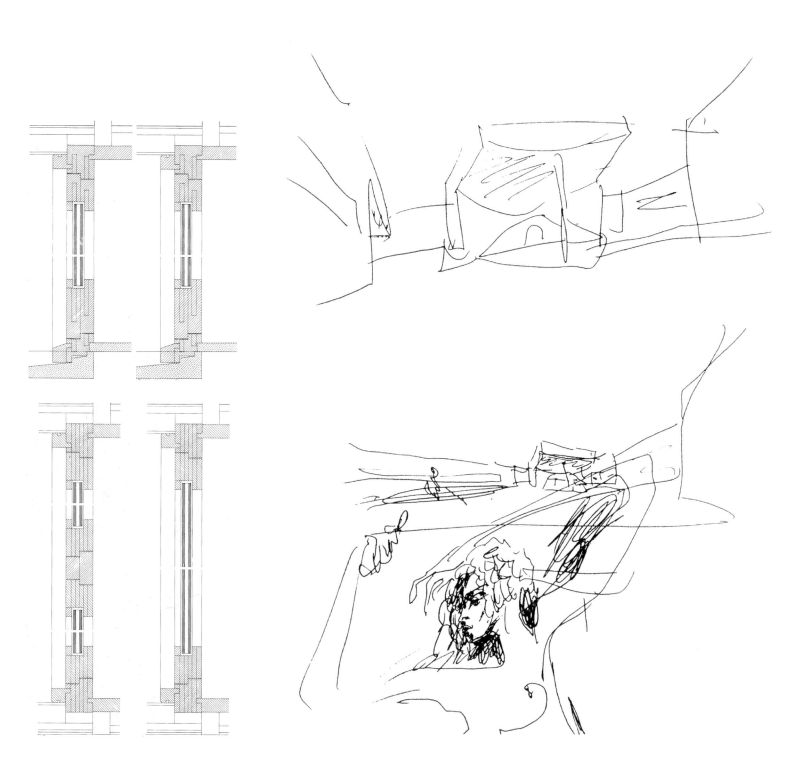

Casa Luís Figueiredo

Valbom, Gondomar, Portugal

Client: Luís Figueiredo

Collaborators: Peter Testa, Luisa Penha,
Carlos Castanheira, Clara Bastai, Cristina Ferreirinha,
Angela Jiménez, Sara Almeida, Fariba Sephernia
Landscape architect: Teresa Andersen

Lot area: 1025 sq. m.
Roofed area: 162 sq. m.
Ground floor: 127 sq. m.
Second storey: 103 sq. m.
Garage and annexes: 35 sq. m.

Casa Figueiredo

In a strongly stimulating setting, this house assumes the condition of an object – a boat near the waters of the river Douro.

But the wall is too close, the garage can't help but melt into it or stand away from it.

In some way, the house is a product of the garage, the point of arrival or departure, relationship with the street and the neighbourhood and a boundary point.

Therefore, this house is neither an object nor a piece of furniture.

Houses are immobile, and they form part of a setting that is fixed at all times.

Each one of us, however, by moving, transforms everything. And so, like a photographer's lens, or like a photographer equipped with a lens, we choose.

Álvaro Siza
Oporto, 1 October 1996

2. *Plan of the roof, of the ground floor and of the second storey (1:250)*
(Source: Álvaro Siza Archives, undated, original scale 1:50)

3. *Elevations (1:250)*
(Source: Álvaro Siza Archives, 1989, original scale 1:50)

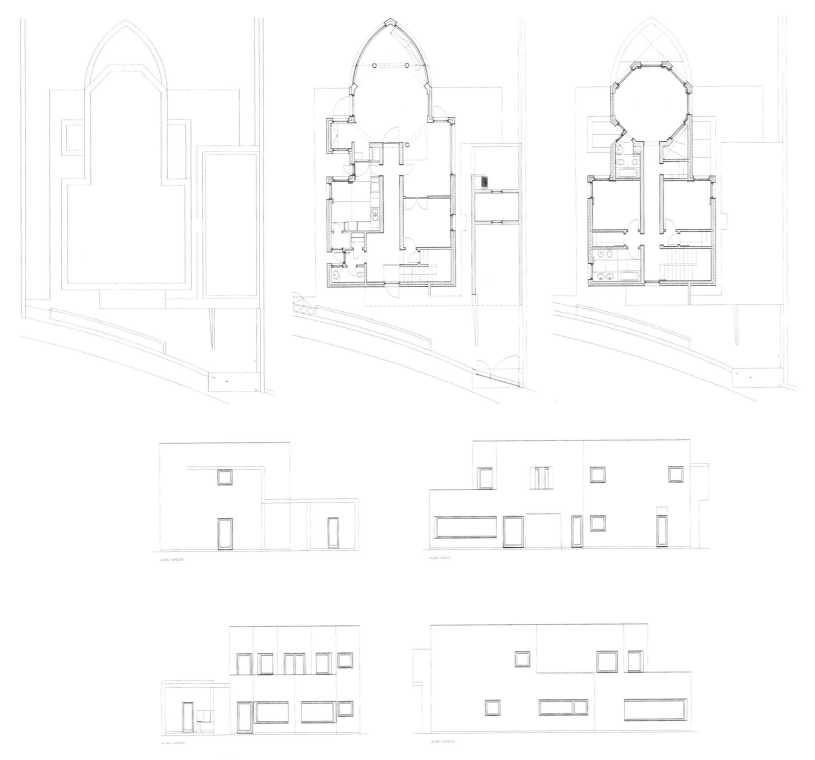

4. *Detail of the curved bench in the living-room*
(Source: Álvaro Siza Archives, August 1982,
May 1993, March 1993, original scale 1:10)

5. *Cross section (1:100)*
(Source: Álvaro Siza Archives, 1989,
original scale 1:50)

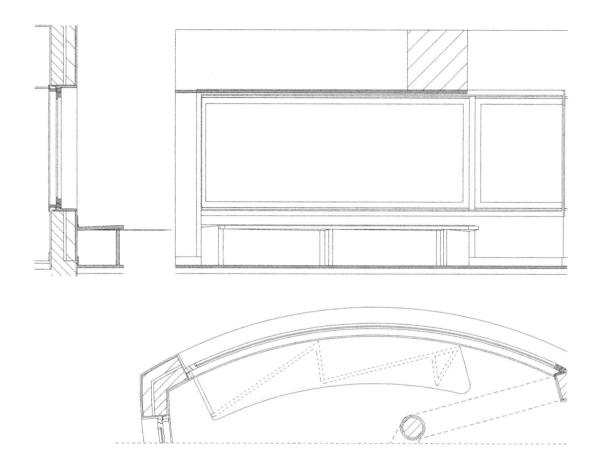

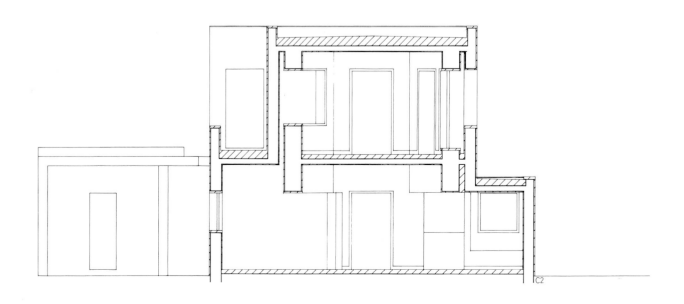

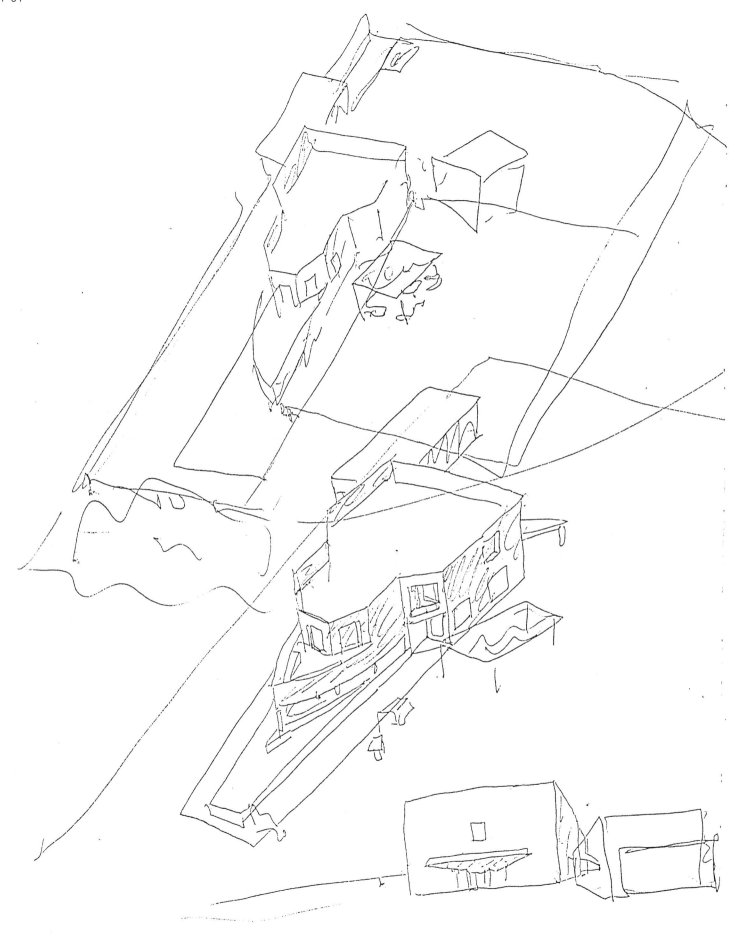

Descriptive Note

Casa Luís Figueiredo has the appearance of an elegant cruise ship from the 1930s, with its prow jutting towards the Douro. We toured it on a luminous day in November, with strong light. This was in Valbom, near Oporto, along the river.

The house occupies the front section of an elongated piece of land that is aligned with other lots along a desolate, slightly uphill road. The neighbouring buildings are definitely ugly: the topography and the proximity of water, however, make the setting pleasant, less hostile than the setting of other suburban houses realised by Siza. The building is articulated on two levels, reworking the typology of the suburban villa with several storeys: it is an autonomous architectural object, in which the theme of intimacy coexists with that of "representation". The project is sharply characterised by the presence of strong geometric forms: the octagon and the tapered bay window in the shape of a prow. The conjunction between the two geometries, central and symmetrical, directs the volume towards the Douro. The building is essentially symmetrical, defined by a principal axis of passage running longitudinally, which penetrates the house from the entrance to the point, without the intervention of any obstacle. A service entrance set along the side façade defines a transverse movement. This two-fold crossing, transverse and longitudinal, is already present in the Casa Duarte. Another element that we find once again is the theme of the double front, the identification of two opposite main façades. The more plastic façade is the one opposite the entrance, while on the road the house appears to be closed, with two openings in the central axis; the continuous awning that connects the façade to the separate structure of the service-rooms constitutes the eccentric feature which unbalances the symmetry. Towards the street, the design is characterised by awnings: one protects the entry gate, joined to the enclosure wall, a second one leads off from the garage and rises to protect the entry front, then turns and also protects the narrow passageway between the house and the garage. In order to provide light to the openings that overlook it, the awning has holes on a line with the windows and remains slightly separate from the house for the whole distance.

On the ground floor is located the central hall with views of the garden, while the corridor is split into two identical parts, one half service (kitchen, bathrooms, side entrance), the other occupied by dining-room and den. The upper floor was reserved for bedrooms; from the room with an octagonal floor plan, you entered a panoramic balcony. The staircase that linked the two levels of the residence was located in a corner, close to the entrance. In a single point we find a small double-height space that allows the master bedroom to overlook the dining-room. In contrast with Ovar, this is a triangular space resulting from the geometries utilised and their contiguity: it is not a cross section open to all the levels that empties the volume on the interior, but an accident of the smallest dimensions. Even the fireplace, set between kitchen and hall, or great room, which organises two very small adjoining sitting spaces, linked by an internal window to the kitchen, is another singular moment, measured on the domestic scale and very important to the equilibrium of the interior spaces. The hall is in fact an important space, articulated in different and balanced environments, in which the strong geometries, the round pillars and the curvatures are contrasting and integrated elements. From the exterior this complexity is lost and the geometric motifs appear much more evident and immediate. The construction system adopted is made up of a double wall, the most interior wall being a load-bearing one with the window frames placed continuously, a middle space and an exterior wall. This is a system that appears consistently in all the holes, protected on four sides by a sort of continuos marble feature.

The colour and the materials define the difference between a pure exterior space and an interior space that is soft, welcoming and tactile. The definition of the volume – dry and compact – is reiterated by the white plaster: the zinc flashing resolves the protection of the façades and a block hollowed out into the marble, at the same time protection and moulding, the attachment to the ground. The walls of the balconies are instead protected by slabs of light-coloured stone, like the flooring. The windows are either casement or swinging vertically, and the window frames are painted light yellow, while on the interior they are left in natural wood.

On the interior, wood dominates, for the floors, the mouldings, the window frames, and for much of the custom-designed and built furniture, such as the fine bench in the hall, that accompanies the curvature of the wall; the wood is juxtaposed against the satin-finished white plaster. Marble is present, without excess. The tone of the interiors is pleasant, very natural and absolutely unostentatious. The furniture has been selected and placed carefully, the sign of a certain affinity between the client and the architect, seen also in the courtesy and stories of the owner.

AC/EM
(Travel Notes, November 2001)

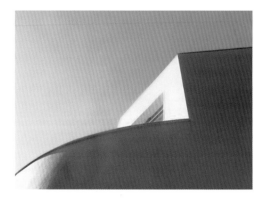

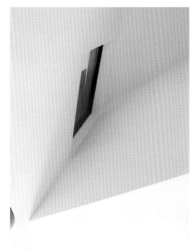

Casa César Rodrigues

1. *Overall view (1:2000)*
(Source: Camara Municipal do Oporto, CD-Rom)

2. *Plans of the ground floor, second storey and attic (1:250)*
(Source: Álvaro Siza Archives, July 1995, original scale 1:200)

Oporto, Portugal

Client: César Rodrigues

Collaborators: José Salgado, Carlos Castanheira, Robert Levit, Cristina Ferreirinha

Lot area: 1750 sq. m.
Built area, ground floor: 120 sq. m. + portico, 15 sq. m.
Built area, second storey: 120 sq. m. + terraces, 25 sq. m.
Garage and storage: 120 sq. m.

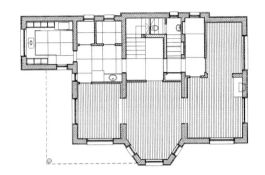

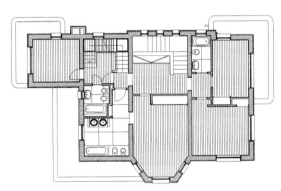

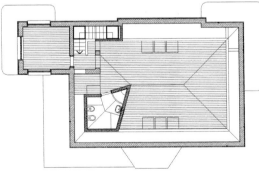

3. *General floor plan (1:500)*
1. Driveway entrance / 2. Walkway entrance /
3. Garage / 4. New shed roof / 5. House /
6. Storage area / 7. Swimming pool (not built)
(Source: Álvaro Siza Archives, July 1995, original scale 1:200)

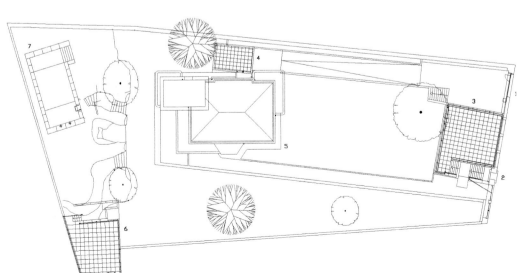

Descriptive Note

Siza's work began with a consultation
on the purchase of the house, built in the
1940s, which would then be adapted to the
new client's needs. The intervention was
prolonged for almost ten years, and entailed
the construction of a new wing on the
street, used as a garage, the arrangement of
the paths and the garden and the complete
renovation of the house.

The property is located in the fine
residential zone of Foz, along the ocean
coastline. In contrast with other projects,
Casa Rodrigues was not built from scratch,
but to all intents and purposes it can be
included among the suburban houses
designed and built after 1980, inasmuch
as it is similarly configured.

All of the interiors were completely redone
and the materials are those used in Siza's
houses in that period. The tone of the
interiors is extremely serene, discreet and
luminous.

The execution is almost perfect, but,
perhaps, slightly impersonal. By eliminating
an artisanal practice that left room for
doubt, revision, invention, it substantially
changes the way the architecture is done.
Siza responded to this reality by fixing,
with a bit of insistence, certain building
solutions, continually modified and adapted,
which lead to a constant and reliable
quality. Details have been normalised
and the solutions are evolutions or direct
repetitions of other projects.

On the exterior there are few new openings:
in fact, the project focuses on giving new
proportions to the existing windows.

The colour selected for the plaster, originally
white, is the pink tone already used in Casa
Serralves, an important building in Oporto
from the same period which Siza knew
quite well.

EM

(Travel Notes, April 2002)

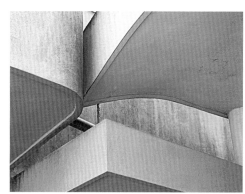

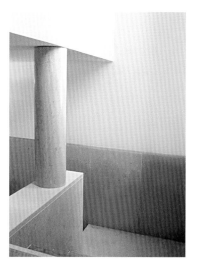

Casa Javier Guardiola

Puerto de Santa Maria, Spain

Client: Javier Guardiola

Collaborators: Joan Falgueiras, Luis Mendes, Carlos Castanheira, Elisiario Miranda, Jun Saung Kim

Lot area: 1250 sq. m. (parcel D)
House, lower storey: 200 sq. m.
House, upper storey: 150 sq. m.
Garage: 80 sq. m.

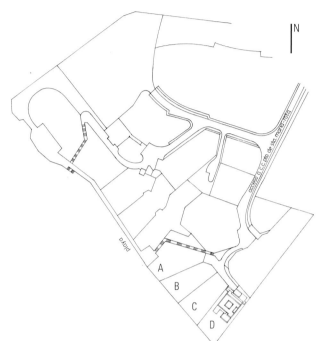

1. *Overall context: parcel A: Frank Gehry; parcel B: John Hejduk; parcel C: Peter Eisenman; parcel D: Álvaro Siza*

2. *Situation, plan of the roof (Source: Álvaro Siza Archives, September 1988, preliminary design, original scale 1:100)*

3. *Photos of the model (Source: Álvaro Siza Archives, undated)*

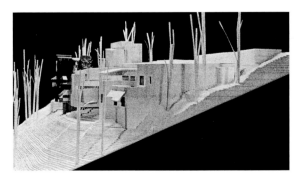

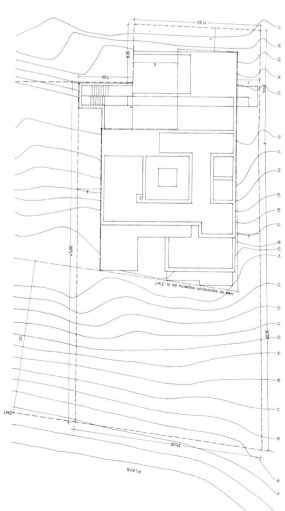

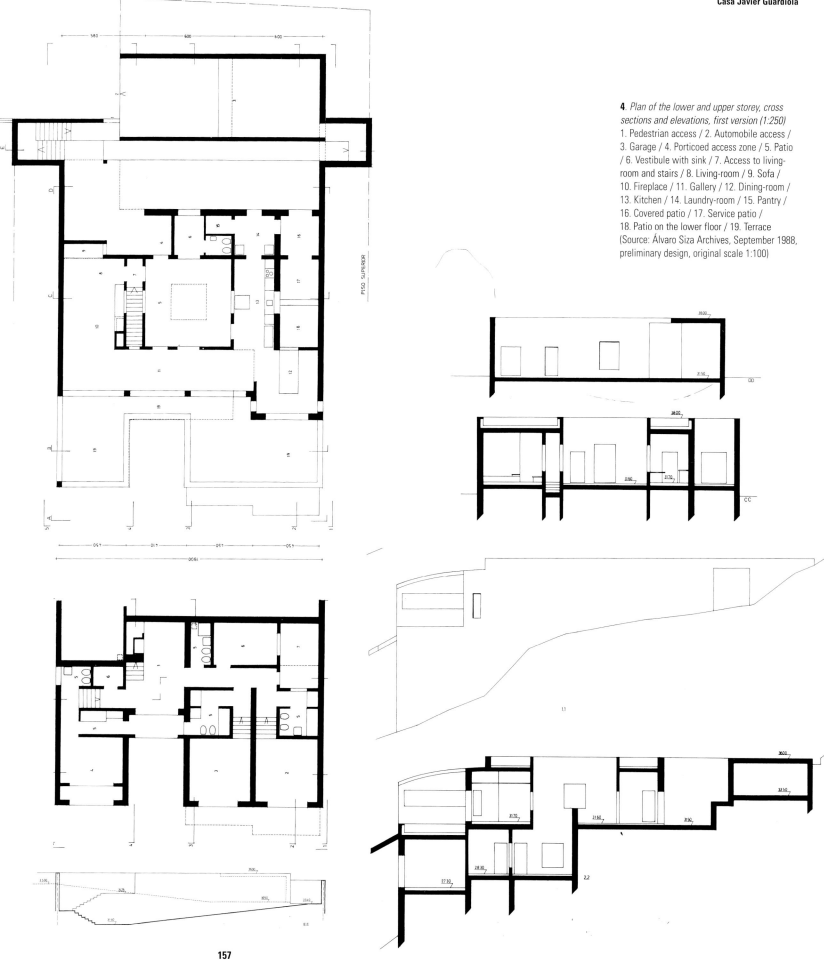

4. *Plan of the lower and upper storey, cross sections and elevations, first version (1:250)*
1. Pedestrian access / 2. Automobile access / 3. Garage / 4. Porticoed access zone / 5. Patio / 6. Vestibule with sink / 7. Access to living-room and stairs / 8. Living-room / 9. Sofa / 10. Fireplace / 11. Gallery / 12. Dining-room / 13. Kitchen / 14. Laundry-room / 15. Pantry / 16. Covered patio / 17. Service patio / 18. Patio on the lower floor / 19. Terrace
(Source: Álvaro Siza Archives, September 1988, preliminary design, original scale 1:100)

PISO SUPERIOR

Quinta de Santo Ovídio

Aveleda, Lousada, Portugal

Clients: Ana Costa, Manuel da Silva

Collaborators: José Luís Carvalho Gomes, Ashton
Richards, Sofia Thenaisie Coelho, Anton Graf,
Matthew Becker, Francesca Montalto, Raffaele
Leone, Mitsonuri Nakamura

Lot area: 30,000 sq. m.
Roofed area: 672 sq. m.
Built area:
Farmhouse: 300 sq. m. (ground floor, 173 sq. m.
+ second storey, 127 sq. m.)
Pool and facilities: 196 sq. m.
Chapel: 43 sq. m.
House renovation: 589 sq. m. (ground floor, 233 sq. m.
+ second storey 329 sq. m. + laundry-room, 27 sq. m.)

Project Description

Renovation of the house, adjoining buildings and gardens, and construction of a covered swimming pool, garage, tennis court and chapel.

1. Description of the estate and its buildings (house, agricultural annexes and house of the custodian of the wine cellars).

The house at Santo Ovídio was once at the centre of a large farming and foresting estate. Presently, its area has shrunk to about 3 hectares, with enclosure walls around the house and the vineyard.

A boulevard of linden trees on the exterior, lined by two walls, leads to a portal with a heraldic crest, from which you reach a square enclosed by a wall, by the interior enclosure wall of the estate, and by the main house.

In the plaza, there is a prominent Baroque fountain next to the retaining wall of a sharply sloping piece of land, bounded at the highest point by old farm buildings.

The vineyard lies to the south and is crossed lengthwise by a road that links the plaza to the wine cellars and the service entry to the estate. Around the house lies a garden with belvedere.

The house, two storeys tall, featured two separate zones, not in communication one with the other: the ground floor, used for storage, office and garage, and the upper floor, with living quarters.

An external staircase leads to the atrium. A succession of alcoves, bedrooms and halls, or great rooms, linked by a corridor, ended in the kitchen at the far end.

2. Intervention

2.1 *House*

The unused spaces, once dedicated to venerable agricultural functions, have been incorporated into the residence, and a connection has been created between the two storeys. The main access on the second storey, where a sequence of spaces set aside for living-room, library, dining-room and kitchen has been maintained. The stairs that lead to the lower storey are now in the space of the library. Between the atrium and the living-room, a courtesy bathroom and a wardrobe. On the ground floor is a living-room, a game-room and bedrooms with a private.

2.2 *Annexes: laundry-room*

Near the kitchen is a small annex that has been set aside for use as a laundry-room, a storage-room with a gas boiler.

2.3 *Indoor pool*

The old custodian's house integrated a wing of buildings adjoining the estate wall, at the highest point of the land.

The covered swimming pool and the dressing-rooms make use of part of this wing, extending it, but separated from the residence by a patio. The renovation preserved the existing rooms, the gable covered with slate, the stone walls and the pitched roofs. The roof over the swimming pool is horizontal and is integrated with an opening skylight. The materials used include zinc and granite on the exterior, marble, wood and *azulejos* on the interior.

2.4 *Chapel*

It appears that a very old chapel dedicated to the saint in question, Santo Ovídio, was demolished at the behest of a former owner.

The new chapel, set among the trees, is situated alongside the linden lane at the high point of the land.

The sacristy juts out from the whitewashed structure of the chapel, and constitutes an entry portico into the holy space before the steps leading to the church courtyard.

2.5 *Garden: belvedere*

The state of neglect of the garden made it impossible to understand exactly the original design. Despite this, the most important elements were present: three high walls and a low wall, belvedere *de conversadeiras*; a portal and a gate at the far end, which describe a longitudinal axis; a pond, a table, an horizontal pergola, trees and a few ruins of a stone irrigation canal.

The intersection between the longitudinal axis and a second perpendicular axis forms a zone of shadow and rest, with a small body of water, surrounded by boxwoods and camelias.

A twisting, "haphazard" path runs through the *parterre*, running around a slate table and over a granite channel. This little canal brings water through the garden to the neighbouring land.

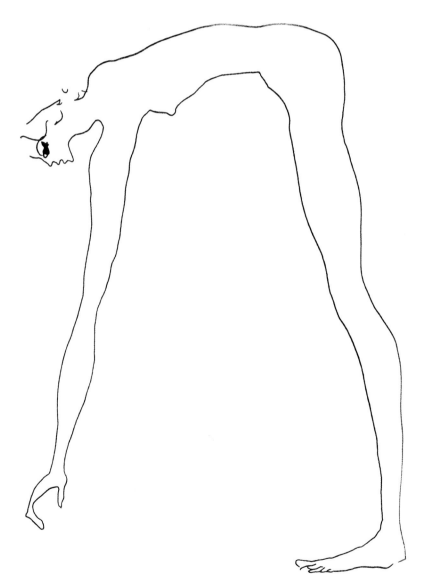

Next to the portal stands an old Chinese wisteria tree near a pergola with stone pillars.
From the pond, on higher land, another pergola runs to the vineyard.

2.6 *Garage*
The solution to reconciling the project (garage for six cars near the house) with the character of the built complex consisted of creating an opening in the retaining wall, near the Baroque fountain, giving access to a patio measuring 6 × 6 metres and a covered space measuring 17 × 8 metres.
A staircase with jutting steps inserted into the walls, like the terracing on the river Douro, leads directly to the high part of the wall.

2.7 *Tennis court*
Adjoining the house and sheltered by the interior enclosure wall of the estate, it is bounded by a granite guide and by netting, with iron supports and steel tensors in the corners.

2.8 *Garden in the hills and barbecue*
The path traced by the square runs past the chapel, climbs up to the level of the swimming pool and the restored house, and then runs down to the level of the main house. This garden has an informal character, with vegetation that is appropriate to the sharp slopes that fill and consolidate the inclines, alternating meadow with shrubbery. In the high zone, continuing from the house but detached, was built the last project requested: the barbecue. These are two granite platforms on offset levels with fireplace and grill, working surface and table. The zinc covering perches on boards and steel pillars.

Álvaro Siza
Oporto, December 2001

1. *General planimetric view (1:1000)*
1. Chapel / 2. Swimming pool / 3. Farm house /
4. Pergola and barbecue / 5. Laundry-room
/ 6. House / 7. Underground garage / 8. Garden
/ 9. Tennis court
(Source: Álvaro Siza Archives, undated,
original scale 1:400)

2. *Swimming pool: longitudinal cross section
(1:100)*
(Source: Álvaro Siza Archives, October 1999,
working design)

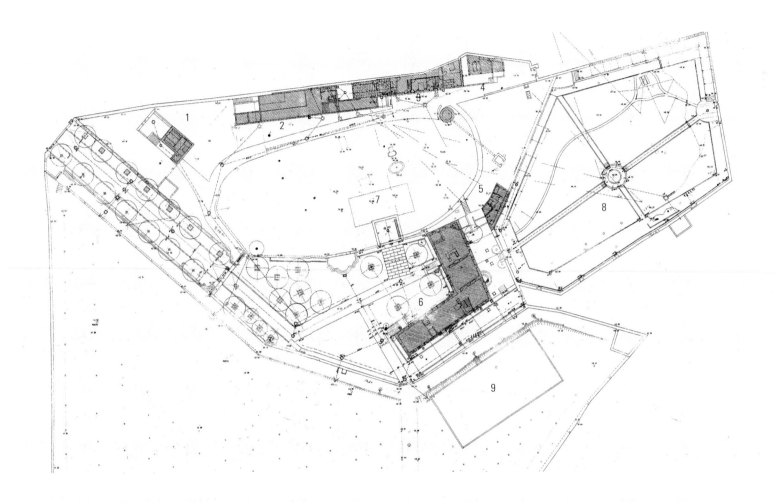

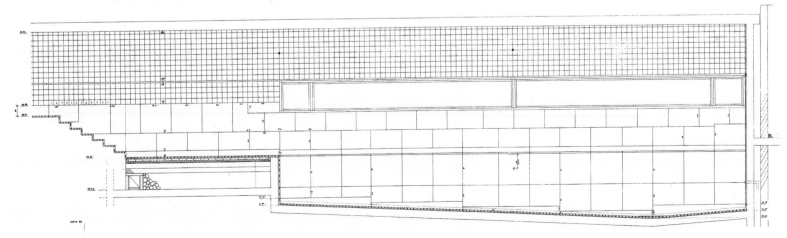

3. *Farm house and covered pool:*
ground floor plan (1:500)
(Source: Álvaro Siza Archives, April 1998
[2001], working design, original scale 1:100)

4. *Chapel: floor plan and elevations (1:200)*
(Source: Álvaro Siza Archives, November 1999,
working design, original scale 1:50)

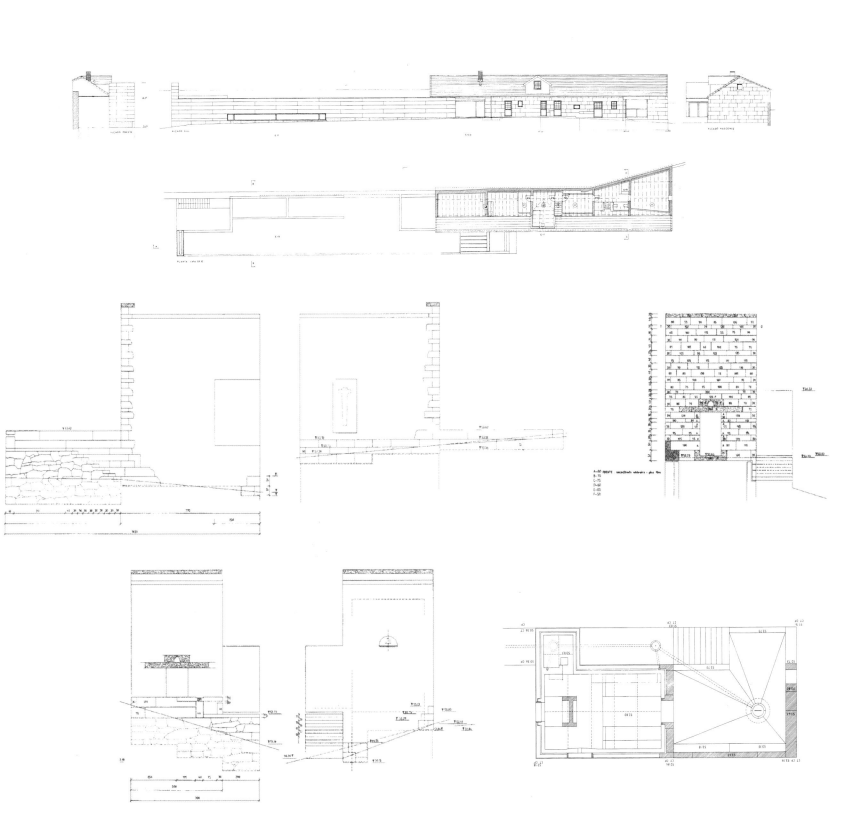

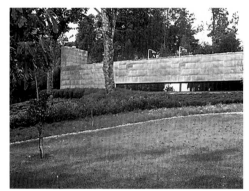

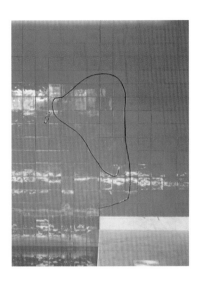

Casa Pereira Ganhão

Tróia, Portugal

Client: Pereira Ganhão

Collaborators: Sandra Vivanco, Carlo Castanheira

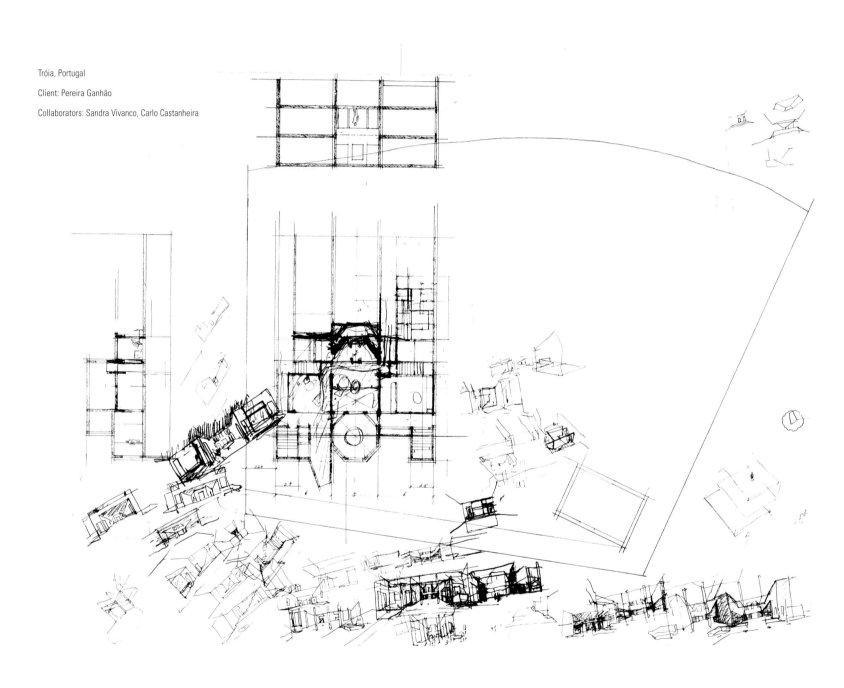

1. *Design sketch*
(Source: Álvaro Siza Archives, undated)

Casa Van Middelem-Dupont

Oudenburg, Ostend, Belgium

Client: Van Middelem-Dupont

Collaborators: Roberto Cremascoli, Andrea Smaniotto, Ueli Krauss, Daniela Antonucci, Maurice Custers
Associates: Christian Kieckens, Kristofel Boghaert, Karen Van de Steene, Pilip Verbeke

Land area: 80,000 sq. m.
Roofed area: 1050 sq. m.
New construction: 330 sq. m.
Rebuilding existing buildings: 710 sq. m.

1. *Floor plan, elevations and transverse cross sections (1:1000)*
1. House (new construction) / 2. House (restoration) / 3. Gallery / 4. Garage / 5. Storage
(Source: Álvaro Siza Archives, January 1998, original scale 1:300)

2. *Overall aerial photo*
(Source: Álvaro Siza Archives)

3. *Photo of the model*
(Source: Álvaro Siza Archives)

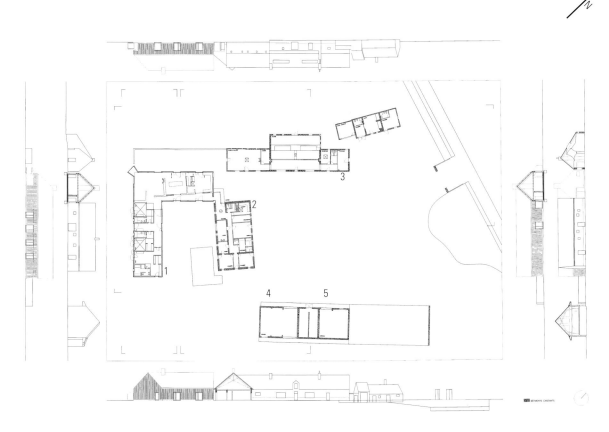

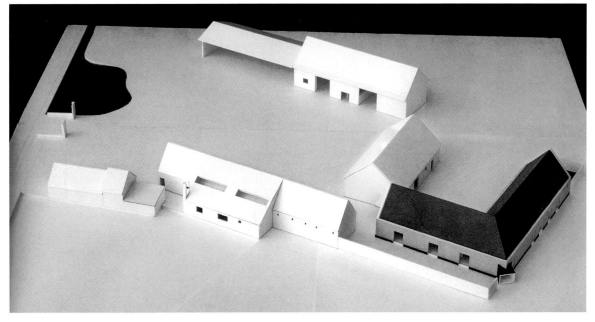

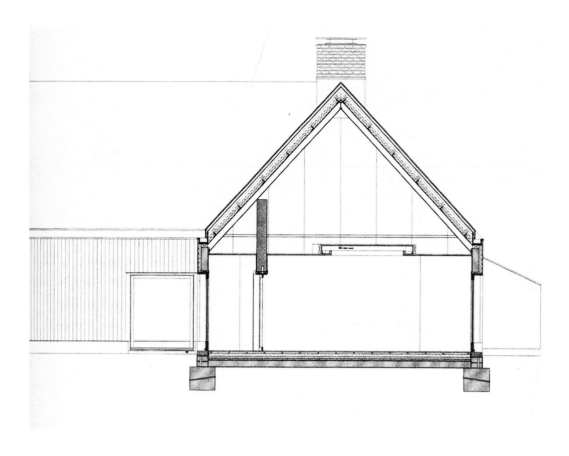

4. *Transverse cross section, dining-room (1:100)*
(Source: Álvaro Siza Archives, undated)

5. *Floor plan of the house (1:250)*
(Source: Álvaro Siza Archives, March 1998)

6. *Working details of the gutter (1:10)*
(Source: Álvaro Siza Archives)

7. *Working details of the window frames (1:10)*
(Source: Álvaro Siza Archives, January 1998
[05.08], original scale 1:4)

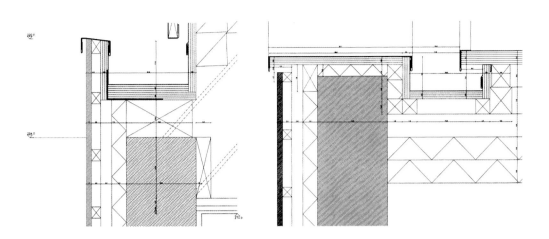

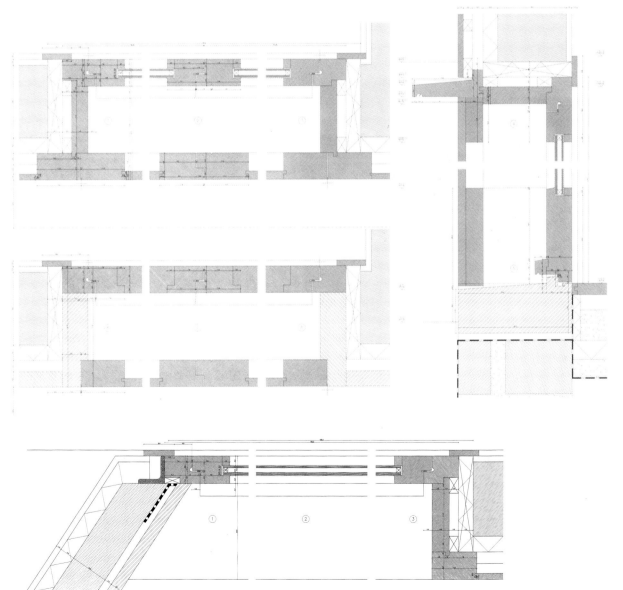

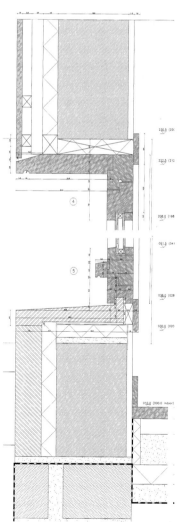

Descriptive Note

The Van Middelem-Dupont House is the first house by Siza built outside of Portugal. It is in Oudenburg, a small town not far from Ostend: the landscape is that of the Flemish *polder*, made up of plains and water, crisscrossed by canals and windswept. The intervention consisted of the renovation and partial transformation of an old farmhouse and the construction of a newly planned residence. The complex is situated on the interior of a very large property, agricultural land reclaimed at the beginning of the eighteenth century. There remains, to commemorate it, a small pond near the entry point. Both the farmhouse and the lands surrounding it have belonged to the client's family for more than two centuries. I visited the house on a rainy day in November, in a milky light; construction had been completed a few months before, with the exception of a part, where renovation was still underway, and which would become a guest house. We see once again the theme of the addition or expansion and thus, the relationship between existing and new construction, taken on and resolved, for instance, already in the Casa Alcino Cardoso. Siza here chose a different strategy, interpreting the new buildings as the growth of a unified complex. The form and the measurements of the new buildings are identical with the existing ones: maximum roof height, pitch of the roof, width of the structures. In fact, while for the placement strategy adopted, the final planimetric layout proves to be almost impossible to decipher in its chronological expansion, the material quality defined for the new structure expresses, in its diversity, the succession of interventions. The existing building is a "U"-shaped compound consisting of three structures, independent one from another, while the addition has an "L"-shaped configuration, which in relation to the existing structures establishes a second, rotated "U." The position of the house and its volumetric and formal relationship with the existing structures creates a final composition that can be interpreted as the growth of a single gene; the use of traditional materials – immediately distinguishable from old ones – differentiates instead the old from the new with a discreet emphasis. The material of the existing buildings is local terracotta brick. One of the three structures – once the house of the client's parents – has been transformed into an art gallery (Madame Van Middelem-Dupont is a psychoanalyst, a collector of contemporary art and a gallery owner); the restoration is executed with respect for traditional rural Flemish typologies, with brick walls painted white, the moulding in black, the window frames in wood that has been painted bright red. The interior was an occasion for research on the theme of structuring space to receive artworks. Various versions have been developed for this part of the project: one of the first saw at the centre of the environment an isolated column combined with a skylight; in the definitive version this element was suppressed in favour of a simpler and more relaxed volumetrics. At the time of our tour, the gallery was hosting a fine exhibition of watercolours and paintings by Helmut Dorner. The structure opposite the gallery has preserved its agricultural function, the walls are visible brick, the roof is in tiles, the window frames are still in bright red. The house with the new floor plan develops from one of the existing structures. The point of attachment between the old structure and the new one is resolved by a small entrance, low and light. The curved glass, on the interior corner, is an especially significant detail. The light rotation of the older structure continues into the new one through the wall that separates the distribution space from the kitchen, dining-room and living-room. In this wing of the house, the spaces follow one another with fluidity, the openings are arranged in keeping with the axes that penetrate the structure from side to side, allowing enfilade views of the surrounding landscape through the house. The other wing of the "L" houses the bedrooms and the bathrooms. All of the window frames are flush with the interior, made of wood painted white on the inside and left natural on the outside, in continuity with the covering of the façades. The living-room is defined by the presence of a large "stereometric" alcove-window covered on the exterior with light-blue stone: this is an addition, a structure grafted on, open to the plain: you can sit in it and admire the horizon. You can see in the floor plan that this element, chiefly expressive in nature, is situated in the exterior corner of the "L", open like an eye in the direction of the countryside. The house is very simple in volumetric terms, with few architectural events and few evident details; what prevails on the interior is an impression of chilly, neutral rigour, a homogeneity of tone. The dominant colours are the light grey of the large slabs of *pietra serena* on the floors in the zone of distribution and the kitchen and a light oak for the other rooms: white for window frames and walls, grey leather for the seat in the window and light-blue lava stone for the fireplace. The homogeneity of the tone continues in the colour of the sky and contrasts with the bright green of the grass. Perhaps a neutrality that makes it possible to project oneself into the landscape, to feel this very present meadow, to perceive a continuity with the atmosphere of the fields, the grain of the earth, the height of the sky. On the exterior the walls are sheathed in vertical planks of red cedar, the same material as was used in the window frames and the shutters fastened to the exterior, which, once they are weathered, will take on a typical silvery colouring; only the entry façade has a sheathing in visible bricks, to better fit in with the adjoining façades. The pitched roof is covered with lead sheets; the gutter, made of the same material, is integrated into the roof. The socle on the ground is made of grey stone. The volume appears completely unitary, elegant; each of the three different materials resolves a specific technical problem. For Siza, the effect, the final image, so important, is not obtained through the use of a single material to cover the entire volume: this is not a reasonable option, but a superficial and not too natural simplification. The construction requires precise choices and, in each point, it is necessary to make use of the best suited material. On the interior, as in other recent projects, one senses the absence of a slow, careful work with the carpenters, with the artisans, but by now this is an old question; he makes up for it on the exterior with the selection of materials that easily take on a certain patina, that take in water, that are affected by time, thus introducing into a design and construction process that must be increasingly normalised, an element of imperfection and fragility and the sensation that the new construction has "always" existed.

AC

(Travel Notes, November 2002)

Restoration of Villa Colonnese

1. *Location. Planimetric view and profiles
of the complex (1:2000)*
(Source: Álvaro Siza Archives, December 1999,
overall rough design, original scale 1:500)

Arcugnano, Vicenza, Italy
Project commencement: 1998, under construction

Client: Domus srl – Patrimoni Immobiliari

Collaborators: Barbara Rangel, Michele Gigante,
Francesca Montalto, José Carlos Oliveira, Francisco
Reina Guedes, Bradford Kelley, Angela Princiotto,
Andrea Smaniotto, Axel Baudendistel, Kenji Araya

Project management: Futura Progetti

Lot area: 32,520 sq. m.
Planned area:
447.40 sq. m. (unit F4)
447.76 sq. m. (unit F5)
450.54 sq. m. (unit F6)
752.52 sq. m. (unit F7)
487.30 sq. m. (unit F8)
566.17 sq. m. (unit F9)
566.17 sq. m. (unit F10)

Plan for restoration of the villa
Volumetrics before the restoration project:
18,955 cubic metres
Volumetrics after the restoration project:
12,045 cubic metres

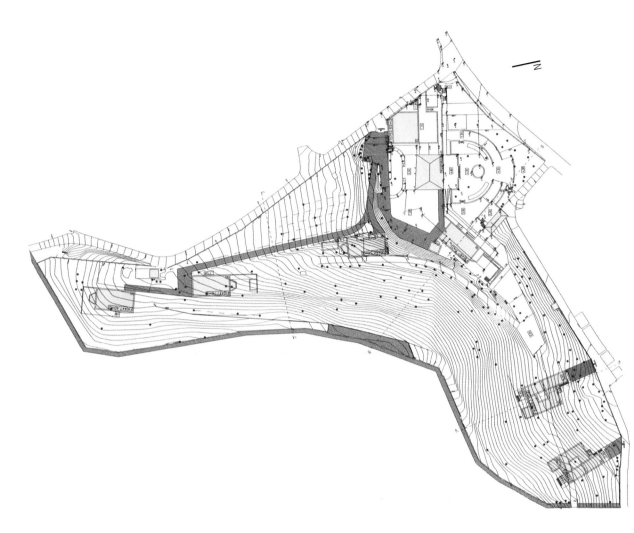

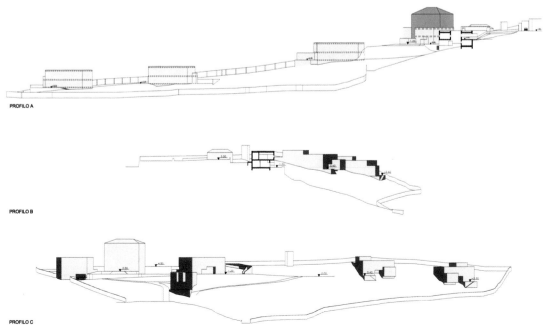

PROFILO A

PROFILO B

PROFILO C

2. *Villa 3 (Unit F8): ground floor plan, second storey, roof, elevations and longitudinal cross section (1:500)*
(Source: Álvaro Siza Archives, January 2000, overall rough design, original scale 1:100)

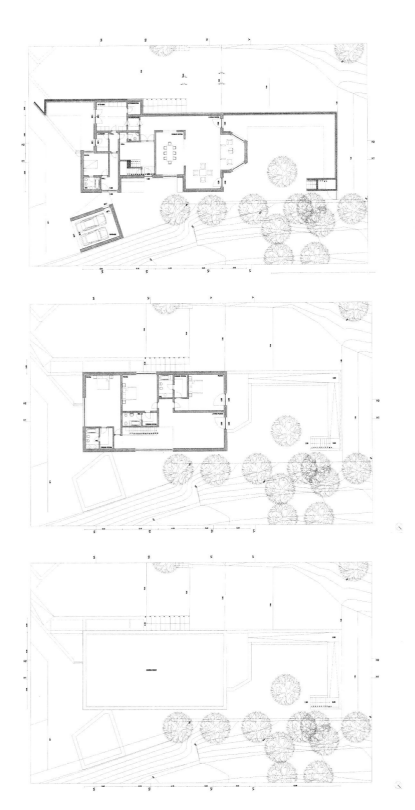

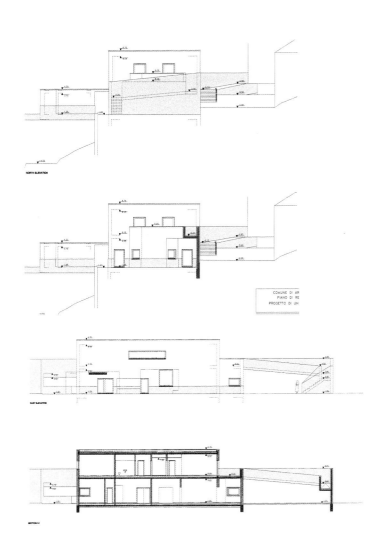

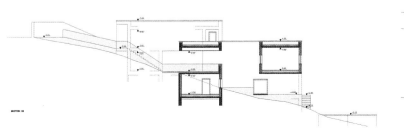

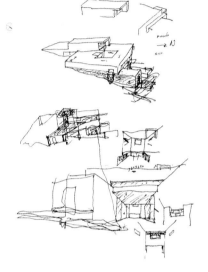

3. *Villa 1 (Unit F10): floor plans, longitudinal cross sections, cross sections (1:750)*
(Source: Álvaro Siza Archives, January–February 2000, overall rough design, original scale 1:100)

4. *Design models of the patio house*
(Source: Álvaro Siza Archives, undated)

Descriptive Note

The project includes the restoration of Villa Colonnese (1681), an oratory with adjoining chapel, dating from the eighteenth century, and the garden surrounding them, situated on the Berici Hills, just south of Vicenza. As far as the historic villa is concerned, there was a decision to opt for a significant reduction of the existing volumetrics, by means of the demolition of the volumes adjoining the central nucleus: a reduction that made it possible to build new houses. The villa thus recovered its "original" state as an isolated, dominant building.

In general terms, the seven new-built houses, all multi-storeyed, are situated at a lower elevation than that of the historic villa. The terrain is not subdivided into different properties, but taken as a single environment. The houses are pure volumes inserted into the hillside, the points of access follow existing, consolidate paths, to keep from altering the topography. There are two distinct typologies: the patio-house and the compact house. The new buildings are organised into groups: a first group (House 1, House 2) consists of the two patio houses, situated in the highest part of the lot. A second group (House 5, House 6, House 7) consists of three almost identical houses, located along the narrowest part of the land. Close to the historic villa is located, on the one hand, a house (House 3) and on the other side a building with three apartments that echo the disposition of the demolished structures.

1. *Landscape*

The structure of the paths and the trees, a number of abandoned buildings or the signs of other existing traces, all is gathered and evaluated, as Siza habitually does: the reasons are understood and the design is rooted solidly in the context and in its history. We are told that Siza, before visiting the construction

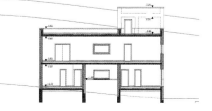

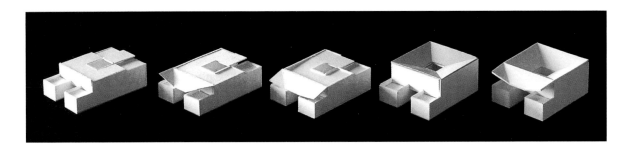

site, has initially designed a plan that concentrated all the buildings on the west side. But the day that he visited the lot for the first time he asked for rubber boots and to be left alone for a few hours. This winter inspection allowed him to identify a new strategy based on the distribution of isolated volumes. The "white boxes" that Siza arranged on the lot have dimensions and positions that do not alter the landscape – hill and villa. As if to say, a strategy for intervention that rendered intelligible what existed, or the essence of what had basically always been there: the shape of the hill. Anyone who walks around the walled property and follows the paths between the houses, and then climbs up onto the flat roofs, looks out of the windows of a house to the exterior, and then turns towards the successive or previous house, is immersing himself or herself in an intact and unitary world, made evident continually by these and other presences. They feel that the distance is measured to be distant and close, adequately separate in the whole, they feel that the elevation of the ground coincides with the height of the gaze (and it is established by the elevation of the structures), they feel that, like nature, a construction too can remain in equilibrium.

2. Houses

The second important question is the nature of the operation: build houses to sell them, and not one, but many houses, a new experience of Siza. This entails the necessity of a greater degree of neutrality in the design and the absence of the entire relationship of constraints and stimuli between client and architect. The client here is the developer/builder, not the home owner, and it offers a type of interaction, also interesting, but entirely different. In general terms, the project moves between typological definition and the definition of the minimal identity of

each house (reduction is the essence of the project).

Patio house. The two patio houses are built on sharply sloping land, in which the elevation of access to the street is about 10 metres higher than the level of the swimming pool. The projects of Casa Bahia and Casa Guardiola are a point of departure, inasmuch as they identify a principle of construction in similar conditions. In this case the project represents a further version and, because it is under construction, there is also the possibility of putting to the test the intuitions expressed in the two preceding projects. The floor plan is square, but composed of two volumes, stacked and overturned, in the form of a "C": on the upper floor, opening out towards the hill, inverted downhill on the lower storey. It is a symmetrical layout, with two staircases at opposite corners which give the house a vertical continuity. The volume of the garage that breaks the square to link up with the street is balanced by a volume jutting downhill. Since they are identical and mirror images, it is worth noticing that the two pools are separated by the jutting volume, suspended about the earth, which protects the setting. The hall extends out along the principal front, in which a long ribbon window frames the entire city.

Compact house. The other houses are simple volumes with rectangular plans, and with distribution on two floors. All share a common gene, both in dimensional and in plan terms: from each volume a part is later removed – in order to protect the entryway – and a bay window is added on the short side – to give a direction and to arrange the courtyard with swimming pool. Through these two operations, the volumes take life and begin a dialogue based on common themes. In relation to the terrain and the reciprocal distance, each house overlooks in one direction or the other the views and the intimacy of the open spaces. The distributive scheme insists on the

division into homogeneous spaces adjoining one another, rectangular in shape, wide, linked without hallways, only occasionally mediated by smaller spaces; the staircase is always supported on the side of the entrance. The fronts are simple: the wall is pierced by openings of various sizes. Each of the openings seems to possess an autonomy of its own and the equilibrium of the composition is not merely construction and has the task of identifying one house from another. From the interior these cuts in the wall or photographic compositions all have proportions and views that are very lovely. The composition of the fronts (vaguely Loosian) and the bay window represent for Siza the necessary signs, aside from the initial typological choice. The relationship with the exterior is punctual and takes place through the views: only the entrance is physically linked to the elevation of the existing terrain. The courtyard with the swimming pool is the only open-air private setting, defined by retaining walls. The theme of the pools has taken on its own precise function in acoustic terms as well: the noise of the highway, which runs at the foot of the hill, reaches up to the villa. The current intention, they tell us, is to utilise the falling water as a noise to cover the noise of the highway, through the study of sounds frequencies. The house near the historic villa is characterised by the ramp-staircase that embraces and protects the courtyard and is important as a volume in the central compound, composed of three different structures: the historic villa, the new villa, the apartment building. Only in this case, Siza had the possibility of interacting with the client, and he brought the project to changes that have slightly distinguished this house from others. The hermetic front that overlooks the villa is very important, characterised by a distinct horizontality and a single central opening: the stone socle extends towards the villa, establishing a common elevation that links the two buildings

and, on the other side, extends and twists to support the ramp-staircase around the swimming pool.

The cubic volume of the three-unit apartment building, also close to the historic villa, is understood as the restructuring of an existing construction, which has maintained its position but with a rationalisation of layout and the design of the fronts. The construction system is traditional, with load-bearing walls and flat roofs. The materials utilised were high-quality, carefully chosen. The brick walls were always double, with a load-bearing wall in reinforced concrete only where necessary for overhangs. The system of layouts utilised the ceilings as a technical water element to produce heat and cold: an additional duct system brought more air in through narrow fissures in the ceilings, always without grillwork. On the interior, then, all the space was given lofts, defining different heights: the walls were satin-finished plaster and, in continuity with the ceilings, they gave uniformity to the spaces. The floors are made of oak. The white fixtures swing open horizontally or with casement windows, with remarkable dimensions. As is customary, the meeting points between the various materials and their attachments are all resolved with great precision. The construction system is secure and effective. On the exterior, the fronts are plastered, the socle on the ground is lined with stone and the flashings are resolved with a slab of the same stone, about 8 centimetres thick, carved into a "C" shape, reversed and placed against the walls with a slight incline towards the interior. All of the construction is thus resolved with only two materials: plaster and stone. The work focuses upon the measurements of each of the construction elements and on the reciprocal relationship, reducing everything to its essence, both in technical and expressive terms.

EM (Travel Notes, June 2003)

House on Majorca

Island of Majorca, Spain

Collaborators: Atsushi Ueno, Francisco Silvestre

Land area: 3,587 sq. m.
Gross project surface area:
House: above ground, 250 sq. m.
Sub-basement, 310 sq. m. (excluding garage and facilities)
Total: 560 sq. m.
Guardian's house: 75 sq. m.

From the Project Report

1.

The lot for which the commission was given, polygonal in shape, has a surface area of 3587 square metres. To the west, it adjoins a city park, to the east, private property, to the north it is bounded by a street, and to the south by the Mediterranean Sea.
The project is developed on a lot with a pronounced slope and with vegetation composed of pines and other native species.

2.

The house is situated within the limits indicated for construction. The building is set back 5 metres with respect to the surrounding street, as established by the terms of the plan. There also remains a distance of 20 metres with respect to the escarpment, above the line of the beach. Access to the building comes from the street on the west side, at an elevation of 26 metres. The solution adopted consists of three structures placed upon a principal platform at an elevation of 22 metres. Each of these volumes has two storeys, in this way respecting the elevation indicated by regulations.
The private zones of the programme, constituted by the master bedrooms and the guest bedrooms, are located in the upper section of each of the volumes, while the common zones, hall, or great room, dining-room, kitchen, technical and service areas, are developed in the lower platform.
The decision to propose a green roof accentuates the integration of the complex into the landscape in which it is located.

Álvaro Siza
Oporto, May 2003

1. *Planimetric view (1:1000)*
(Source: Álvaro Siza Archives, undated)

2. *Photo of the model*
(Source: Álvaro Siza Archives, undated)

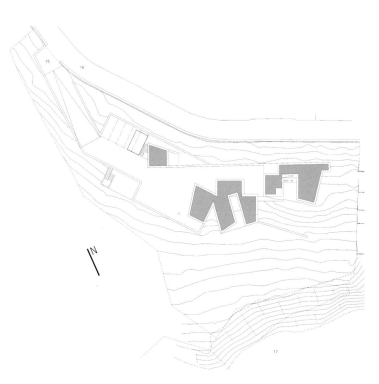

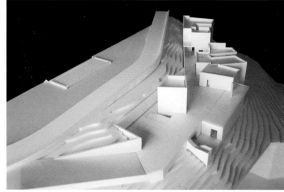

3. *Floor plans (1/500). Level 15.4, 18.6, 22.1, 25.6*
1. Hall, or great room / 2. Dining-room /
3. Kitchen / 4. Closet / 5. Laundry-room /
6. Pantry / 7. Entryway / 8. Access-room /
9. Bedroom / 10. Dressing-room / 11. Terrace /
12. Storage-room / 13. Technical room /
14. Lift / 15. Access / 16. Street / 17.
Mediterranean Sea
(Source: Álvaro Siza Archives, undated)

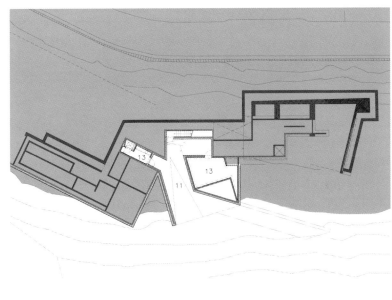

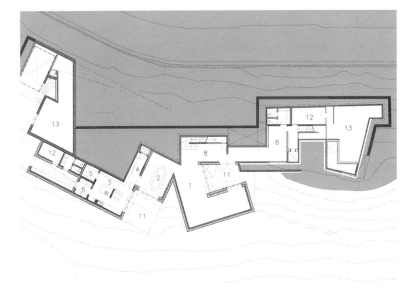

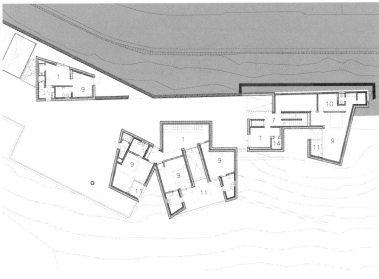

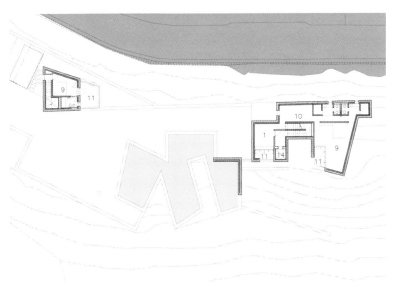

4. *Elevations (1:500)*
(Source: Álvaro Siza Archives, undated)

5. *Transverse cross sections (1:500)*
(Source: Álvaro Siza Archives, undated)

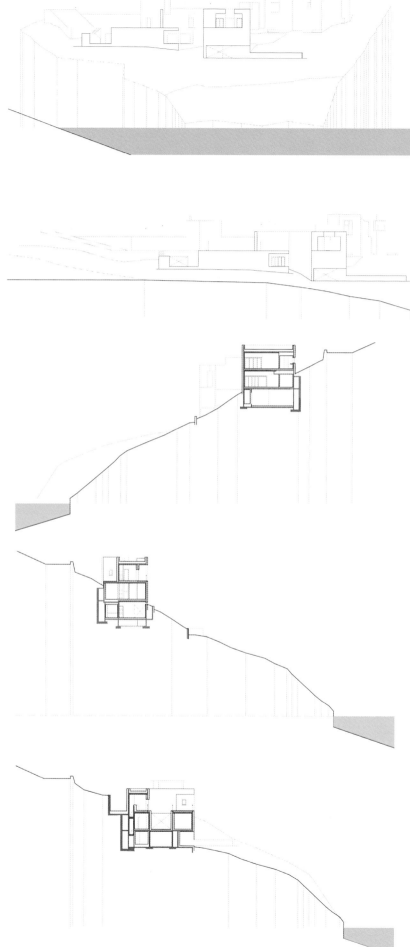

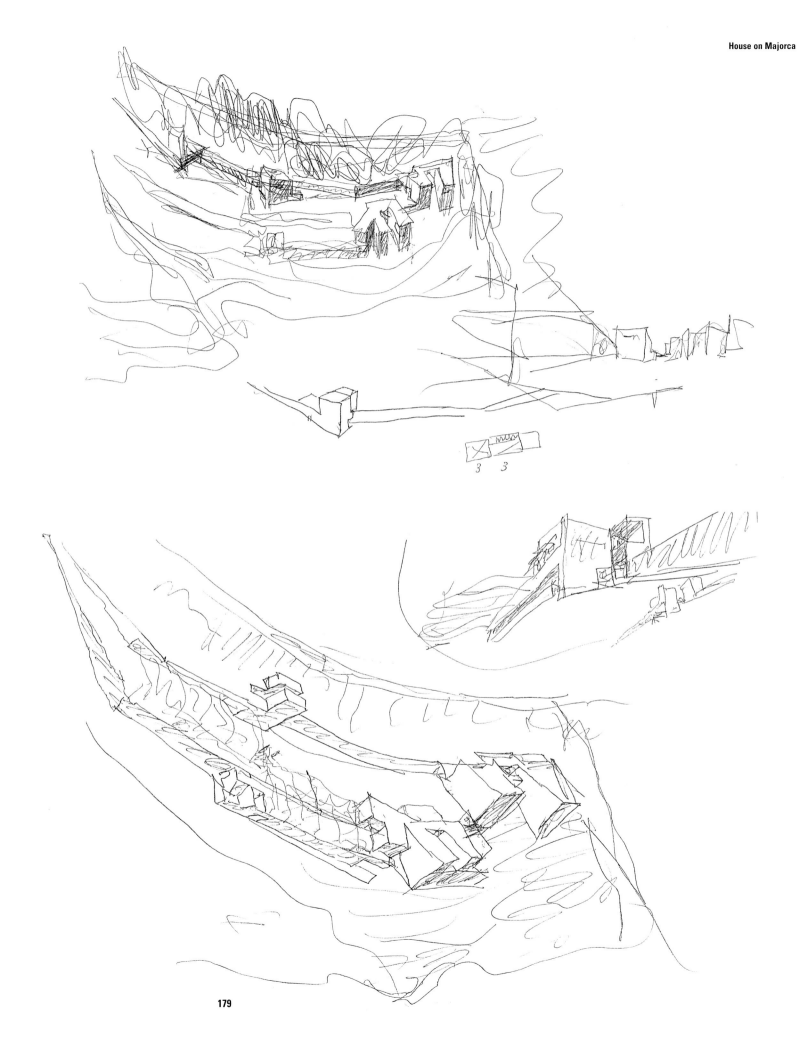

11 Houses, Photographs

Roberto Collovà

Casa Carneiro de Melo, Oporto
1957–59

Casa Ferreira da Costa / Miranda Santos,
Matosinhos
1962–65, 1988–93

Casa Alves Costa, Moledo do Minho
1964–68

Casa Alves Santos, Póvoa de Varzim
1966–69

Casa Manuel Magalhães, Oporto
1967–70

194

Casa Alcino Cardoso, Moledo do Minho
1971–73

Casa Carlos Beires, Póvoa de Varzim
1973–76

Casa António Carlos Siza, Santo Tirso
1976–78

Casa Maria Margarida, Arcozelo
1979–87

Casa Avelino Duarte, Ovar
1981–84

215

Casa Luís Figueiredo, Gondomar
1984–94

Bibliography

Four Houses at Matosinhos

Various Authors, "Álvaro Siza: Professione poetica", in *Quaderni di Lotus*, Electa, Milan 1986, p. 26.

"Álvaro Siza 1954-1988", in *A+U*, extra edition, A+U Publishing Co. Ltd., Tokyo, June 1989, p. 198.

Frampton, Kenneth, *Álvaro Siza. Opera Completa*, Electa-Elemond Editori associati, Milan 1999.

Casa Carneiro de Melo

Martins Barata, Paulo, *Álvaro Siza. 1954-1976*, Blau, Lisbon 1997, pp. 18, 21.

Frampton, Kenneth, *Álvaro Siza. Opera Completa*, Electa-Elemond Editori associati, Milan 1999, p. 81.

Casa Rocha Ribeiro

Flores, Carlos, "La obra de Álvaro Siza Vieira", in *Hogar y Arquitectura*, no. 68, Madrid 1967.

Teixidor, Pepita, "Casa Luis Rocha", in *Quaderns d'Arquitectura i Urbanisme*, no. 159, Barcelona, October–December 1983, pp. 24–27.

Various Authors, "Álvaro Siza: Professione poetica", in *Quaderni di Lotus*, Electa, Milan 1986, p. 47.

"Álvaro Siza 1954-1988", in *A+U*, extra edition, A+U Publishing Co. Ltd., Tokyo, June 1989, p. 201.

Rodrigues, Jacinto, *Álvaro Siza, obra e metodo*, Livraria Civilização, Oporto 1992, pp. 66–71.

Dos Santos, Jose Paulo, *Álvaro Siza: Obras y Proyectos 1954-1992*, Gustavo Gili, Barcelona 1993, pp. 22–25.

Martins Barata, Paulo, *Álvaro Siza. 1954-1976*, Blau, Lisbon 1997, pp. 66–77, 203.

Frampton, Kenneth, *Álvaro Siza. Opera Completa*, Electa-Elemond Editori associati, Milan 1999, p. 95.

Casa Júlio Gesta

Martins Barata, Paulo, *Álvaro Siza. 1954-1976*, Blau, Lisbon 1997, p. 203.

Casa Ferreira da Costa/Miranda Santos

Flores, Carlos, "La obra de Álvaro Siza Vieira", in *Hogar y Arquitectura*, no. 68, Madrid 1967.

Various Authors, "Álvaro Siza: Professione poetica", in *Quaderni di Lotus*, Electa, Milan 1986, p. 48.

Rodrigues, Jacinto, *Álvaro Siza, obra e metodo*, Livraria Civilização, Oporto 1992, pp. 82–87.

Cazzaniga Luca, Cerri Pierluigi, "Álvaro Siza. Un laboratorio di mobili 1987-94", in *Domus*, no. 759, Milan, April 1994, pp. 51–69.

Martins Barata, Paulo, *Álvaro Siza. 1954-1976*, Blau, Lisbon 1997, pp. 92–103.

Frampton, Kenneth, *Álvaro Siza. Opera Completa*, Electa-Elemond Editori associati, Milan 1999, pp. 103, 319.

Arnardottir Halldora, Sanchez Merina Javier, "Las edades del arquitecto", in *Blanco y Negro Cultural*, 6-9-2003.

Casa Rui Feijó

RA, Rivista da Faculdade de Arquitectura da Universidade do Porto, Year I, no. 0, October 1987, pp. 60–63.

Frampton, Kenneth, *Álvaro Siza. Opera Completa*, Electa-Elemond Editori associati, Milan 1999, p. 103.

Casa Alves Costa

"Casa Alves Costa", in *Controspazio*, no. 9, Milan, September 1972, p. 30.

Mateo, Josep Lluis, "Casa Alves Costa", in *Quaderns d'Arquitectura i Urbanisme*, no. 159, Barcelona, October–December 1983, p. 35.

Various Authors, "Álvaro Siza: Professione poetica", in *Quaderni di Lotus*, Electa, Milan 1986, p. 48.

"Álvaro Siza 1954-1988", in *A+U*, extra edition, A+U Publishing Co. Ltd., Tokyo, June 1989, pp. 141–144, 215.

Álvaro Siza architectures 1980-1990, 30 May–3 September 1990, Centre de Création Industrielle/Centre Georges Pompidou, exhibition catalogue, pp. 18–19.

Rodrigues, Jacinto, *Álvaro Siza, obra e metodo*, Livraria Civilização, Oporto 1992.

Martins Barata, Paulo, *Álvaro Siza. 1954-1976*, Blau, Lisbon 1997, pp. 104–113.

Frampton, Kenneth, *Álvaro Siza. Opera Completa*, Electa-Elemond Editori associati, Milan 1999, pp. 104–105.

Casa Adelino Sousa Felgueira

Frampton, Kenneth, *Álvaro Siza. Opera Completa*, Electa-Elemond Editori associati, Milan 1999, p. 111.

Casa Alves Santos

"Casa Alves Santos", in *Quaderns d'Arquitectura i Urbanisme*, no. 159, Barcelona, October–December 1983, pp. 32–34.

Various Authors, "Álvaro Siza: Professione poetica", in *Quaderni di Lotus*, Electa, Milan 1986, p. 50.

Rodrigues, Jacinto, *Álvaro Siza, obra e metodo*, Livraria Civilização, Oporto 1992, pp. 94–97.

Martins Barata, Paulo, *Álvaro Siza. 1954-1976*, Blau, Lisbon 1997, pp. 114–125.

Frampton, Kenneth, *Álvaro Siza. Opera Completa*, Electa-Elemond Editori associati, Milan 1999, pp. 106–107.

Casa Manuel Magalhães

"Abitazione unifamiliare a Porto, 1967-70", in *Controspazio*, no. 9, Milan, September 1972, pp. 28–30.

"Casa unifamiliare a Porto, 1967-70", in *Lotus International*, no. 9, Milan, February 1975, pp. 54–55.

Huet, Bernard, "Maison, Av. dos Combatentes, Porto, 1967/70", in *L'Architecture d'Aujourd'hui*, no. 185, Paris, May–June 1976, p. 47.

Gregotti, Vittorio (edited by), *Álvaro Siza-Architetto 1954-1979*, Edizioni Padiglione d'Arte Contemporanea di Milano & Idea Editions, Milan 1979.

"Manuel Magalhães House", in *A+U*, no. 123, A+U Publishing Co. Ltd., Tokyo, December 1980, pp. 23–26.

"Casa Manuel Magalhães", in *Quaderns d'Arquitectura i Urbanisme*, no. 159, Barcelona, October–December 1983, pp. 39–42.

Various Authors, "Álvaro Siza: Professione poetica", in *Quaderni di Lotus*, Electa, Milan 1986, pp. 52–53.

"Álvaro Siza 1954-1988", in *A+U*, extra edition, A+U Publishing Co. Ltd., Tokyo, June 1989, p. 206.

Álvaro Siza architectures 1980-1990, 30 May–3 September 1990, Centre de Création Industrielle/Centre Georges Pompidou, exhibition catalogue, p. 20.

Rodrigues, Jacinto, *Álvaro Siza, obra e metodo*, Livraria Civilização, Oporto 1992, pp. 98–101.

Dos Santos, Jose Paulo, *Álvaro Siza: Obras y Proyectos 1954-1992*, Gustavo Gili, Barcelona 1993, pp. 26–29.

Martins Barata, Paulo, *Álvaro Siza. 1954-1976*, Blau, Lisbon 1997, pp. 126–135.

Frampton, Kenneth, *Álvaro Siza. Opera Completa*, Electa-Elemond Editori associati, Milan 1999, pp. 114–116.

Casa Carlos Vale Guimarães

Frampton, Kenneth, *Álvaro Siza. Opera Completa*, Electa-Elemond Editori associati, Milan 1999, p. 117.

Casa Alcino Cardoso

"Casa Alcino Cardoso a Moledo do Minho, 1971", in *Lotus International*, no. 22, Milan, 1979, pp. 56–59.

Gregotti, Vittorio (edited by), *Álvaro Siza-Architetto 1954-1979*, Edizioni Padiglione d'Arte Contemporanea di Milano & Idea Editions, Milan 1979.

"Cardoso House", in *A+U*, no. 123, A+U Publishing Co. Ltd., Tokyo, December 1980, pp. 38–43.

"Maison Alcino Cardoso", in *L'Architecture d'Aujourd'hui*, no. 211, Paris 1980, pp. 18–20.

"Vacation house at Moledo do Minho", in *Parametro*, no. 121, November 1983, pp. 56–57, 63.

"Casa Alcino Cardoso", in *Quaderns d'Arquitectura i Urbanisme*, no. 159, Barcelona, October–December 1983, pp. 50–58.

Various Authors, "Álvaro Siza: Professione poetica", in *Quaderni di Lotus*, Electa, Milan 1986, pp. 58–60.

"Álvaro Siza 1954-1988", in *A+U*, extra edition, A+U Publishing Co. Ltd., Tokyo, June 1989, pp. 34–43, 208.

"Casa Cardoso", in *Lotus International*, no. 63, Milan 1989, pp. 118–121.

Álvaro Siza architectures 1980-1990, 30 May–3 September 1990, Centre de Création Industrielle/Centre Georges Pompidou, exhibition catalogue, p. 27.

Rodrigues, Jacinto, *Álvaro Siza, obra e metodo*, Livraria Civilização, Oporto 1992, pp. 102–109.

Dos Santos, Jose Paulo, *Álvaro Siza: Obras y Proyectos 1954-1992*, Gustavo Gili, Barcelona 1993, pp. 30–35.

Fleck, Brigitte, *Álvaro Siza*, Chapman and Hall, London 1995, p. 35.

Martins Barata, Paulo, *Álvaro Siza. 1954-1976*, Blau, Lisbon 1997, pp. 136–149.

Frampton, Kenneth, *Álvaro Siza. Opera Completa*, Electa-Elemond Editori associati, Milan 1999, pp. 127–128.

Casa Marques Pinto

Frampton, Kenneth, *Álvaro Siza. Opera Completa*, Electa-Elemond Editori associati, Milan 1999, p. 138.

House at Azeitão

"Maison à Azeitão, Setúbal 1973", in *L'Architecture d'Aujourd'hui*, no. 211, Paris 1980, p. 27.

Frampton, Kenneth, *Álvaro Siza. Opera Completa*, Electa-Elemond Editori associati, Milan 1999, p. 136.

Casa Carlos Beires

"Maison Beires-Póvoa", in *L'Architecture d'Aujourd'hui*, no. 185, Paris, May–June 1976, pp. 48–49.

"Casa Beires a Póvoa, 1973-75", in *Lotus International*, no. 22, Milan 1979, pp. 53–55.

Gregotti, Vittorio (edited by), *Álvaro Siza-Architetto 1954-1979*, Edizioni Padiglione d'Arte Contemporanea di Milano & Idea Editions, Milan 1979.

"Beires House", in *A+U*, no. 123, A+U Publishing Co. Ltd., Tokyo, December 1980, pp. 50–56.

Huet, Bernard, "Maison Beires", in *L'Architecture d'Aujourd'hui*, no. 211, Paris 1980, pp. 34–37.

Burkhardt, Françoise, "Traumhaus 6-Arcadia von Póvoa", in *Bauwelt*, no. 47, Berlin, December 1982, p. 1917.

Bru, Eduard, "Casa Beires", in *Quaderns d'Arquitectura i Urbanisme*, no. 159, Barcelona, October–December 1983, pp. 43–47.

Various Authors, "Álvaro Siza: Professione poetica", in *Quaderni di Lotus*, Electa, Milan 1986, pp. 66–70.

"Álvaro Siza 1954-1988", in *A+U*, extra edition, A+U Publishing Co. Ltd., Tokyo, June 1989, pp. 52–59.

Álvaro Siza architectures 1980–1990, 30 May–3 Septembre 1990, Centre de Création Industrielle/Centre Georges Pompidou, exhibition catalogue, p. 32.

"Beires Wohnhaus in Póvoa de Varzim", in *Bauwelt*, special issue, vol. 81, no. 29/30, August 1990, pp. 1473–1474.

Rodrigues, Jacinto, *Álvaro Siza, obra e metodo*, Livraria Civilização, Oporto 1992, pp. 114–117.

Dos Santos, Jose Paulo (edited by), *Álvaro Siza: Obras y Proyectos 1954-1992*, Gustavo Gili, Barcelona 1993, pp. 36–41.

Martins Barata, Paulo, *Álvaro Siza. 1954-1976*, Blau, Lisbon 1997, pp.160–173.

Frampton, Kenneth, *Álvaro Siza. Opera Completa*, Electa-Elemond Editori associati, Milan 1999, pp. 141–145.

House at Francelos

"Maison Francelos", in *L'Architecture d'Aujourd'hui*, no. 211, Paris 1980, p. 55.

Frampton, Kenneth, *Álvaro Siza. Opera Com-*
pleta, Electa-Elemond Editori associati, Milan 1999, p. 158.

Casa António Carlos Siza

"António Carlo's House", in *A+U*, no. 123, A+U Publishing Co. Ltd., Tokyo, December 1980, pp. 73–77.

"Maison António Carlos Siza", in *L'Architecture d'Aujourd'hui*, no. 211, Paris 1980, pp. 56–59.

"Casa António Carlos Siza", in *Quaderns d'Arquitectura i Urbanisme*, no. 159, Barcelona, October–December 1983, pp. 66–69.

Various Authors, "Álvaro Siza: Professione poetica", in *Quaderni di Lotus*, Electa, Milan 1986, pp. 110–112.

Testa, Peter, "Tradition and actuality in the António Carlos Siza House", in *Journal of architectural education*, no. 40, Washington, D.C.1987, pp. 24–30.

"Álvaro Siza 1954-1988", in *A+U*, extra edition, A+U Publishing Co. Ltd., Tokyo, June 1989, pp. 141–144, 215.

Álvaro Siza architectures 1980-1990, 30 May–3 September 1990, Centre de Création Industrielle/Centre Georges Pompidou, exhibition catalogue, p. 22.

"António Carlos Siza Wohnhaus in Santo Tirso 1976–78", in *Bauwelt*, special issue, vol. 81, no. 29/30, August 1990, pp. 1470–1472.

Rodrigues, Jacinto, *Álvaro Siza, obra e metodo*, Livraria Civilização, Oporto 1992, pp. 126–127.

Dos Santos, Jose Paulo, *Álvaro Siza: Obras y Proyectos 1954-1992*, Gustavo Gili, Barcelona 1993, pp. 42–45.

"Casa António Carlos Siza", in *El Croquis*, monographic work, vol. 13, no. 4, 68/69, Madrid 1994, pp. 72–75.

Fleck, Brigitte, *Álvaro Siza*, Chapman and Hall, London 1995, pp. 33, 38–39.

Martins Barata, Paulo, *Álvaro Siza. 1954-1976*, Blau, Lisbon 1997, pp. 188–198.

Frampton, Kenneth, *Álvaro Siza. Opera Completa*, Electa-Elemond Editori associati, Milan 1999, p. 159.

Casa Maria Margarida

"Maison Maria Margarida", in *L'Architecture d'Aujourd'hui*, no. 211, Paris 1980, p. 68.

Various Authors, "Álvaro Siza: Professione poetica", in *Quaderni di Lotus*, Electa, Milan 1986, p. 113.

"Álvaro Siza 1954-1988", in *A+U*, extra edition, A+U Publishing Co. Ltd., Tokyo, June 1989, pp. 145, 218.

Cortés, Juan Antonio, "Los desplazamientos de Álvaro Siza", in *Anales de Arquitectura*, no. 4, Valladolid 1992, pp. 193–199.

Rodrigues, Jacinto: *Álvaro Siza, obra e metodo*, Livraria Civilização, Oporto 1992, pp. 144–147.

Dos Santos, Jose Paulo (edited by), *Álvaro Siza: Obras y Proyectos 1954-1992*, Gustavo Gili, Barcelona 1993, pp. 46–49.

Frampton, Kenneth, *Álvaro Siza. Opera Completa*, Electa-Elemond Editori associati, Milan 1999, p. 159.

Casa José Manuel Teixeira

Various Authors, "Álvaro Siza: Professione poetica", in *Quaderni di Lotus*, Electa, Milan 1986, p. 114.

"Maison J.M. Teixera", in *L'Architecture d'Aujourd'hui*, *Álvaro Siza*, no. 278, Paris, December 1991, pp. 132–135.

Rodrigues, Jacinto, *Álvaro Siza, obra e metodo*, Livraria Civilização, Oporto 1992, pp. 152–155.

Dos Santos, Jose Paulo, *Álvaro Siza: Obras y Proyectos 1954-1992*, Gustavo Gili, Barcelona 1993, pp. 50–55.

Frampton, Kenneth, *Álvaro Siza. Opera Completa*, Electa-Elemond Editori associati, Milan 1999, pp. 204–205.

Casa Avelino Duarte

"Casa Avelino Duarte", in *Quaderns d'Arquitectura i Urbanisme*, no. 159, Barcelona, October–December 1983, pp. 72–73.

"Álvaro Siza. Avelino Duarte House near Ovar", in *Architectural Design*, no. 54, November–December 1984, pp. 60–62.

"Maison Duarte-Ovar", in *AMC Architecture, mouvement, continuité*, no. 7, March 1985, p. 18.

Wang, Wilfried, "House in Ovar, Portugal, 1984", in *9H*, no. 7, 1985, pp. 53–59.

"Álvaro Siza Vieira, Casa Duarte e appartamento Teixeira", in *Casabella*, no. 514, Milan, June 1985, pp. 4–13.

Collovà, Roberto, "La casa a Ovar", in *Casabella*, no. 514, Milan, June 1985.

Frampton, Kenneth, "Al punto fermo del mondo che ruota", in *Casabella*, no. 514, Milan, June 1985.

Wang, Wilfred, "House in Ovar", in *A+U*, no. 191, August 1986, pp. 107–114.

Various Authors, "Álvaro Siza: Professione poetica", in *Quaderni di Lotus*, Electa, Milan 1986, pp. 115–120.

Testa, Peter, "Unity of the discontinuous. Three projects", in *Assemblage*, no. 2, February 1987, pp. 46–95.

"Álvaro Siza 1954–1988", in *A+U*, extra edition, A+U Publishing Co. Ltd., Tokyo, June 1989, pp. 90–101, 220.

Bottero, Maria, "Portogallo. Ovar 1981-85. Casa Duarte", in *Abitare*, no. 286, Milan, June 1990, pp. 114–120.

Zabalbeascoa, Anatxu, *Houses of the century*, Cartago, London 1990.

Rodrigues, Jacinto, *Álvaro Siza, obra e metodo*, Livraria Civilização, Oporto 1992, pp. 156–159.

Dos Santos, Jose Paulo, *Álvaro Siza: Obras y Proyectos 1954-1992*, Gustavo Gili, Barcelona, 1993, pp. 58–65.

"Casa Avelino Duarte", in *El Croquis*, monographic work, vol. 13, no. 4, 68/69, Madrid 1994, pp. 88–93.

Fleck, Brigitte, *Álvaro Siza*, Chapman and Hall, London 1995, p. 37.

Dubois, Marc, *Álvaro Siza. Dentro la città*, Federico Motta Editore, Milan 1996, pp. 24–33.

Frampton, Kenneth, *Álvaro Siza. Opera Completa*, Electa-Elemond Editori associati, Milan 1999, pp. 211–216.

Casa Fernando Machado

"A Casa do Dr. Fernando Machado/A casa interronpida", in *Obradoiro*, no. 8, Santiago de Compostela, March 1983, pp. 7–13.

Various Authors, "Álvaro Siza: Professione poetica", in *Quaderni di Lotus*, Electa, Milan 1986, p. 114.

Frampton, Kenneth, *Álvaro Siza. Opera Completa*, Electa-Elemond Editori associati, Milan 1999, p. 221.

Casa Aníbal Guimarães da Costa

Frampton, Kenneth, *Álvaro Siza. Opera Completa*, Electa-Elemond Editori associati, Milan 1999, p. 223.

Casa Mário Bahia

"Abitazione a Gondomar", in *Case da vendere*, Como, December 1983.

"L'effect réglementaire. Habitation particulière", in *L'Architecture d'Aujourd'hui*, no. 235, Paris, October 1984, pp. 8–9.

"Casa Baia", in *Quaderns d'Arquitectura i Urbanisme*, no. 163, Barcelona, October–December 1984, pp. 60–64.

Various Authors, "Álvaro Siza: Professione poetica", in *Quaderni di Lotus*, Electa, Milan 1986, p. 133.

"Álvaro Siza 1954–1988", in *A+U*, extra edition, A+U Publishing Co. Ltd., Tokyo, June 1989, p. 224.

Dos Santos, Jose Paulo, *Álvaro Siza: Obras y Proyectos 1954-1992*, Gustavo Gili, Barcelona 1993, pp. 66–67.

Fleck, Brigitte, *Álvaro Siza*, Chapman and Hall, London 1995, pp. 40, 94.

Frampton, Kenneth, *Álvaro Siza. Opera Completa*, Electa-Elemond Editori associati, Milan 1999, pp. 227–230

Casa Mário Bahia, Gondomar, in *Álvaro Siza. Scultura Architettura*, Skira, Milan 1999, pp. 44–49.

Casa Pascher

Various Authors, "Álvaro Siza: Professione poe-

tica", in *Quaderni di Lotus*, Electa, Milan 1986, p. 136.

Frampton, Kenneth, *Álvaro Siza. Opera Completa*, Electa-Elemond Editori associati, Milan 1999, p. 251.

Casa Álvaro Siza

Molteni, Enrico, *Álvaro Siza. La Malagueira a Evora*, Edicom, 2000, p. 119.

Castanheira, Carlos, Porcu, Chiara (edited by), *As Cidades de Álvaro Siza*, exhibition catalogue, Figueirinhas, Lisbon 2001.

Casa David Vieira de Castro

Various Authors, "Álvaro Siza: Professione poetica", in *Quaderni di Lotus*, Electa, Milan 1986, p. 137.

"Álvaro Siza 1954-1988", in *A+U*, extra edition, A+U Publishing Co. Ltd., Tokyo, June 1989, pp. 141–144, 215.

"Maison Vieira de Castro", in *L'Architecture d'Aujourd'hui*, no. 278, Paris 1991, pp. 126–131.

Rodrigues, Jacinto, *Álvaro Siza, obra e metodo*, Livraria Civilização, Oporto 1992, pp. 166–171.

Dos Santos, Jose Paulo, *Álvaro Siza: Obras y Proyectos 1954-1992*, Gustavo Gili, Barcelona 1993, pp. 68–71.

"Casa Vieira da Castro", in *El Croquis*, vol. 13, no. 4, 68/69, Madrid 1994, pp. 126-135.

Castanheira, Carlos, De Llano, Pedro (edited by), *Álvaro Siza-Opere e progetti*, Centro Galego de Arte Contemporánea, Electa, Milan 1995, pp. 96–99.

Casciani, Stefano, "Case e Architetture. Diverse per scale. Uguali per qualità", in *Abitare*, no. 379, Milan, December 1998, pp. 84–91.

Siza, Álvaro, *Una casa*, in *Álvaro Siza. Immaginare l'evidenza*, Laterza, 1998, pp. 25–37.

Frampton, Kenneth, *Álvaro Siza. Opera Completa*, Electa-Elemond Editori associati, Milan 1999, pp. 253–260.

"Habitar el paisaje: Casa David Vieira de Castro, Vila Nova de Famalicão, Portugal", in *Ar-quitectura Viva*, no. 65, March–April 1999, pp. 98–101.

"Vieira de Castro House, Vila Nova de Famalicão, Portugal", in *A+U*, special issue, *The House*, no. 4 (355), Tokyo, June 1999.

Banz, Claudia, "House in Vila Nova de Famalicão", in *Detail: Innenräume,* vol. 41, no. 2, March 2000.

"Casa David Vieira de Castro, Vila Nova de Famalicão, Portugal", in *GA Houses*, no. 64, May 2000, pp. 10–23.

Futagawa, Yukio (edited by), "Casa David Vieira de Castro, Vila Nova de Famalicão, Portugal", in *GA Houses*, special issue 2002, *Masterpieces 1971–2000*, Tokyo, November 2001.

Casa Luís Figueiredo

Castanheira, Carlos, De Llano, Pedro (edited by), *Álvaro Siza-Opere e progetti,* Centro Galego de Arte Contemporánea, Electa, Milan 1995, pp. 92–95.

"Casa a Valbom, nella Valle del Douro", in *Domus*, no. 778, Milan, January 1996, pp. 30–35.

Frampton, Kenneth, *Álvaro Siza. Opera Completa*, Electa-Elemond Editori associati, Milan 1999, pp. 261-264.

Casa César Rodrigues

Frampton, Kenneth, *Álvaro Siza. Opera Completa*, Electa-Elemond Editori associati, Milan 1999, p. 318.

Casa Javier Guardiola

Sanmartin, Antonio, "Tres casas verdaderas. La casa Guardiola en el Puerto de Santa Maria", in *Basa*, no. 14, Santa Cruz de Tenerife, April 1991, pp. 76–101.

"Maison Guardiola, Puerto de Santa Maria", in *L'Architecture d'Aujourd'hui*, no. 278, Paris, December 1991, pp. 124–125.

Frampton, Kenneth, *Álvaro Siza. Opera Completa*, Electa-Elemond Editori associati, Milan 1999, p. 355.

Quinta de Santo Ovídio

Frampton, Kenneth, *Álvaro Siza. Opera Completa*, Electa-Elemond Editori associati, Milan 1999, pp. 374–375.

"Quinta de Santo Ovídio-Douro", in *arq./a revista de arquitectura e arte*, ano II, no. 7, Lisbon, May–June 2001, pp. 25–33.

"Santo Ovidio estate, Douro, Portugal 2001", in *A+U*, no. 5, Tokyo, May 2002, pp. 8–18.

Stocchi, Attilio, "Álvaro Siza Vieira a Santo Ovídio (Portogallo). Esercizio di Stile", in *Abitare*, no. 415, Milan 2002, pp. 112–114.

Van Middelem-Dupont Casa

Kieckens, Christian, "Álvaro Siza, Maison Van Middelem-Dupont", in *GA Houses*, no. 55, 1998, pp. 129–131.

Frampton, Kenneth, *Álvaro Siza. Opera Completa*, Electa-Elemond Editori associati, Milan 1999, pp. 553–554.

"Casa Van Middelem-Dupont", in *El Croquis, Álvaro Siza. 1995-1999*, no. 95, Madrid 1999, pp. 216–223.

"Self-confident owners-8 family houses: in Belgium-near Ostende (Álvaro Siza)", in *Bauwelt*, vol. 93, no. 37, October 2002, pp. 30–33.

Dubois, Marc, "La semplice retorica della domesticità", in *Casabella*, nn. 706-707, Milan, December–January 2002/2003, pp. 36–47.

"Casa van Middelem-Dupont", in *Area*, no. 70, September–October 2003, pp. 148–153.

Villa Colonnese

Bassi, Alberto, Cevese, Renato, *Le case di Álvaro Siza nel parco di Villa Colonnese*, Vicenza, October 1999.

Frampton, Kenneth, *Álvaro Siza. Opera Completa*, Electa-Elemond Editori associati, Milan 1999, pp. 582–584.

"Villa Colonnese, Vicenza", in *GA Houses*, special issue, *Project 2000*, no. 63, Tokyo, March 2000, pp. 58–63.

"Villa Colonnese housing project, Vicenza, Italy 1998", in *A+U*, special issue, *Álvaro Siza-recent works*, no. 4 (355), Tokyo, April 2000, pp. 122–129.

Dubois, Marc, "Kontinuität statt Kontrast", in *Deutsche Bauzeitung (db)*, no. 1, Jg. 137, 2003, pp. 27–31.

Dubois, Marc, "Een Portugese ode aan Vlaanderen", in *Kunsttijdschrift Vlaanderen*, no. 294, Jg. 52, February 2003, pp. 64–65.

Maddaluno, Raffaella, "Álvaro Siza Vieira. Sette case nel parco di Villa Colonnese", in *d'Architettura*, no. 20, Milan 2003, pp. 158–165.

Collaborators, since 1956

Orlando Varejão, Alexandre Alves Costa, Beatriz Madureira, *António Madureira, Francisco Guedes de Carvalho, Francisco Lucena, Adalberto Dias, Edgar Castro, Nuno Ribeiro Lopes, Miguel Guedes de Carvalho, Eduardo Souto de Moura, Maria Manuela Sambade, Graça Nieto, José Paulo dos Santos, Teresa Fonseca, Bruno Marchand, Jean Gèrard Giorla, Chantal Meysman, Luisa Brandão, *Luisa Penha, *José Luis Carvalho Gomes, Peter Brinkert, Ramiro Gonçalves, Zahra Dolati, Jorge Nuno Monteiro, Mateo Corrales, Roberto Collovà, V. de Pasquale, Oreste Marrone, Viviana Trapani, Anna Alí, Sabina Snozzi, Hughes Grudzinski, Angela Jimenez, André Braga, Susana Afonso, Pier Paolo Mincio, João Pedro Xavier, José Manuel Neves, Helena Torgo, Peter Testa, Pascale De Weck, Carlos Castanheira, Eduardo Marta da Cruz, *Avelino Silva, Luis Filipe Mendes, Humberto Vieira, Tiago Faria, Joan Falgueras, Robert Levit, Alfredo Jorge Ascenção, Mona Trautman, Francisco José Cunha, Joelke Offringa, José Fernando Gonçalves, Christian Gaenshirt, Cristina Guedes, Maria Clara Bastai, *Cristina Ferreirinha, Guilherme Páris Couto, Elisiário Miranda, Jotta van Groenewoud, Antónia Noites, Anton Graf, António Angelillo, João Gomes da Silva, Wilfried Wang, Jun Shuang Kim, John Friedman, José Salgado, Giacomo Borella, Brigitte Fleck, Jan van de Voort, Jorge Carvalho, Teresa Gonçalves, Salvador Vaz Pinto, Matthew Betmaleck, Ashton Richards, Alessandro D'Amico, Sandra Vivanco, Jane Considine, Yves Stump, *Maria Chiara Porcu, Ana Williamson, *Edite Rosa, João Sabugueiro, Pascale Pacozzi, Cecilia Lau, José Eduardo Rebelo, *Clemente Menéres Semide, Sofia Thenaisie Coelho, Sara Almeida, Carles Muro, Colm Murray, Ulrike Machold, Matthew Becker, Rui Castro, Fariba Sepehrnia, *Miguel Nery, Raffaele Leone, Joaquim Conceição, Karine Grimaux, Peter Cody, Daria Laurentini, Gonzalo Benavides, Carlos Seoane, Rudolf Finsterwalder, Maria José Araújo, *Marco Rampulla, Luis Diaz-Mauriño, Roberto Cremascoli, Daniela Antonucci, Andreia Afonso, Edison Okumura, Paul Scott, Taichi Tomuro, Hana Kassem, Abílio Filipe Mourão, Luís Antas de Barros, Maite Brosa, Maurice Custers, Dirk Sehmsdorf, Susana Correia Leite, Joana Soares Carneiro, Bárbara Rangel Carvalho, Francesca Montalto, Michele Gigante, Marco Ciaccio, Lia Kidalis, *Tatiana Berger, *António Dias, Mariel Suarez, Pedro Rogado, Petra Katarina Alankoja, Francisco Reina Guedes de Carvalho, Vitor Oliveira, Angela Princiotto, Roger Lundeen, Maria Moita, Ueli Krauss, Bradford Kelley, Carolina Albino, Andrea Smaniotto, Filipa Guerreiro, Mitsunori Nakamura, Ameet Sukhthankar, *Atsushi Ueno, *José Carlos Oliveira, *Kenji Araya, *Benjamin Bancel, Angel Esteve, Antje Kartheus, Nuno Abrantes, Victor Navarro Dias, Axel Baudendistel, Markus Elmiger, Emílio Sanchez Horneros, Verónica Martinez, Gabriel Flórez, *Matthias Heskamp, *Pedro Polónia, Pedro Quintela, Claudia Vogel, Cecilia Alemagna, *Tomoko Kawai, Francisco Silvestre, *Simon Lanza Olmi, *Hans Ola Boman, *Wesley Hindmarch, *António Mota, Paula Nascimento, Laura Menéndez, *Saurabh Malpani, Andrea Araguas, Asako Kuribara, *Rita Amaral, *Natacha Viveiros, *Biatriz Tarazona, *Ren Ito, *Vânia Miranda, *Pablo Elinbaum

Archives
*Maria Chiara Porcu

Library
*Isabel Castro

Secretariat
Teresa Godinho, Ivone Sobral, Dinora Rodrigues, *Anabela Monteiro, Angelina Gomes, *Maria João Sousa

* *current collaborators*

231